Principles of language and mind

T. P. Waldron

Principles of language and mind

Foreword by
Ashley Montagu

Routledge & Kegan Paul
London, Boston, Melbourne and Henley

First published in 1985 by Routledge & Kegan Paul plc

14 Leicester Square, London WC2H 7PH

9 Park Street, Boston, Mass. 02108, USA

464 St Kilda Road, Melbourne Victoria 3004, Australia and

Broadway House, Newtown Road,
Henley-on-Thames, Oxon RG9 1EN, England

Set in Baskerville
by Hope Services, Abingdon
and printed in Great Britain by
St Edmundsbury Press Ltd,
Bury St Edmunds, Suffolk

Library of Congress Cataloging in Publication Data

Waldron, T. P.
(Terence Patrick), 1926–

The principles of language and mind.
Bibliography: p.
Includes index.
1. Languages—Philosophy. 2. Human evolution.
3. Thought and thinking. I. Title.
P106.W28 1985 401 84–11667

British Library CIP data available

ISBN 0–7102–0323–3(C)

Contents

What is man, what does his nature possess which others lack, what qualities affecting action and experience? PLATO

Any hypothesis which pretends to discover the ultimate original qualities of human nature ought at first to be rejected as presumptuous and chimerical. HUME

It has often and confidently been asserted that man's origin can never be known: but ignorance more frequently begets confidence than does knowledge: it is those who know little, and not those who know much, who so positively assert that this or that problem will never be solved by science. DARWIN

Those other faculties, which seem proper to man only, proceed all from the invention of words and speech. HOBBES

Here, as elsewhere, we shall understand things best if we consider them as they emerge from their origins. ARISTOTLE

Foreword

Good wine needs no bush. But this is so excellent a book I really feel privileged to share my enthusiasm for it with the reader. I should say at once that it is the book I would very much like to have written. Ever since my studies more than half a century ago with Franz Boas, and my discovery that language is the best possible means to understanding the minds of those who use it, I resolved that in due time I would write upon the subject, not because of any great or original contribution I might be able to make, but because the subject was in itself so fascinating.

With the years the fascination grew stronger and wider to embrace the origin and evolution of speech. In various books and articles I briefly discussed the subject, but never developed it at any great length. The pressures of adjacent interests increasingly made it apparent that I would never get round to the book I had hoped to write. Hence my delight on discovering that such a book — the present study — was being written.

Principles of Language and Mind is a masterly performance, and I regard it as the best book that has been written on the evolution of language. It is indeed the sanest statement of the problems concerning the nature and function of language that I have read in the whole contemporary debate about these matters. The author has taken a very complex subject and made it clear in its relations to origins, evolutionary development, behaviour, psychology, logic, philosophy of mind, and even the foundations of mathematics. In addition to its criticism of contemporary linguistics, the book will serve the very useful purpose not only of enlightening readers of every kind, but also of acting as a whetstone upon which the more careful reader may sharpen his wits.

It is a book which is not in the least technical, yet it deals with highly technical matters: no less than the origin and evolution of language, and the processes by which language assisted in the favouring of those changes which resulted in the development of the human mind. There has been no book which even remotely approaches the success with which the author has carried out his investigation into the relation between the development of language and the emergence of mind. I cannot recommend his work too highly.

Princeton, New Jersey — Ashley Montagu
26 January 1984

Preface

The purpose of the present work is to provide a systematic account of the principles which enable us to understand the origin, primary functions, and later development of human language, and to clarify the manner in which this development underpins another: that of the distinctively human form of intelligence which we call mind. This aim can be achieved only if we place the language problem in its proper evolutionary perspective. This will enable us to see how the originative principles of language emerge, naturally and intelligibly, from their behavioural and perceptual antecedents, in the context of common experience. Thereafter, the progressive complications of both language and conceptual thought—from common speech and everyday thinking to the highest forms of scientific discourse and understanding—become amenable to perfectly clear theoretical explanation. So also do the many causes of error and confusion to which ignorance of our own most distinctive faculty renders us liable. Each stage in the development of human language and thought brings with it also a new potential for error and misunderstanding. This is the chief reason why we need a valid theory of language.

Academic orthodoxies in the three fields—linguistics, psychology, philosophy—most concerned with the theory of human language (as distinct from the study of individual languages) are for the most part non-evolutionary or even anti-evolutionary in orientation. Hence their failure to clarify the nature either of language or of thought, and the ceaseless polemics which characterize these fields of inquiry. But equally, evolution theory has so far proved inadequate to account for the higher mental faculties which so obviously set humankind apart from all other species. Evolutionary speculation on language, mind, and human culture in general has tended to be reductionist in character, thus leaving evolution theory defective in the very area which concerns us most.

The virtue of an evolutionary theory of language, then, is that it fills serious gaps both in the field of the humanities and in natural science. It also enables us to effect the long-desired rapprochement between these two areas of inquiry. It alone can provide a sure guide for the solution of theoretical problems in psychology and epistemology, since linguistically formulated categories and logical constructs are the very foundation of human reason and understanding. By the same token, only such a theory of language can provide existent evolution theory with the principles needed to explain in purely naturalistic terms the emergence of mind, and to account for the intellectual faculties and ethical values of human life. Since the presentation of the theory in question is, to borrow Darwin's phrase, one long argument from the beginning to the end, and one in which many points must be touched on before they can be adequately developed, a brief outline of the direction, import and scope of the argument may be of assistance to the reader.

If we are to have a valid theory of language, one which will clarify its essential role in the development of human intelligence, we need to understand (among other things) why we have not had one so far, especially since many of the principles needed for the elaboration of such a theory have long been a matter of public record. The nature of the present inquiry, therefore, is essentially theoretical and critical, as befits any investigation in the field of the humanities, that is, in any discipline in which human knowledge, thought, understanding, purpose and action constitute the very subject matter of the inquiry. An underlying theme of the book is, indeed, the essential difference between all such forms of inquiry and empirical science. The present work is not primarily concerned with physical *phenomena* as such. The aim is, rather, to clarify universal *principles* of semantics and epistemology which are implicit in all human knowledge (including, of course, empirical science), and to show how they are interconnected. The fundamental problems—psychological, linguistic, logical, epistemological—with which we are here concerned cannot be solved in isolation one from another. Nor can they be solved in any other than an evolutionary framework. Before this can be demonstrated, however, we need to consider certain recurrent misconceptions concerning the nature of language, and to show how these exemplify misconceptions within the three philosophical traditions—idealism, naturalism, scepticism—which have now engaged in repetitious and sterile debate for well over two thousand years.

These shortcomings in the humanities are matched by comparable misconceptions in contemporary biology and evolution theory. Chief among these is the notion that evolution theory is on a par with other theories in natural science. Logically, however, evolution theory is unique. For it correlates the findings not of *one* single scientific discipline, but the established findings of many quite disparate disciplines, and much more: virtually everything we know about life in general (not excluding our own). To achieve this, evolution theory must integrate a vast number of utterly heterogeneous and incommensurable factors within a single explanatory framework which can make their interrelations intelligible. In this, evolution theory most resembles the study of the humanities: the study of human history, for example, which faces similar problems. It is indeed the methodology of the humanities, and not that of empirical science, which is appropriate to evolution theory. Moreoever, until human knowledge and culture are adequately accounted for in evolutionary terms, evolution theory itself will remain defective and vulnerable to the kind of attack to which it has traditionally been subjected. A theory of evolution which cannot explain the emergence of human knowledge, and a theory of knowledge cut off from its biological roots, are equally useless for an understanding of human nature or the human mind.

Biology, then, is clearly the area where we must seek the

crucial links between natural science and the higher mental faculties of man. That these faculties must be rooted in human physiology is obvious enough. However, contrary to certain modish hypotheses about the genes and the brain, we cannot leap straight from physiology to conceptual thought and mind. We must pass through the intermediate zones of perception and behaviour, of psychology and semantics. What has been even less appreciated is that to bridge the gap we also need a systematic theory of language: one which explains its antecedents, its origin, its development, the distinctive nature of its semantic function, and the many and complex ways in which words may refer to non-linguistic fact. Such a theory alone can throw light on two momentous transitions: the transition from pure physiology to animal psychology, and the transition from animal intelligence in general to the distinctively human kind. The first is the evolutionary shift from behaviour triggered by *immediate* physical stimulation to behaviour which is semantically *mediated*, that is, dependent on the interpretation of signs. The second is the shift from sign-mediated behaviour in general to behaviour dependent on conceptual thought, human understanding, and rational control, all of which first emerge with the learning and use of language.

The relation between biology and mind, then, is no simple physiological matter. As Sherrington, Eccles and others have noted, mind, unlike brain, is not a physiological concept at all. (This does not mean, however, that mind is a mystical concept, or an insoluble problem, as many have thought.) But neither can mind be accounted for in simplistic terms of adaptation between organism and environment. There are many distinct modes of adaptation and biological levels at which it occurs. Behavioural adaptations, which vary greatly between individuals, are infinitely more complex than organic adaptations which characterize all members of a given species. They differ also from social adaptations, which characterize many different forms of life, and from those cultural and intellectual means of not merely adapting to the environment but of actually controlling it. How these higher and more complex faculties originate, how they develop and interact, and how they make possible a uniquely human way of life is the main concern of psychology, of semantics, and of epistemology. Only when these matters have been explained can the links between physiology and human consciousness be clarified, and the antique body-mind problem be resolved in a manner at once naturalistic and rational. We shall then be able to see that evolution theory, far from implying or supporting modern dogmas of psychological determinism, is in fact the only theory capable of explaining not only biological novelty in the organic sense, but also the emergence of conceptual thought, consciously controlled behaviour, and that degree of freedom of choice which these faculties make possible and which is uniquely human. The notion that evolution theory implies any 'law of necessary development' was expressly disavowed by Darwin.

It should by now be clear that language theory is concerned, not with the countless different languages which exist or have existed, but with a universal faculty, or rather with a complex of interrelated faculties. Different languages constitute psychological barriers—though not insurmountable ones—dividing human societies one from another, but the possession of language as such—any language—is what constitutes our common humanity and most distinguishes the human species from all others. To understand the nature and origin of this unique faculty, then, we must begin, not with existent languages (whose forms and their uses are innumerable), but with the two fundamental semantic principles, implicit in *all* languages, and indeed in all intelligence, both animal and human. These are the principles of *semantic efficacy*, the origin of which in purely instinctive behaviour was clarified by Darwin; and the principle of *sign perception* (as distinct from object perception), the original dependence of which on purely physiological stimulation was first clarified by Pavlov. Language originates with the emission of vocal *signals*, which initially were no more than the expression of emotion, but which become associated with objects of sense experience and thus come to be interpreted as *signs* of such objects. When the usage of such signals which are also signs becomes stabilized, by virtue of their referential utility and socializing effect, they automatically acquire a normative function as objective, socially accepted terms of reference.

Since a similar sequence of events occurs in rudimentary form even in animal behaviour, the theoretical explanation of how language originates is less problematic than the task of explaining the complexities of its development. Yet there is complexity in language from the start. As each individual learns to use them, the basic words or *symbols* of language simultaneously acquire many quite distinct functions which radically differentiate them from mere signs and signals. Verbal symbols are indeed uttered as signals and responded to as signs. But they do not merely become *associated* with objects. We consciously use words to *refer* to objects. And we achieve this, not by having a separate word for every object of experience (which is clearly impossible), but by the adoption of a finite number of category words whose meanings combine, overlap, and reciprocally define one another in countless different ways. The many uses of such category words underlie the conceptual thought of each individual, promoting both analytic finesse and keener understanding, and also innovatory conceptual synthesis, suggestive of novel possibilities both of thought and action. In addition, they make possible a uniquely human kind of symbolic communication, utterly distinct from animal communication of any other kind. They also have mnemonic and heuristic functions. We do not merely react to objects present. We may refer to objects absent, or even no longer existent. We may also refer to objects and situations which do not yet exist but which, as a result of prior symbolic projection or 'conception', may later be brought into being.

When words become syntactically combined into sentences, and when sentences are concatenated into continuous discourse, these complex and interrelated functions, already operative in language from the start, create ever more complex modes of reference, both to real objects and situations and to others which are purely notional. Moreover, since our verbal categories may be not only more generally categorized but also more restrictively defined, language creates many different kinds and levels of conceptual abstraction. These in turn combine, even in common speech, to produce many kinds and degrees of logical complexity. Conceptual abstraction and logical complexity, assimilated unawares by each individual in the learning and use of language, are indeed the main problem areas which language theory and logic must clarify.

We should not forget, however, that underlying these conceptual and logical complexities are more basic physiological factors without which neither language nor human thought would exist: the peculiar ability of the human mouth to produce a limitless number of subtly articulated sounds, and of the human brain to accommodate a vast amount of information associated with them. If we fail to see the implications of these two factors we are likely to remain for ever ignorant of the central function of human language: the manner in which it *mediates* between sense experience and conceptual thought. This comes about for the good reason that language belongs to both spheres at once. Words are themselves perceptible, like many things with which they are associated. But they only have meaning insofar as they are interpreted and understood. Words also become associated, in the silent thought of each individual, with other words, and through these with other elements of experience, in an ever expanding zone of consciousness which we usually speak of as mind. Language, then, is by no means the simple thing which familiarity with it often leads us to believe. It is not merely a means of animal communication along with others, as many theorists have thought. It is also the vehicle of human thought and the key to human understanding. With the learning of language, and with increasing proficiency in its many, diverse, and complex uses, we build up a novel *symbolic consciousness*, which is quite distinct from the purely *sensory awareness* common to animal life at large; and is indeed the precondition of human thought, rational discourse, culture and civilization. If we fail to grasp this fact, we are in constant danger of detaching human *thought* from human *experience* of the world in which we live, creating an ever greater number of insoluble 'metaphysical problems' in the process. Here as elsewhere, the salutary virtue of an evolutionary methodology is that it seeks to begin at the beginning. In language theory, psychology, and epistemology, we must not begin with the adult mind in all the complexity of its evolved state. We must begin with its antecedents, or, as Kant would say, with the preconditions of its possibility.

Before considering more closely how the symbolic function of language enables each individual to reduce the constant and often chaotic influx of sense experience to intelligible order, attention must be given to the basic theoretical concepts on which semantics and epistemology ultimately rest: stimulus, sign, signal, symbol. Critical scrutiny of these concepts enables us to trace what is doubtless the most momentous evolutionary development of all: that which begins with mindless animal reaction to physical stimuli, and leads—by way of unconscious association, animal expression, and interpretation of signs—all the way to language, human understanding, and conscious thought. The transition from immediately stimulated behaviour to sign-mediated behaviour greatly augments the amount of information available to animal life. It is, perhaps, the point at which it first makes sense to speak of information, of learning, and thus of animal intelligence (which in an ever changing and often hostile environment is most simply defined as the ability to learn from experience).

With semantically mediated behaviour, then, we move from the realm of pure physiology into that of psychology. Such behaviour may take two directions. It may remain unconscious and simply lead to the more successful fulfilment of animal needs and desires (but also, as often happens, to their frustration: since error also enters the scheme of things at this point). Or, with the development of the symbolic functions of language, it may lead to conceptual thought and human consciousness, to theoretical understanding and rational control. This development can be understood only if we trace its stages in the order of their emergence. Before this can be undertaken, however, we need to grasp the two fundamental distinctions referred to above: that between physiology (which is a branch of empirical science) and the study of animal intelligence; and the distinction between animal intelligence in general and the uniquely human kind, which does not merely utilize language, but would not exist without it.

The multiple functions of the linguistic symbol have already been noted. But what most distinguishes language from all other forms of semantic behaviour is the sheer diversity of its modes of reference. Linguistic reference is characteristically effected by the use of category words, and of such others as are needed to combine them syntactically. For the referential utility of our category words is greatly enhanced by our ability both to conjoin and modify their already complex functions in countless ways. This not only makes possible more precise forms of reference but, given the constant interplay between sensory experience and conceptual thought, is suggestive of novel possibilities of thought and subsequent action. The skill with which we exploit the more innovatory or creative aspects of the use of language largely determines the distinctive consciousness and understanding of each individual. But equally, the illogical use of language is a constant source of conceptual error, misunderstanding, and irrational behaviour. Hence the need not only for a positive theory of language but also for an understanding of the ways in which it may be unwittingly misused, and lead us astray.

In common speech and everyday thought about matters of immediate concern, the misuse of language rarely causes insuperable difficulties, though error does of course occur even here. Once we move into the area of continuous discourse, however, and especially into abstract and theoretical discourse, the possibilities of error increase dramatically. For not only are *empirical* and *psychological* checks (present in person-to-person speech in actual situations) now left behind, but many *logical* complexities (implicit in language from the start) now create problems of quite a different kind. We need therefore to establish what occurs in the transition from common speech to continuous discourse. Here three points need emphasis. First in coherent discourse the meaning of words and sentences depends not only on that to which they refer, but also on the meaning of the other words and sentences with which they are conjoined. Problems of logical consistency and consequentiality first obtrude themselves at this level. Second, even apparently simple forms of discourse, such as narrative and description, almost imperceptibly take on an *explanatory* function, and may indeed eventually develop into systematic theory, both in physical science and in the humanities. Third, long before this stage is reached, primitive and purely speculative attempts at explanatory theory—myth and metaphysics—often become established as orthodoxies, and become serious obstacles to theoretical advance. All such problems can be remedied only through an understanding of logic, which is thus an integral part of language theory and (contrary to traditional belief) cannot be studied as an independent discipline in its own right.

The emergence of *written* forms of language, and their diffusion in space and time, have had incalculable effects on human culture and civilization. So much so that this relatively late development in the history of language has often been mistaken for the thing itself. The 'decontextualized' forms of the written language are still commonly thought to be the subject matter of language theory as such. (The whole mystique of modern 'structuralism' is based on this illusion.) This error exemplifies the type of reification which language itself first makes possible. We unconsciously place our own symbolic constructs on the same logical or ontological level as that to which they are meant to refer. We constantly treat words as if they were things like any others. It is important to realize why this is so. It is this very confusion which first gives words their meaning and which enables infants to learn to speak. Words signify things, but equally things suggest the words we refer to them by. Inevitably, in the early stages of learning these two levels of awareness become as one. Indeed, confusion of word and thing is what enables language to get off the ground in the first place, and is simply a special case of that unconscious association of A with B (and, of course, of B with A) on which all signification, meaning, consciousness, language and thought ultimately rest. However, unconscious association, which in the early stages of learning may be an inestimable advantage, becomes at the level of systematic theory a serious liability.

On the credit side, apart from the relative permanence of written texts as against the evanescent nature of speech, the advent of written forms of language had other important effects. The gradual emergence of *alphabetic* writing first made possible the phonological analysis and re-synthesis of the pre-existent spoken language: writing and reading as we know them. This in turn facilitated study of the complex relations between form and function in individual languages, and eventually the theoretical study of language in general.

Ancient analyses of the so-called parts of speech, which range from the exclamation (which is a conventionalized expression of emotion) to the purely logical connectives of theoretical discourse, anticipated Darwin's insight that 'language still bears the stamp of its gradual evolution'.

Growing awareness of the complexities of conceptual thought eventually led ancient thinkers to seek out logical principles by which rational discourse and theory might be regulated. Despite some initial success, however, this endeavour has remained largely frustrated by ignorance of the manner in which language mediates, in complex but quite unmysterious ways, between sense experience and conceptual thought; and of the fact that it is our verbal categories which make conceptual thought possible in the first place. Before approaching logic in the more specialized sense, therefore, we must consider the logical complexity of language in general. This brings us to the very core of language theory, and to a number of closely related problems. These concern the special nature of linguistic meaning (as distinct, say, from pre-linguistic meaning); the great variety of ways in which language relates to non-linguistic fact; the *categorial* function of the linguistic symbol; the different kinds of universal concept which our verbal categories create; and the fundamental distinction between *empirical* and *modal* reference: that is, the distinction between linguistic reference to objects of immediate sense experience and *all other uses* of language whatever. To establish the temporal and logical priority of empirical reference as the original bond between external fact and conceptual thought, and the dependence of all other uses of language on this fundamental semantic link, is the prime task of both language theory and logic. Once this is grasped, the progressive complications of language and conceptual thought, as we move to the more abstract (and hence logically more complex) modes of reference, cease to be problematic.

For if language *begins* with reference to the empirically given, it by no means ends there. As already noted, mnemonic and heuristic functions are implicit in its very use. We may refer not only to the real but also to what is 'ideal' or purely notional. This in no way validates metaphysical idealism. Among other things, it simply draws attention to the obvious fact that we refer not only to actualities but also to possibilities, some of which later may be realized. We may even refer to impossibilities, and we may utter contradictions and other absurdities. Language enables us to talk nonsense as well as sense. All this gives some insight into the logical complexity which lies just beneath the surface even of common speech: a complexity which in everyday usage we unconsciously take in our stride, but which in the more abstract and theoretical uses of language (especially those concerning human problems) is a constant source of confusion and error. It is at this level that we find ourselves in need of logical theory.

The unhappy history of the discipline of logic is largely explained by the fact that there has never been consensus among its practitioners as to what the subject is about. This is a serious matter, since logic is concerned with nothing less than the difference between sense and nonsense. More precisely, logic is concerned with the *normative* function of language (implicit in our first verbal categories); and, in a narrower sense still, with the principles and rules which regulate its more abstract and theoretical uses. Norms are conventions or agreed terms of reference by which other things are judged or regulated. This is obvious enough in the case of material norms (such as weights and measures), and of practical norms (such as rules and laws). But underlying all others are the logical norms which are built into language, without which there could be no rational judgment or thought whatever.

Logic, then, is our means of distinguishing between human reason and irrationality: in the social uses of language, in conceptual thought, and in the conscious pursuance of human ends. Only when we understand this may we approach logic in the narrower sense and consider the three stages of its development. First came positive theory construction, which began with primitive attempts to understand the workings of nature (the starting point of empirical science), or to solve problems concerning human life and society (the origin of the humanities). Second, logical criticism of primitive theory, which inevitably ran into problems for which, initially, the only solution seemed to lie in mythical modes of thought, which are notoriously tolerant of contradiction, inconsequentiality and imaginative leaps in the dark. Third, the search for principles which might be invoked to render theory proof against logical inconsistency. (Other kinds of error, due to ignorance of fact, misinformation and so on are not the immediate concern of logic, and need to be attended to separately.) Although the relevant principles—those of logical identity, logical contradiction, and logical implication—were discovered long ago, their true significance and their close interdependence have not been generally recognized. Nor has the distinction between the purely logical use of these terms and other quite proper but logically irrelevant uses been widely understood. As a result, while naive mythical discourse has often been supplanted by the more sophisticated metaphysical kind, this has not brought any advance in explanatory theory, least of all in the study of human affairs: a field in which modes of argument long since discredited elsewhere are still accorded academic respectability.

Although metaphysical doctrines and preconceptions have long hindered a proper understanding of logic, perhaps the main obstacle has always been the confusion of logic with the type of deductive argument which is peculiar to mathematics. Mathematics, however, is a highly specialized *post-linguistic* symbolism, humanly designed to make possible calculation, and therefore deduction, in the clearly delimited area of physical magnitudes and relationships. (Calculation and deduction are here correlative terms, as we learn in the solution of problems in elementary arithmetic.) Logic, by contrast, has for its province all human discourse whatever, covering the entire field of human experience. To make mathematics the paradigm of logic, therefore, or to view logic as a mere aspect or subdivision of mathematics is to put the cart before the horse. Without the logical function of language and the rational *human* activities of counting and measuring, there would be no mathematics at all. The only way to eradicate this ancient fallacy is to examine the similarities and differences between language and mathematics, to examine the different ways in which each symbolism initially relates to empirical fact, and to see how they develop, in quite different directions, to serve quite different human ends.

If misconceptions concerning the nature of logic, not least the attempt to subordinate all logical discourse to the mathematical model, have seriously obstructed theoretical progress in the humanities, another major obstacle to human self-understanding has been the persistent attempt to reduce psychology to the status of physical science, in the mistaken belief that physical science is the only form of rational inquiry known to man. Here we have another anachronistic absurdity, since physical science is itself a *product* of human thought and human understanding directed at the study of natural phenomena. The whole of science, Einstein noted, is nothing more than a refinement of everyday thinking. It is the nature and origin of the latter which constitute the central problem of human psychology and epistemology. And since language is what first enables us to refer to physical phenomena and so order, systematize, and exploit our knowledge of nature, and also the means by which we refer to many things which are *not* given in nature, but which may be brought into being through intelligent human action, it is clear that language, with its many functions and uses, is central to human psychology. It is indeed the psychological factor which most distinguishes our species from all others.

The full scope and import of language theory thus becomes evident when, as is here proposed, we trace the gradual development of language from its simple beginnings, scarcely distinguishable from animal signalling and response to signs, to the higher forms of theoretical discourse, both in physical science and in the humanities. Conceptual thought, symbolic consciousness, human understanding, rational theory, science, technology, the ability to make intelligent provision for the future, of individuals, of communities, of the entire human race: all this ultimately depends on the uniquely human faculty of speech and the psychological and intellectual faculties which come in its wake. This thesis is by no means new. In its essentials it is as old as antiquity. What we need, however, is not a thesis but a theory: one which will explain in naturalistic terms exactly how this momentous evolutionary development came about. But one also which explains how ignorance of these language-dependent faculties leads us not only into theoretical error, but since theory (good or bad) underlies all human action of any complexity, into practical absurdities also; and worse, into horrors and atrocities which no other animal species would be capable of perpetrating. It is ironic that ours, the only species capable in large measure of determining its own destiny, has proved to be the most self-destructive. Modern technology, itself a product of human rationality, has of late given this irony a more sinister twist. Since only an evolutionary theory of language can provide us with a rational theory of mind, with an understanding of what makes us human and, alas, inhuman also, the relevance of such a theory to our present plight should not be too difficult to see. Except, of course, for those who have vested interests in seeing things otherwise.

A theoretical treatise which must take account of many areas of inquiry at once cannot be armed at all points. And given the range of divergent opinion on virtually every topic treated, detailed polemic is out of the question. Only good theory can oust bad. Inevitably, then, what may appear obvious to one reader in any given context may well be problematic to another. It can only be hoped that the coherence of the whole will compensate for any gaps in the exposition of the parts. The book is meant to be read as a self-contained critical essay. While many of the quotations from other authors exemplify important theses which the book develops and correlates, these authors are in no sense invoked as 'authorities'. They do, however, enable us to see that the problems treated are by no means so novel, nor their solution so intractable, as many modern theorists would have us believe. And of course, when it occurs, the consensus of distinguished thinkers from many different disciplines must be more impressive than the inconclusive wranglings which so often characterize debate in the individual fields of inquiry with which we are here concerned. The Notes are not essential for an understanding of the text, and are mainly designed to clarify or develop certain theoretical and historical topics which may be of interest to the reader. The Appendix is in part a glossary of theoretical terms and in part a summary of certain theses which are central to the theory proposed.

December 1982

Acknowledgments

The author is deeply indebted for advice and encouragement to Kathleen McCarthy, Marian Sugden, Luis de Sousa Rebelo, and Stephen F. Walker. The final version of the book owes much to the critical interest and friendly exhortation of the distinguished anthropologist and humanist who has kindly consented to write the Foreword.

1

The nature of the inquiry

> If what you say is true, there must be some one theoretical discipline which provides theory not only of itself and of the other disciplines, but even a critique of bad theory as well. PLATO

> The inquiry is not exhausted in the statement of its purpose, but in that purpose being carried through; nor do the findings embody the whole truth of the matter, but the findings along with the process of arriving at them. HEGEL

There was an ancient quarrel between empirical science and the humanities which haunts us still. In former times natural phenomena were commonly explained in what we now see to be ludicrously anthropomorphic or mythical terms. In the long run this did not prevent the emergence of mature empirical science. But now it is common practice to treat the humanities as though they were themselves branches of empirical science, with the disastrous consequence that they have all but ceased to perform their proper function: to teach people to think critically and humanely about human affairs, and to promote the rational solution of human problems. It is paradoxical that one of the most remarkable achievements of human rationality, empirical science, should now have become a major source of confusion and stultification in the study of man himself. The tail now wags the dog.

How might this state of affairs be remedied? The only way, it seems, is to trace the roots of human rationality—which itself underlies our understanding of nature and all else—and establish the principles on which it rests. For if we ask why the empirical sciences flourish while the humanities are in a state of theoretical chaos, the answer is that in empirical science care is taken to establish the principles of each discipline and to articulate them into a systematic theory, which is at once explanatory of the known facts and a heuristic device for further inquiry, which in turn may necessitate formulation of new principles and extension of the theory. And so matters progress. In the humanities, by contrast, principles are either neglected altogether, or trumped up *ad hoc* when things become problematic, or dragged in from alien disciplines and blindly imposed where they clearly do not apply. It is even held that the humanities differ from empirical science in that only the latter admits of general principles, while in the humanities all that is possible is description of fact. This view, which is widespread, would deprive the study of human affairs of rational explanatory theory altogether. Theory is rational only insofar as it *is* based on coherent general principles, which must be made explicit on demand. Such principles are themselves human formulations, constructed out of the symbolic forms of human language. Unfortunately, descriptivism still dominates large areas of anthropology, psychology and linguistics, with the result that the more that is known, the less is understood, as ever more facts are discovered and described. The situation is not helped by the proliferation of ever new categories and modes of description which ensure that the descriptive task will remain permanent. Yet it is precisely when the amount of data is overwhelming that we need, not new ways of describing them, but well-founded principles and theory to make them intelligible.

Principles are starting points, the elements or rudiments in a given field of inquiry. They may be substantive, theoretical, or methodological, this depending on whether they refer to the fundamental facts, the theoretical formulations, or the basic procedures of inquiry, on which all other such factors in that area depend. Until such principles are established there can be no serious theory in any area of inquiry, but only description and surmise. Principles are like concepts in that they are universals: that is, they serve to bring many similar cases under a single head. But they differ from simpler concepts in that they may refer not only to objects and processes but also to recurrent *relations* between objects and processes. Principles thus acquire great explanatory value inasmuch as all theoretical understanding, as distinct from mere perceptual familiarity, is a question of grasping relationships. To understand is to correlate, to see something in its relationships with other things. This is a ceaseless process since such relationships are many, complex and variable, and the things that may be related are limitless. Yet in any field of inquiry some relationships are more fundamental than others: to isolate such basic principles and articulate them into a logically coherent system is what constitutes the theory of that subject. Most fundamental of all, of course, are the principles of human knowledge and understanding, on which all other principles necessarily depend. Here we reach, as it were, epistemological rock-bottom. Here we come up against such ultimate theoretical problems as the nature and reliability of perception and knowledge, the meaning of meaning, the understanding of understanding, the theory of theory.

A moment's reflection makes clear that any inquiry in this area is not only expressed in language, but would be quite impossible without it. The formulation of any principles whatever is a use of language, and without linguistically formulated principles there can be no critical inquiry or theory at all. Language, then, is far from being a mere adjunct of our theoretical understanding, but is one of its essential preconditions. All higher theoretical formulations rest ultimately on the more basic and familiar formulations of ordinary language, just as all higher forms of theoretical knowledge rest ultimately on common perception and experience. Neither of these facts has been adequately understood, and the intimate relation between them hardly at all. What is even less understood is that human consciousness—as distinct from mere animal awareness which we also possess—is inseparable from the linguistic formulations which structure and constitute it. Ordinary language provides, as it were, the informal theory of common experience, inasmuch as it enables us—however unconsciously—to monitor that experience, to analyse it and reflect on it. The new symbolic consciousness that each individual builds up as he or she learns the use of language becomes so intertwined with our basic sensory experience that initially these two levels of awareness—experience and thought—become virtually indistinguishable. This initial confusion does little or no harm at the level of common speech and common-sense thought. Indeed, as we shall see, it is a precondition of both. If undetected, however, such confusion will later become a source of endless mischief, especially at the level of explanatory theory, and not least in the theory of language. Theory is an extension and a refinement of processes already present in common speech. But at the level of theory all essential factors and principles must be consciously distinguished and made explicit.

Language, then, is a unique, distinctively human, complex and important affair. A common error has always been to think it simple and trivial. We learn to speak at so early an age that we soon take language, and all that it makes possible, quite for granted. Yet when we begin to theorize about the subject we soon find ourselves in deep waters, as the polemics of contemporary philosophy, psychology and linguistics amply demonstrate. Language begins as a form of behaviour having clear affinities with signalling activity and sign interpretation in the animal world at large, but before we get very far in the study of it we find ourselves engulfed in epistemological problems concerning what we know, how we know, what kinds of knowledge there are, how human knowledge differs from animal knowledge, and how far language aids or distorts more primitive sources of knowledge. To cope with all this we soon find we need not only a theory of language but also a theory of mind: more precisely, that the two are inseparable. Moreover, if language begins as a form behaviour linked with the perception and interpretation of signs, our theory must embrace these areas also, since if we are to understand how language originates, and what distinctive novelty emerges with it, we must go beyond language to trace its antecedents and preconditions in general animal psychology.

The aim of the present essay, then, is to examine a complex of problems variously referred to as linguistic, psychological, logical and epistemological (and quite a few others that have become entangled with these); to show that they are so interrelated that they can only be solved together or not at all; to explain why they can be solved only in the context of a naturalistic, that is, an evolutionary conception of human psychology; to demonstrate that this in turn is possible only on the basis of a systematic theory of language; and to provide such a theory. The main problems concern the nature of mind—human consciousness, thought, reason—and the ways in which it differs from all other forms of animal intelligence. The central thesis, which is by no means new, is that all the distinctive features of human intelligence—and indeed its aberrations also—are dependent on the emergence and use of language: that with language man acquires a distinctive symbolic orientation of his own making, which is continuous with, but not reducible to, the purely sensory orientation which is the basis of animal intelligence at large. It is further maintained that the principles of both language and mind are susceptible of a completely rational and natural explanation within an overall evolutionary perspective.

If this be so, the idealist thesis that language is the mere adjunct or tool of some pre-existent mind (the nature of which remains quite unexplained), and the behaviourist thesis that human language and language-dependent behaviour are on all fours with animal behaviour at large, must both be repudiated. The nature of language is here misconceived in opposite ways. The idealist disregards the origin and development of language and thus fails to grasp its constitutive role in the build-up of individual and social consciousness. The behaviourist fails to see that language, while it has obvious behavioural aspects, also has to do with interpretation and understanding. The ability to correlate words and things, which is initially no more problematic than any other kind of association or conditioning, has the remarkable effect that in interpreting and so understanding the words we produce, we orient ourselves more effectively among the things we experience: we literally make sense of them. Even at the lowliest level of language use we thus have two quite separate modes of orientation—sensory and symbolic—which interact, monitor, control and correct one another. What is wrong with the notion of language as 'verbal behaviour' is that language cannot be called behaviour in any ordinary sense at all. Its basic function is not causal efficacy in the physical sense, or even semantic efficacy of the sort found in animal signalling behaviour: display, threat, and the like. Linguistic meaning is not of this kind. Language is *sui generis*, and the new symbolic orientation that emerges with it marks the great divide between animal awareness and intelligence, which may be of a high order, and human consciousness, thought and rationality, which are of a quite different order. To provide a systematic theory of the origin, primary functions and later developments of language, therefore, and to explain its constitutive role in the gradual development of human thought, should be the prime task not only of language theory but also of psychology and epistemology. Without such a theory any other theory in these areas must necessarily be fragmentary and premature, when not plainly false.

But if the proper use of language is the basis of all forms of rational thought and theory, its improper use is, by the same token, the source of the many fallacies and aberrations which have always plagued human thought and had fateful repercussions on human life and history. We need therefore not only a positive theory of language but also, as it were, a pathology of language, a critique of the misuses of language. If all this be true, then there must be, as Plato suggested, some one theory which provides not only the theory of itself and is the key to all others, but also provides a critique of bad theory.[1] And if language is the basis of all theory, then the theory in question can only be the theory of language.

As noted above, the central importance of an understanding of language for an understanding of the human mind is no new discovery. It was a commonplace of Greek antiquity and in the modern age was unequivocally re-stated by Hobbes, Condillac, Herder, Wilhelm von Humboldt, Hegel and others. In the course of the present century the theme has become almost an obsession. We have indeed reached the curious situation that while countless theorists in the most diverse fields are convinced that language somehow holds the key to the solution of their problems, none seems prepared to take the obvious next step, which would be to provide an adequate theory of so important a subject. Why this should be so requires some attention. Obviously, the main obstacles in the way of an adequate theory of language are the many misconceptions which exist concerning the nature of language and the complexity of its relations both with reality and with our own thought. Such obstacles can be removed only by a systematic theory which will clarify these matters. In a preliminary way, however, it may be of use to consider some of the more pervasive and insidious misconceptions which lie in the path of such a theory.

Perhaps the greatest difficulty for most language theorists lies in their inability to grasp the essentially theoretical, non-empirical nature of the inquiry. This failing forms part of the more general confusion between empirical science and the humanities to which reference has been made. First, then, a word on terminology. The term 'natural science' is misleading for three reasons. First, it encourages the belief that there can be systematic theory—which is all the word 'science' means—only about natural phenomena, understood as referring to the world of nature external to man. This in turn gives support to the belief that humanity is somehow external to nature, that human affairs are sacrosanct and immune to theoretical inquiry. The third error is quite different: the belief that any theory concerning the human species must conform to principles established in the field of empirical science. These *theoretical* confusions rest on a more fundamental confusion concerning the *subject matter* in each of these quite distinct fields of study.

The term 'natural science' strictly means physical or empirical science. Its objects of inquiry are by definition physical phenomena in their own right—falling bodies, sparks jumping gaps, living tissue, the behaviour of molecules—studied by empirical methods. But the study of the spoken and written 'phenomena' of language is not empirical in this sense, since they are human conventions, they normally signify things other than themselves, and they differ from one language to another. Their value resides not in their physical existence but in the symbolic functions which they peform. This does not mean that they cannot be understood or systematically studied. On the contrary, they are the very foundation of human understanding, their uses are readily assimilated by children, and their study has long been the subject matter of philology. However, the formal conventions of any given language, or even those of all languages whatever, do not exhaust the subject of language, and in any case they are not the subject matter of language theory. Language is a complex affair. It cannot be explained in terms of its spoken and written forms alone. Its origin needs to be explained in relation to its antecedents. It involves many organs, faculties and processes. Above all, its use has quite remarkable peculiarities and consequences which so radically determine the nature of human intelligence that it would be theoretical folly to disregard them. Language is a form of behaviour which has symbolic efficacy quite unlike causal or mechanical efficacy, or even semantic efficacy of the kind resulting from other forms of animal behaviour. Language depends on and helps illuminate the most elemental form of perception: sign perception—the basis of all higher forms of learning—as distinct from the recognition of objects. Verbal signs like all others need to be interpreted in order to be understood, or even, as commonly happens, to be misunderstood. Language, in short, is intimately tied up with the distinctively human form of intelligence which we call mind. But it is equally tied up with the multiplicity of things—objects, processes, their qualities, aspects, relations and so on—to which the forms of language refer.

At this point it might seem that language is far too complex and heterogeneous a subject to admit of unitary theory. This is because we tend to approach language matters without method and from the wrong end. We attempt to study linguistic complexity without inquiring how it came about. If we adopt an evolutionary approach, however, we shall find that language theory is concerned with a quite small number of interrelated problems, all of which admit of rational solution in completely naturalistic terms. These problems concern the immediate antecedents of language, its originative principles, the nature of symbolization, the progressive complications of language as symbolization develops into syntactic speech and later into various kinds of theoretical discourse, the manner in which this continuous process underpins the parallel development of human intelligence, and various errors and misconceptions which come with language and are liable to undermine this development. Language is a source of both sense and nonsense.

Language theory, then, has a unique subject matter, quite distinct from that of empirical science (and even from that of philology which is not concerned with these more fundamental questions). But not only language, no form of behaviour or thought which is distinctively human can be studied by the methods of empirical science, since all such behaviour and thought are language-dependent, with all the complexity and potential for error that this implies. When we theorize about human thought, action, understanding, motivation, purpose, choice, the adoption of means to achieve determinate ends and so on, we move into a zone of infinite complexity. No physical scientist is called on to make matters as uncertain and heterogeneous as these the very subject matter of his inquiry, although they necessarily form part of his own pyschology. This paradox may illustrate the absurdity of imposing pseudo-empirical methods in the study of the humanities, the futility of perpetual description in an area where what is needed is explanation, and the ludicrous proliferation of ever new schools of thought which explain precisely nothing. By contrast with the steady advance of accepted theory in empirical science, the very multiplicity of conflicting hypotheses in every area of the study of man suggests that while all cannot be right, all could very well be wrong. At best, each may deal with some part or aspect of the truth, exaggerated to the exclusion of many others. We may thus see why theoretical hygiene is even more necessary in human studies than in physical science itself. In physical science bad theory is commonly belied by empirical fact. Here good theory is that which makes sense of the facts and is in turn confirmed by the findings. Moreover there is often a pleasing regularity about physical phenomena which, once one has learnt the rules, makes extrapolation and prediction relatively simple. Human affairs, by contrast, tend to be more complex. The results of human action, whether rational or otherwise, cannot be studied as though they were just 'given' like the phenomena studied in empirical science. But even less can the psychological determinants of human action be so studied. Among these determinants is human language.

Ironically, these fundamental distinctions—between what is given in nature and what is humanly contrived, and between empirical and purely theoretical inquiry—were long ago made explicit by Greek thinkers of both the idealist and the naturalist traditions. Plato and Aristotle commonly distinguished between the phenomena of nature and the results of human action—a distinction which eludes so many modern theorists—and Plato systematically argued the case for a purely theoretical kind of inquiry. He explicitly repudiated the suggestion that such theoretical inquiry is in any way inferior to empirical inquiry or more dependent on 'images'. Plato seems to have been the first to grasp that even empirical science is theory-dependent. Again, the essential role of language as the very condition of rational thought was a leitmotif of Greek philosophy. The link between language and theoretical knowledge, which is implicit in the word *logos*, was more than hinted at by Plato, but in the naturalist tradition it became fully explicit. For the Epicureans there were two main types of inquiry: one deals with things, the other being 'purely linguistic'. Even in the later theological tradition the insight was not lost. For Aquinas, knowledge of things *in verbo* (i.e. conceptualized knowledge) was more thorough and complete than knowledge of things *in propria natura* (i.e. pre-conceptual knowledge.)[2]

Failure to grasp the essentially theoretical nature of the inquiry is the basic error of modern language theory and accounts for the bogus empiricism that now dominates human studies in general: so fundamental is a proper understanding of language to all else in this area. This error, however, is supported by many others that have taken on the character of orthodoxy. Among these is the refusal to study language as part of the general study of human life, behaviour and culture, and in the larger context of animal behaviour and intelligence in general; or, where the attempt has been made, the failure to set such studies in a proper evolutionary perspective. Many theorists insist on studying language as though it were a pure formalism or abstract system, divorced not only from its origins—a problem we shall find to be much less intractable than is usually thought— but also from its vital associations and multiple connections: with human purpose, other people, and the vast range of things, situations, possibilities and so on to which our words relate. This error comes from taking as the subject matter or basis of language theory, not live speech, but the decontextualized forms of written language, a late arrival in the history of our subject.

Not unrelated to this view, which presents language as a ready-made system, is the notion that language is somehow isomorphic with the reality to which it refers. A naive version of this view is that language simply copies reality, rather as reality, in a similarly naive theory of perception, simply imprints itself on the mind, as on a photographic plate. A more sophisticated version is that isomorphisms exist between all three: language, reality, and mind or thought. This way of thinking is closely related to the visual bias and reliance on neat analogies which dominate so much of our thought, and which explain the proliferation of image and picture theories in psychology and epistemology. Ironically enough, serious theorizing about language began with the refutation of all such notions by Gorgias, the ancient Sophist. What we *say* cannot really be like what we *think*, and what we *think* cannot really be like what we *see* or otherwise experience. How, he asked, can an individual *say* in words what he *sees* with his eyes, and so communicate or transfer to others what is in fact merely his own subjective experience? Here for the first time in the western tradition the complexity of the relationship between language, thought, and reality was explicitly referred to, along with the attendant problems of the subjective nature and relativity of knowledge. Gorgias raised, but did not solve, the very problems with which any serious epistemology or language theory must concern itself.[3]

In response to this challenge, which made the inescapable subjectivity of personal experience an argument against the possibility of objective thought, the more subtle thinkers, idealists and naturalists alike, saw that there must be 'a third something'—a term used by both Plotinus and Kant—which somehow mediates between sense experience and thought, and lays the foundation of objective knowledge and rational discourse. But while the idealists left this 'third something' a metaphysical mystery, many naturalist thinkers such as Hobbes and Condillac grasped that this mediating function was initially effected by signs, and, at the human level, by words, by language.[4]

Here, however, a new problem arose. For the difference between signs, to which animals and humans respond alike, and words or symbols, which are the distinctive constituents of human language, remained obscure. Here neither faction had a monopoly of the truth. The idealists saw the difference between animal and human behaviour in this area but failed to see any continuity. The naturalists saw the continuity but failed to see any essential difference. There is much to be learned from this age-old antagonism. Indeed, if we consider the three main traditions of western thought—idealism, naturalism, scepticism—we discover that each has a great strength and a great weakness. The sceptics of all periods raise the most radical and critical problems, but seem committed to the belief that they are insoluble. The great idealists rightly seek to protect human knowledge and ethical values against the corrosive effect of scepticism, but the rational standards they seek to establish rest on nothing better than vaporous metaphysics and flights of mysticism, which cut man off from his roots and from the rest of nature. The naturalists rightly seek to ground human knowledge on a firm basis, tracing it back to its origins and antecedents, but tend to be epistemologically naive, confusing human knowledge and rationality with animal intelligence at large. These three traditions have always traded on one another's weaknesses, whereas what is needed is to combine their virtues and discard their absurdities. Only then may we lay the ghost of idealism, while still accepting its lofty ideals; dismiss the sceptics, while acknowledging the radical importance of the problems they raised; and embrace a naturalism that no longer wears the mask of Caliban.

Returning to our catalogue of errors, perhaps the most common of all is the failure to grasp that language is *sui generis*, or the attempt to make it a form of something else: of expression, communication, behaviour, or animal intelligence. The error here is failure to see that while language emerges as a unique combination of all these things, and much besides, it cannot be reduced to any one of its ingredients or functions; nor can it be understood in terms of any one of its derivatives: writing, grammar, mathematics. Language can be understood only when we identify its originative principle, symbolization, trace its antecedents, and follow its developments.

In contrast to such reductionist views is the hypothesis that language is indeed *sui generis*, being a free creation of the human mind. However, if we make any serious distinction between mind and animal intelligence, and if it turns out that the learning and use of language are constitutive factors in the genesis of what we call mind, then clearly this view must be wrong. Moreoever, if true, it would leave us with two insoluble problems since the concept of mind, no less than that of language, would then become immune to theoretical explanation. To make matters worse, this old metaphysical doctrine, which made language a mysterious emanation of mind or soul, has been reformulated in modern pseudo-scientific versions. In one of these, language (the nature of which is left conveniently undefined) is the product of some putative speech area of the brain. In another, language is identified with a mysterious universal grammar, allegedly common to all languages and embedded in all minds, and an emanation, no longer of the soul, but of the genes. These views are reminiscent of an earlier doctrine according to which thought was 'a secretion of the brain', but one which, unlike other secretions, proved recalcitrant to empirical scrutiny. Modern irrationalism is due, in no small measure, to the importation of such pseudo-scientific notions into the humanities.

This brings us back to our initial theme, the relation between empirical science and the humanities. More precisely, to the difference between the study (by man) of natural phenomena in general, and the study (by man also) of those subjects in which man himself, human motivation and purpose, human aspirations and limitations, human knowledge and understanding, human welfare and survival, are not merely incidental to the inquiry but constitute its very subject matter. We thus come to what has been called the problem of demarcation between natural science and the humanities, but is really the problem of bridging the gap between them. For if man is part of nature, and also the student, not only of impersonal physical and biological processes, but also of his own nature and faculties, then there must be a point at which the conventional barrier between natural science and the humanities breaks down. There are in fact two theories that converge at this very point. One is the theory of evolution, which takes for its province the systematic study of all biological phenomena whatever, and which, in Medawar's phrase, 'permeates and supports every branch of biological science'.[5] The other is the theory of language, a biological 'phenomenon' which permeates and supports the life of man, and is the precondition of his distinctive intellectual faculties: being the means by which all theories, including the theory of evolution, are formulated, and so make intelligible the matters with which they deal.

How this more special theory relates to the more general one is a matter that has not been sufficiently considered. The result is that we have not only an imperfect theory of evolution, which has so far proved inadequate to account for the mental and intellectual faculties of man; but we also lack an adequate theory of language, the complexities of which become intelligible only when viewed in an evolutionary perspective. The marriage of these two disciplines—evolution theory and language theory—promises, therefore, to be of advantage to both. Moreover, since an adequate theory of language is the principal prerequisite for an adequate theory of knowledge in general, the fruits of the proposed union promise to be of more than merely academic interest.

2

Language and evolution

What we need is not description of phenomena, but disclosure of the principles of their development. PAVLOV

Much that is puzzling about man can be understood only when man is considered as evolved and evolving. A thorough knowledge of the principles and mechanisms of evolution is therefore a prerequisite for the understanding of man. ERNST MAYR

After 123 years, Darwinism is still a controversial issue. WILMA GEORGE

No two subjects have been more disastrously misunderstood than language and evolution. For if language plays a key role in the emergence and development of human thought and understanding, evolution theory provides the only scientific explanation of the emergence and development of human life as such. No two subjects could be of greater human importance. Yet the relation between them has never been clarified. We possess no systematic theory of language; and as for the psychological side of human evolution, the subject remains very largely where Darwin left it a century ago. Indeed, some of Darwin's finest insights have been widely neglected, and others misconstrued. And while modern genetics has richly confirmed and developed one part of evolution theory, over-emphasis on genetic factors to the exclusion of others has led to serious distortions of the finely balanced theory that Darwin proposed.

The situation is doubly paradoxical. For although the importance of language is a dominant theme of modern thought, where this importance lies seems to elude all theorists. And while we are assured that no serious biologist doubts the validity of evolution theory, its impact on the serious study of human life has been negligible, although it has often been made to subserve the most absurd and nefarious doctrines for purely ideological purposes. There is scarcely any topic in either language theory or evolution theory on which the most discordant views are not canvassed by supposedly competent persons. To make matters worse, language theory has lately become infected with ill-conceived notions of genetic determinism, while the true evolutionary importance of language—understanding of which is needed to expel such notions—remains quite unaccounted for. To remedy this state of affairs we require not new facts—we have as many as we need—but better theory, based on sound principles.

In order to relate language theory and evolution theory we have only to seek out the area where they meet. In evolutionary terms this is *adaptation*, a term that covers all that mediates between life and the world around it. More especially, and in psychological terms, we are concerned with two distinctive forms of adaptation: perceptual orientation and behavioural control. Unlike fangs, claws and furry coats, which are genetically determined *organic* adaptations, perception and behaviour permit the emergence of progressively more complex *functional* adaptations, so different in kind from purely organic adaptation that they demand quite new theoretical principles if they are to be understood. Their adaptational effect, for example, may be immediate, is highly variable, and may come progressively under a creature's own control, thus conferring high survival value on individual intelligence; whereas organic adaptations may take millions of years to arrive, and are what a creature is born with and cannot change. Together, perceptual orientation and behavioural control constitute the most distinctive adaptations of all higher forms of life. Although dependent on more basic organic factors and instinctual adaptations, they cannot be reduced to these. Where we are concerned with the emergence of novelty, as in evolution theory, the patent absurdity of reductionism hardly needs to be stressed. Perceptual orientation is much more than sensation, and behavioural control much more than reflex action. The combined effects of these faculties we call knowledge, which is at once a store of information and a repertoire of skills and strategies. The ability to acquire new knowledge we speak of as learning, and the ability to learn, and so expand the store of knowledge, is what we call intelligence, whether animal or human.

All learning and all higher forms of knowledge come about as a result of behaviour which is sign-mediated, that is dependent on signs and signals which enable animals not only to communicate and receive information from one another, but also to acquire information from their environment. It is this complex of pre-existent and interrelated factors—perception, behaviour, signs, signals, learning ability, communication—that sets the stage of language. Even before we see how language originates, then, we would expect that it will be a complex, emergent phenomenon, the origin and nature of which can be understood only within its evolutionary context. Also that it will be in every sense a synthetic phenomenon, quite unlike any pre-existent forms of perception, behaviour, or communication, out of which it is compounded. This is confirmed by the facts that language is clearly a late arrival on the evolutionary stage, serving no immediate vital need; that its function is not directly causal but symbolically mediated; that its effect is likewise mediated, being dependent not on a physical stimulus as such, but on some stimulus which is *interpreted as significant* of something else; and finally, that each of the organs involved in the production and interpretation of language has a biological function which is prior to, and independent of, its function in the build-up of language. Hence, recent attempts to make language a ready-made genetic endowment, rather than the end-product of a complex learning process, betray ignorance both of the complexity of language and of the nature of evolutionary processes. Likewise, the temptation to make human consciousness or mind a simple function of the brain reveals a failure to grasp the dependence of human intelligence on language, itself a complex outgrowth of prior perceptual and behavioural factors, these in turn largely determined by experience of the external world.

Such theories are in fact more primitive than the crude behaviourist view of language which at least took note of its behavioural origin. Behaviourists however are notoriously weak on perception, which is another precondition of language. What most theorists fail to grasp is that language is neither genetically determined nor empirically given, neither a ready-made system to be passively acquired nor a form of behaviour to be simply mimicked. It is something that has to be built up out of the perception, behaviour and experience of each individual, with whatever aid he or she receives from other members of the same speech community. Only in such a process do the verbal forms of any given language come to have meaning. These forms, which differ from one language to another, have no intrinsic meaning. They are devices established by use and convention which, in addition to their utility for communication, are the means by which each individual learns, well or ill, to monitor, reflect on and understand his own experience. In so doing we acquire a new symbolic orientation which augments, refines, and utterly transforms the initial sensory orientation that comes with perceptual awareness and feedback from behaviour.

Fortunately, therefore, if we are to explain the origin and nature of language we must turn, not to genetics and neurology, which are the preserve of the few, but to much more familiar areas of experience. These however need to be understood in their proper evolutionary context, and it is here that difficulties arise. Before approaching the language problem proper, therefore, we must look at the present state of evolution theory and some of its ills.

Nothing broadens the mind like the theory of evolution, for it is—or rather should be—the theory of life itself, in all its aspects. Only physics and cosmology have a broader sweep, and they do not touch us quite so directly. Contrary to popular misconception, evolution concerns not only the fossil record of reptiles but also the future of man; not only the origin of species but also their survival and extinction, topics which daily take on new significance. The theory however has never been widely accepted and has rarely been understood. As Darlington said, it had a rough time in the nineteenth century and has not had a much easier passage through the twentieth.[1] Today, opposition to the theory is as strong as ever, and ignorance of its true significance almost universal, even among biologists. Opposition to evolution theory has always been strong in philosophical circles, a fact which accounts for the anachronism and irrelevance of most writing in this field over the past century. Wittgenstein affirmed that the Darwinian theory had no more to do with philosophy than any other 'hypothesis of natural science'.[2] Human thought was thus cut off from its biological roots and philosophy made safe for futile speculation. Yet we shall later see that the central epistemological and ethical questions of philosophy cannot be intelligently asked or answered in any other than evolutionary terms.

The influence of Wittgenstein is still strong. But even Popper, who deplores this influence and claims to be a philosopher of science, plainly states that he does 'not think highly of the theoretical or explanatory power of the theory of evolution', which he describes as a 'metaphysical research programme'.[3] More alarming is the steady stream of physicists, chemists, biologists and other natural scientists who propose non-natural explanations in biology, or wish to make some special exception to normal explanatory procedures in the case of man or of human consciousness. Others, by contrast, overplay their biological hand, hypostatize all higher mental faculties, and attribute them without more ado to some area of the brain; or, more modishly, to the genes.[4] Thus Lorenz assures us, without adducing a shred of evidence, that language learning is 'based on a phylogenetic programme which ensures that the child's innate power of abstract thought is integrated with the vocabulary that belongs to its cultural tradition'.[5] And J. Z. Young opines that we are 'programmed' not only for language but even for worshipping.[6]

All such speculation is anti-evolutionary in character. The

gradual emergence of the higher faculties and more complex forms of behaviour cannot be explained in this way. Evolution theory is at all times concerned with life-forms interacting with their environments. This means that environmental factors are as important as purely physiological ones; and further, that we cannot assess the evolutionary importance of either kind in isolation from the various *mediating* factors that link them. In all higher forms of animal life perceptual and behavioural kinds of mediation assume ever greater evolutionary importance. One complex and uniquely human kind of mediation is language, which is not only a means of social communication but a vehicle of thought, as well as an instrument of analysis and thus of more refined knowledge of the world about us. It is clear that the means of transmission of human culture from one generation to another is to be sought, not in the genes, but in language and derivative symbolisms.[7] But language and its derivatives account for more than the mere transmission of human culture: they enable us to account for its distinctive nature. Central to this essay is the thesis that all human culture and thought presuppose the existence of human language, that all the functions of language are rooted in human speech, that speech emerges quite naturally out of prior forms of behaviour and perception, and that it develops to become an indispensable constituent factor in human consciousness and rationality.

Those who wish to exclude man from the evolutionary scheme, or to make human consciousness a special exception outside that scheme, betray lack of understanding of the most basic principle of evolution, namely that everything in evolution *is* a special case. The theory was initially devised to account for the origin of special cases, usually referred to as species. Being a special case already, then, man no longer needs to be made a special exception. What is needed is not to establish man's special nature, which is obvious enough, but, as Plato saw long ago, the nature of his special faculties. It would, however, be disingenuous to attribute opposition to the theory of evolution to obscurantist misrepresentation, which undoubtedly exists, without noting that as much obscurantism has been generated by advocates of the theory as by its opponents, from Darwin's day down to the present.

Many inferences which even today are drawn from the theory border on absurdity and often overstep the mark. The truth is that the theory of evolution is anything but a well-established theory. As it stands, it is inadequate not only because all its principles and mechanisms have not been clarified, but because in this incomplete state the existing principles and mechanisms are made to do service where they clearly do not apply. This is most obviously the case in all that concerns animal intelligence and human reason. Only recently has this fact become a matter of serious debate. Contrary to popular belief, then, the modern theory of evolution is very modern indeed. It dates in fact from the 1960s when, after the startling revelations of modern genetics had been assimilated, it began to be appreciated that evolution theory was indeed the only basis for an understanding of all forms of life, including our own. Seen in this sense, the theory becomes an education in itself, a veritable philosophy of life: for it must account for *all* that is peculiar to life, and not just its physical basis and genetic origins. That this was the vision of Darwin there can be no doubt, for he followed up *The Origin of Species* with two other notable studies: one dealing with human evolution, the other with those forms of animal and human behaviour that culminate in the emergence of language.[8] In so doing, Darwin clearly indicated the direction in which evolution theory—as we ought to call it at this level—should be developed. Why so few have followed his lead, and with so little success, is a matter that calls for investigation.

One reason has already been touched on. Since modern genetics came of age there has been a tendency to see evolution theory as a mere appendage of molecular biology. Thus the one theory that could effect a rapprochement between natural science and the humanities was made a new barrier between them. Major responsibility for this, however, lies not so much with the biologists as with theorists in psychology, linguistics, and epistemology, who seem to be utterly unaware of the relevance of evolution to their chosen disciplines. As a result, the main deficiency of contemporary evolution theory is failure to account for what must be two of the most dramatic evolutionary shifts of all: the emergence of animal intelligence, and of human rationality. One advantage of an evolutionary theory of language is that it helps solve both problems at the same time, since rationality can be explained only in terms of language theory, and the origin and function of language can be explained only in terms of more general principles of animal intelligence.

Before we come to this, however, we need to consider other errors and misconceptions which have come to cluster around evolution theory like a mythology. (Similar mythologies sprang up around classical mechanics, relativity, and quantum theory, doing them no harm whatever. But in the case of evolution, the errors have become a serious obstacle to advance within the theory itself.) First is the belief that evolutionary thinking was the invention of Darwin or his immediate predecessors. In fact it is implicit in totemism and much primitive mythology, and was a commonplace of Greek naturalism and all schools of thought influenced by it down the centuries. We understand things best, said Aristotle, if we trace them back to their origins and then follow them in their development. This is a basic principle of all historical inquiry, and indeed of common sense, not to mention geology which played so crucial a role in the genesis of Darwin's theory. Darwin's stroke of genius was to apply this principle systematically to the entire field of biology.

Another error is the belief that evolution theory is descriptive but hopelessly incomplete. This view reveals total incomprehension of the nature of theory. The function of theory is not to describe but to explain: to explain, on the basis of clearly formulated and coherent principles, whatever needs to be explained in a given area of inquiry; if need be, by the discovery of supplementary principles. All good theory makes provision for its own improvement. If contemporary evolution theory is defective, then it is up to the evolutionists to discover the missing explanatory principles: most importantly, those which will account for the origin of language and the emergence of mind.

Yet another misconception is the belief that evolution theory deals exclusively with organic aspects of evolution. This runs counter to Darwin's life-long concern with the behavioural and mental aspects of the theory, with problems of animal behaviour, mind and man. Equally unfounded is the notion that evolution theory implies determinism. It is in fact the only theory capable of explaining the emergence not only of rationality, but of that kind of rational choice we call freedom. It is indeed the most curious of all misconceptions of evolution theory to think that it has no place for value, meaning, purpose, freedom, ethics or reason, since it is the only theory that can dispel the metaphysical fog that surrounds these concepts, explain each individually, and clarify their systematic interconnection. To begin this task, something must here be said on the nature of evolutionary causality and explanation, and on the notion of value.

The distinctive feature of evolutionary explanations, unlike those in physics but very like those in history, is less to trace the regularities and continuities which clearly underlie all change, than to account for critical developments and turning-points which create new and quite unforeseeable possibilities.[9] Evolutionary causality is quite unlike physical or mechanical causality in that it must explain novel and often extremely complex developments in terms of a mix of factors so heterogeneous and incommensurable that no physical scientist would dare approach. Such explanation is achieved by showing that each of these factors is a necessary precondition for the emergence of some given development. The emergence of human language, consciousness, mind and reason must be explained in just this way.

Since the theory of evolution was expressly designed to explain events which occurred long ago, it is one of the more bizarre misconceptions of the theory (and indeed of science) to deny it scientific status on the ground that it does not admit of prediction. But the fact that evolutionary explanations account for the emergence of novelty only *after* the event is not to be construed as a weakness. For the understanding they bring provides insight into a vast range of new possibilities, into a limitless range of possible consequences. Thus, to understand language is, potentially, to understand all that it makes possible: nothing less than the totality of human culture, and much besides. For part of human culture is of course natural science, our understanding of nature itself.

Next a word about value, its place in evolution theory, and the modern confusion concerning value judgments. It is curious that while Samuel Alexander once described evolution theory as 'the natural history of value',[10] many modern evolutionists seem to think value has no place in the evolutionary scheme at all. Yet value is implicit not only in conscious human choice, and in animal goal-seeking behaviour (since goals are values): it is implicit in *all* behaviour, and in the interest most creatures have in their own survival. Life is a process deeply committed to its own continuance. In biological terms, survival or the continuance of life is the value or end to which all other things are necessarily viewed as means. The formula *omnis natura vult esse conservatrix sui* was quoted by Cicero as already an ancient maxim.[11] Sherrington speaks of self-conservation as a principle 'innate in the individual' and 'implicit in life'.[12] Moreoever, insofar as the concept of behaviour is distinguishable from mere animal movement, it can only be defined in terms of some value or end, with reference to which other things are defined as means. The higher we ascend in the evolutionary scale, the greater the complexity of behavioural means to achieve ever more complex ends, and the greater the importance of perceptual orientation, and ultimately of rational thought, to discover not only new means to achieve the same ends, but also new ends and values. Naturally these processes are instinctive long before they become consciously controlled. The greater the need therefore to distinguish between different grades of behaviour: instinctive reflex action, behaviour dependent on perceptual awareness and learning at the animal level, behaviour which is under conscious but uncritical human control, and behaviour which is the result of rational contrivance. Only when we grasp the continuity between these different forms of behaviour, how each stage develops out of a more primitive one, does the barrier between natural science and the humanities begin to crumble. The notion of science, so long identified with the principles of physical science, must be expanded to accommodate principles adequate to the study not only of the organic aspects of life, but also of such important matters as behaviour, learning, intelligence and reason.

The situation initially appears paradoxical. Both physical and biological science are in fact manifestations of human rationality. Yet rationality must itself be brought within the ambit of biological theory if we are to understand its nature. The paradox thus disappears, to become the evolutionary problem of the origin and nature of human thought and reason. Until this problem is solved we shall remain unsure about the nature of human intelligence, but equally we shall have a defective theory of evolution. Only when we see evolution theory as the theory of life in *all* its aspects, from its remote origins to its highest manifestations, will the long-desired unification of sciences and humanities become feasible. The notions of value, purpose and meaning are here crucial, as we shall see. For while they have no part in the subject matter of purely physical science, they acquire ever greater importance in biology and evolution theory. If Samuel Alexander referred to evolution theory as the natural history of value, it remains to be shown that the same theory can provide what may be called 'the natural history of mind'.

Before leaving the topic of value a word may be said on the positivist superstition that value judgments are sinful: merely emotive, subjective, invalid. This view is utterly misconceived. No judgment, no statement, can be other than subjective, that is, made by a human subject. The question of its objective value or truth is quite a separate issue. Nor is it possible to make any judgment whatever without some criterion, value, norm, standard or principle whereby we judge, and which must be made explicit on demand. Only thus can judgments be validated, or exposed as valueless. Both Plato and Kant grasped that there must be some *a priori* normative element in any valid judgment, but neither was able to explain it in other than metaphysical terms. Yet each came within an ace of seeing that it is the normative function implicit in the use of language which creates our logical and theoretical norms.[13] Theoretical norms, which are wholly language-dependent, are of course more ideal than material norms. Yet even the latter—say a yardstick or a pint measure—are 'ideal' in that their value resides not in their physical nature but in the purposes which, by human convention, they serve. It is perhaps here that the crucial difference between real or empirical *object* and ideal or symbolic *value* is most easily grasped, as well as the manner in which a real object comes to take on symbolic value. The words of language also must have a real existence, but to study them is not empirical science, since their utility and value lie not in their actual forms, which obviously differ from language to language, but in their symbolic meanings, that is, their human utility, which obviously cuts across all language barriers.

Values, then, are by no means the irrelevance the naive empiricist would have us believe. They are not only as fit a subject of systematic study as any other, but in the study of all higher forms of life, value and related concepts—purpose, meaning, symbolic norm—constitute the chief problem area, and cannot be studied as though they were empirical phenomena. The laborious attempt to account for human knowledge and behaviour by techniques proper to physics and chemistry has long been a tedious charade.

The more distinguished evolutionists avoid such crass reductionism. For Darwin 'the advancement of the intellectual powers' of man was part of the evolutionary process. He saw also that his theory alone could provide the basis for a genuinely universal ethic embracing all mankind.[14] Perversions of his theory which reduce man to bestial status suffer from a fatal flaw. It is that while claiming to be evolutionary theories they utterly fail to take note of the distinctive evolution of man. The result is a plethora of determinist hypotheses which attribute anything that smacks of human consciousness or culture directly to the genes or the brain. We have already noted the anti-evolutionary character of such views, which precludes them from offering any rational explanation of the genesis either of human consciousness or of human culture. Since neither is conceivable without the prior emergence of language it is clear that only an evolutionary theory of language can help us here, and this is no task for the geneticist. As for hypotheses which would make consciousness a simple product of the brain, Eccles and other competent specialists have made clear that nothing we know or can hope to know about the brain can throw any light on the problem of consciousness.[15] Sherrington puts the matter bluntly: the body-mind relation is a 'liaison between two incommensurable factors'. Brain and mind belong to utterly different realms of discourse. The brain is a physical organ studied by physiologists, while mind, objectively viewed, is always 'an inference from behaviour'.[16] It is true that Eccles then drew mystical inferences from all this, and Sherrington was content to settle for an ultimate dualism. But neither of these conclusions is necessary once we understand the role of language in the genesis of what we call mind.

Mind, human intelligence, clearly makes man unique in that he not merely adapts to his environment or tampers with it as other creatures do, but radically transforms it by conscious design. Human intelligence, then, is clearly more than mere animal intelligence. But how does it arise? How for that matter does animal intelligence arise? The problem of the relations between awareness, behaviour, intelligence and thought is still unresolved, and the source of endless polemics. Certain assumptions have always barred progress in this field. Human consciousness has either been equated with animal awareness because of the obvious links; or severed from it because of the obvious differences. Both views betray ignorance of the central virtue of evolution theory: that it enables us to understand the emergence of radical novelty on the basis of underlying continuities, to see how new processes and potentialities are based on, continuous with, but not reducible to, others which precede them, and even continue alongside. The most primitive organisms and processes subsist alongside the most evolved.

Another source of error is that awareness and consciousness are commonly divorced from, and even given priority over, behaviour. This is the essential weakness of all philosophical idealism. Yet behaviour, which is initially no more than animal movement, is itself the most basic source of knowledge, through feedback from the environment in which an animal moves: and this long before we come to anything we might call awareness, consciousness, or mind. Behaviour, as Sherrington and Pavlov clearly saw, begins as reflex action, and all higher forms of behaviour develop out of this.

Underlying most of the misconceptions of evolution theory

is a confusion as to the nature of biology as such. The term is ambiguous. Biology in the narrow sense is biochemistry, genetics, physiology and the like, established scientific disciplines of immense importance. The word *bios* however is simply Greek for *life*. Biology in the broader sense is the systematic study of life as a whole, life in the round, life as a multiplicity of processes developing through time in actual environments: each life form needing to be studied in its distinctive character and modes of adaptation to, and control of, such environments. This is the subject matter of evolution theory as distinct from biology in the narrow sense.[17] Among such life processes is our own, which for all its diversity is identifiably of a special kind, and which for all its similarity to other life forms is unquestionably unique. That this more general, evolutionary biology should be deemed less worthy of study than genetics or physiology, or that its study be thought less scientific, is a prejudice among biologists of the narrower sort, who in this give succour to all—and they are many—who would make the study of man the special province of obscurantism. It must be granted, however, that this belief is encouraged by the failure of modern evolutionists to establish this larger discipline on objective principles; by their regrettable habit of applying the principles of organic evolution indiscriminately to all aspects of human behaviour and thought; and by their tendency to provide instant and highly unconvincing explanations of everything in life in terms of 'selection pressures'. Where Darwin saw 'no law of necessary development' in evolution, many of his would-be followers seem to see nothing else.[18] Yet between organic evolution and human culture—institutions, laws, education, technology and the like—there is such a distance that the principles proper to the former—selection, adaptation, fitness—cannot be applied to the latter without more ado. It is no mere matter of time-scale or complexity that is at issue. One cannot leap from the organic to the cultural without some grasp of the difference between *organic adaptations*, like fangs and furry coats, and *behavioural adaptability*, which is virtually synonymous with animal intelligence; nor without a firm grasp of the difference between animal intelligence and human rationality. And insofar as the latter is dependent on the emergence of language, language theory becomes indispensable for any understanding of what is vaguely referred to as 'cultural evolution'. The term, condemned by Darlington, is misleading. It would be more proper to speak of cultural behaviour and adaptations (e.g. wearing clothes, cooking food, living in houses); and, to avoid the myth of automatic progress, of cultural history.

Failure to emphasize behavioural adaptability as a distinctive evolutionary *principle*, quite different from any other form of adaptation, has had unfortunate consequences. For it is only through behaviour and the related concept of *learning* that we can approach the more difficult problems of intelligence and mind. Behaviour also leads us straight into the problem zone of teleology and purpose. While every conceivable misconception of *purpose* has been read into biology and nature at large, it has not been commonly noted that the only thing which is teleological by definition is in fact behaviour. Behaviour is most simply defined as the adoption of *means* towards some *end*. (The double meaning of both *telos* and *end* is no accident.) This is as true of the most instinctive animal reflex action as it is of a human action consciously based on moral principle. It is not the least task of evolution theory to trace the continuity between these two extremes.

The relative neglect of behavioural adaptability is strange for another reason: behaviour is the most obvious characteristic of animal life as such. Unlike trees, animals move about and do things. Ernst Mayr has called behaviour the pace-maker and probably the most important factor in animal evolution, noting that hominid evolution has been especially rich in behavioural shifts, all the way from arboreal habitat to industrial civilization.[19] Despite this, in some surveys of evolution theory behaviour does not even rank as an evolutionary principle at all. The gravity of this omission is only matched by two others: the omission of language theory, which alone can account for the distinctive evolution of human intelligence or mind; and omission of the topic of neoteny, which is a key factor in the evolution of man and in the emergence of language.[20] All this explains why no evolutionary treatise has advanced beyond Darwin in dealing with the higher mental faculties. For Darwin dealt not only with behaviour, but with expressive and communicative behaviour, and even established the dependence of the latter on the former. He further saw that communication by language was 'of paramount importance in the development of man'.[21] In all of which he was a century ahead of his time. He saw that evolution is not merely a continuous development. There are quite distinct *stages* of evolutionary advance, each of which must be described in its distinctive character, explained in terms of the antecedents that make it possible, and understood in terms of the advantages and new potential that come with it.

The truth is that many evolutionists have a weakness for the larger vision. There is of course grandeur in the view which condenses millions of years and the teeming life of innumerable species—extant, extinct, and yet to emerge—within the confines of an abstract formula in which all aspects of all environments become 'the environment', and all conceivable adaptations—physical, behavioural, cultural—are simply 'adaptation'. If however we wish to know what goes on between the origin and extinction of any given species—say our own—then the very vastness of such abstractions becomes a liability. For 'the environment' is nothing less than the totality of factors external to any organism at any time: anything from a louse to an ice age, not forgetting the solar system. Those condemned to work with more precise concepts may well feel envious of such latitude. When, however, we come to 'adaptation' serious ambiguities arise. The term may refer to such critical turning points as the adaptation of sea creatures to the land, or of land creatures to the air, the adaptation of a particular species to an ecological niche, organic adaptations of every sort, the behavioural adaptations of animals, and the cultural adaptations of man. Here, if we are to avoid absurdity, we must first make a radical distinction between organic adaptations, which arise not in response to need but prior to their own utility, which alone decides their survival value; and behavioural adaptations, which admit of limitless variation, flexibility and new developments, may be initiated by individuals as immediate response to environmental challenge, and thereafter imitated, taught or culturally transmitted. It hardly makes sense to speak of organic and behavioural adaptation in the same breath.

But even when we make behaviour an evolutionary topic in its own right our troubles are far from over. For behaviour is a vaster abstraction than either environment or adaptation. Behaviour is any animal movement, or the lack of it, or any aspect of it— inception, continuance, change, cessation—which can be viewed as means to some end or advantage, real or imagined. Behaviour is anything that any creature does, has done, may do, or even not do, at any time in any circumstances. To deal descriptively with all that, and then classify the results, must seem a daunting task to any theorist foolish enough to approach matters in this way. Nothing illustrates better the hopelessness of a purely descriptive approach in psychology and the humanities, or the futility of naive empiricism in such areas. Nothing illustrates better the need for guiding principles in all such inquiry, the need for establishing criteria for the choice of such principles, and the unique validity, in all that concerns the study of life, of evolutionary principles, and of a method which traces things back to their origins and then follows them in the order in which they develop.

In the study of behaviour four criteria seem relevant: the order of emergence of behavioural characteristics, the antecedents of each, its distinctive novelty, and the benefits it confers. It is of course these last, the limitless new potentialities that come with behavioural innovation, that constitute its evolutionary importance and make it imperative that we isolate behaviour as a distinct theoretical principle. Attempts to account for all aspects of life in terms of genetic variation and natural selection have increasingly brought evolution theory into disrepute. Darwin invoked the principles of genetic variation (of which he knew little more than that it occurs, but that was enough for his purpose) and natural selection in order to explain the origin of species, and of course their extinction. The modern mania of attempting to explain all that comes beween these two extremes in terms of the same two principles leads straight to absurdity. For now the notion of adaptation, which initially meant no more than successful adjustment and thus survival, is made to do service where it is both inadequate and misleading. Involved in the complex notion of adaptation are not only organic and environmental factors, but also behavioural factors which *mediate* between the two but cannot be reduced to either. Many of the ills of modern evolution theory are rooted in confusion of these interrelated but quite distinct principles.

Behaviour, then, is of immense importance in evolution theory, since along with perception it brings us to a distinctive kind of adaptation: that which concerns *psychological* forms of mediation between living creatures and their world. Together, behavioural feedback and perceptual information first constitute what we call knowledge. (The verbs *can*, indicating behavioural ability, *ken*, and *know* are all cognate forms.) Knowledge is the chief evolutionary advantage of all higher forms of life, the key to man's evolutionary hegemony and—by one of those ironic turns of fate—to his possible self-destruction.

The greater the need, therefore, to provide a theory of human knowledge which will clarify its origin in simple forms of semantic behaviour and sign perception which combine to produce language, and clarify also how language first creates the possibility of conceptual thought. It is to be regretted, then, that epistemology—the general theory of knowledge—has never been made an evolutionary topic. Epistemology has usually been relegated to metaphysics—a discipline whose subject matter has never been satisfactorily defined—and abandoned to theorists who are either ignorant of evolutionary principles or resolutely opposed to them. Fiercely guarded and utterly bogus specialisms have been created to preserve this *status quo* by the invention of problems which, if set in a proper evolutionary perspective, are seen to be wholly illusory and factitious. To remedy this state of affairs we clearly need a rational epistemology based on evolutionary principles, including those which account for behaviour and perception as the primary sources of learning and knowledge. What has so far appeared less obvious is that we also need an evolutionary theory of *language*, the locus where all these things—behaviour, perception, learning and knowledge—meet and lay the foundations of human intelligence and rational thought.

Darwin wrote of his *Origin of Species* that it was one long argument from the beginning to the end. In this he showed that his grasp of logic was not less than his grasp of fact. He saw that it was impossible to explain the extraordinary wealth of facts that his unceasing research had revealed otherwise than by establishing principles to correlate them, and by then co-ordinating these principles into a coherent theory. In an endeavour of this kind he has never been surpassed, and the magnitude of his achievement has never been adequately appreciated. All scientific theory must be logical, but what distinguishes evolution theory is that it is not the theory of a single discipline, but a logical theory that co-ordinates the findings of many disciplines—botany, zoology, anatomy, physiology, biochemistry, geology, paleontology and so forth—along with all we know about life in general. As Darlington has it, our understanding of evolution feeds on the whole of our knowledge of life, and our knowledge of life is bound to feed on our understanding of evolution.[22] Attempts to discredit evolution theory, strenuous efforts to exclude human life from its purview, have hitherto had the excuse that the theory has so far proved inadequate to account for the higher faculties of man. What is needed, therefore, is to enlarge the theory by the provision of principles—psychological, linguistic, logical and epistemological—adequate to account for the unique nature of human life, mind and reason.

But if this extended theory is to be logically coherent, where might the evolutionist turn for logical guidance? Not to academic philosophy as practised today; least of all to academic logicians, who since the time of Frege and Russell have laboured under the delusion that logic is a branch of mathematics. Academic logic, like academic linguistics, is indeed one of the last bastions of idealist metaphysics. Fortunately, the evolutionist has the solution on his own doorstep, in the theory of evolution itself.

The construction of valid theory, at which Darwin excelled, is itself one main function of logic (the other being critical analysis and correction of existing theory, or of logically connected discourse in general). But there are closer ties between evolution and logic which are far from accidental. Logic, like evolution, is also very much a matter of priorities, preconditions, preclusions, connections, consequences, continuities and discontinuities, of relations between the general and the particular. It is curious to note that these two words—general and particular—have etymological connections with the notions of genesis and birth; and that throughout the Indo-European languages there is a recurrent link-up between words like our *kin*, *ken*, *know*, *kind* (and many others derived from the same root). Human knowledge is not quite so remote from human life as idealist metaphysicians would have us believe: it originates, not as an intellectual affair, but more humbly through familiarity with people and things. This is the source of all our categories, or *kinds* of things, which, once fixed or symbolized in language, form the basis on which all higher knowledge must build.

However, because evolution theory is itself a logical theory—indeed the only theory capable of explaining the genesis of logical or any other kind of human thought—it would be a grave error to think that logic itself evolves. If it did, it would be of no theoretical utility whatever. Logic is the only product of evolution which does not change. Not because of some mystical property, however, but because of the human purpose it is meant to serve. We shall later see that logic is a systematic extension of the normative function which is central to language from the start. Logical consistency in use of terms, and logical coherence in the combination of sentences, are the very conditions of any discourse whatever. True, common speech admits of great latitude in the use of words, intelligibility being the sole criterion. Rational theory demands greater rigour. To understand what constitutes rational theory, we must first understand the nature of language, on which all theory rests. But if language is a distinctively *human* faculty, and the basis of all theory, including that of evolution, the evolutionist here comes full circle: he becomes the object of his own inquiry. Put another way, humanity can be brought within the ambit of evolution theory, and a serious deficiency of the theory could thus be corrected, but only if we enlarge the theory by discovering the principles which make the emergence of language and mind intelligible in evolutionary terms.

It is clear, then, that contemporary evolution theory, which is primarily concerned with the organic aspects of evolution, must be expanded to include principles adequate to account not only for the emergence of human language and reason, but also for the prior emergence of animal intelligence as such. Strangely enough, most of the principles required have been a matter of public record for the best part of a century. Yet self-styled evolutionists even today blindly apply the principles of organic evolution in behavioural and psychological areas, where they are clearly inadequate to explain the known facts, thus bringing the whole discipline into ridicule and disrepute. Every aspect of life is glibly 'explained' in terms of genetic variation and selection pressures. There is a profound irony in this. Darwin arrived at the notion of natural selection partly on the basis of Malthus's shrewd insight into the automatic checks on fertility and survival at work in nature, and partly by analogy with selective breeding as practised by English farmers. He saw nature blindly doing what the farmers did with intent, consciously, purposefully, intelligently. That human consciousness, purpose and intelligence should now be reduced to the same blind workings of nature, or equated with the pre-rational behaviour of other animal species, is the absurdity to which certain would-be evolutionists have now reduced Darwin's great theory. This state of affairs can be remedied only by the provision of principles capable of explaining how animal intelligence emerged from more primitive forms of behaviour and perception, and by a systematic account of the origin, primary functions and later developments of language. Only such a theory will explain how animal awareness and intelligence became transformed into human consciousness and reason.

3

The nature and origin of language

One cannot be content with showing how a language could have been invented. One must show how language must have been invented. FICHTE

The half-art, half-instinct of language still bears the stamp of its gradual evolution. DARWIN

If you solve the problem of the nature and origin of language, we can explain the rest: what culture is, and how it made its appearance. LÉVI-STRAUSS

No theory of language is possible unless we make a radical distinction between human *language* as such and the multiplicity of different *languages* that exist and have existed. Apart from the distinction between being and not being, this is probably the most radical distinction we could make. It is more radical even than the distinction between words and things, between the symbolically formulated and the empirically given. For now we are making a distinction between actual symbolic formulations, which are effectively and often unproblematically used by the entire human race, and the nature of symbolic formulation as such, an unresolved problem which underlies all other theoretical problems in the humanities: not only in linguistics, psychology and epistemology, but in ethics, politics, economics, and above all in education, on which all else in the cultural field depends. If the principles of our educational system are corrupt then our entire culture will be corrupt. Many would argue that this is already the case, but seek to repair the damage by reversion to primitive mythologies and other philosophies of despair. In fact, our educational system is extremely healthy in all that concerns empirical science and technology, and corrupt only in those disciplines which concern the study of man. It is in this area, alas, that decisions are made concerning the use and abuse of modern science and technology. There can, therefore, be no question as to where the main problems arise in human affairs, since here all depends on the use and abuse of human intelligence in the furtherance of human purpose. Many errors, and indeed many human conflicts, stem from genuine confusion and misunderstanding concerning our mental faculties. But many also are caused by conscious sophistry and rhetorical manipulation. Whatever the cause, given the constitutive role of language in the distinctive development of human intelligence and subsequent human action, it is clear that an understanding of the origin, nature and proper use of language, and of the many abuses of its logical function, is a precondition of any enlightenment in this area.

There is another reason why we must distinguish between languages and language as such. Different languages superficially divide and isolate human communities and cultures, but human language is the most important thing they have in common. It is recognizably the same in function and utility in all speech communities; and rational thought, which language alone makes possible, is the only means that humans have of understanding their common humanity and their common interests, not least their interest in common survival. To understand language, therefore, is to understand ourselves, not in the trivial sense of knowing our good and bad points, but in the sense of knowing what it is to be human at all. Paradoxical as this may seem, then, the words and constructions of any given language are quite irrelevant to the general theory of language, which must be concerned with the fundamental principles common to all languages, and not with the features which differentiate one language from another. Hence, when we speak of language, without further qualification, we rightly mean not the formal structures of this language or that, but any language at all, as learnt, spoken, heard, understood and misunderstood, and put to various uses by any ordinary speaker. Language in this primary sense, before academic linguists proceed to its dismemberment, is central to human life, and no mere adjunct to human thought and theory, but the necessary precondition of their existence.

Where should we begin the study of so important a subject? This is the only question in our inquiry which answers itself. We begin by asking where we should begin. If we do not, we shall almost certainly begin in the wrong place: with the speech of adults intuitively familiar with all the complexities of language, but totally ignorant of what was involved in the learning of it, and of the extent to which language progressively affects our conscious and unconscious life from the moment we learn to speak. This is a natural error which at least has the virtue of accepting language as a complex affair with many ramifications. Academic linguists, by contrast, fearful of such complexity, tend to cut language down to size, either by reducing it to some simplistic 'paradigm', or by fragmenting its study into a multiplicity of separate subdisciplines. They often make the written language the basis of their theory (a grave error as we shall see), focus on the oddities of particular languages (which are quite irrelevant to the general theory of language), or on an ever increasing number of 'problems' of phonology and syntax (which are largely the product of their own preconceptions). Many prefer to avoid the central topic of meaning and also the origins problem. Thus cut off from its roots and its function, language becomes a topic for ceaseless metaphysical and pseudo-scientific speculation.[1]

Both these views, the naive and the academic, exemplify the same mistake. They approach the language problem from the wrong end. To rectify this we must begin at the beginning. This however cannot mean replacing speculation about language by speculation about the remote origins of man. Quite the contrary, only an adequate theory of language will finally illuminate the anthropological problem, which in many respects remains more or less where Darwin left it. Many later evolutionists have preferred to give humanity a wide berth. Some have even failed to note any special difference between human mind and animal psychology in general. In a theory concerned with the origin and distinctive characteristics of different species this is, at very least, a flaw.

It would however be an error to go to the other extreme and claim that language explains the origin of man. The advantages conferred on man by the emergence of language doubtless explain his hegemony and even his survival as a species. But language also had its origin: and this origin is intelligible only in terms of certain prior and well established facts of morphology and neoteny which are distinctively human. In broadest outline, there is a complex of interrelated factors without which neither language nor the human species would exist: retention of the foetal angle of the head (cranial flexure), upright posture and bipedal gait, infantile dependency, retarded maturation, a protracted growth and learning period with adult protection and influence, and a relatively large brain, favouring the development of complex behavioural and mental skills. All this is well known. Less noted, however, is another related feature, orthognathy—the retention of a flat face with relatively small dentition—which made the human mouth the ideal and indeed the real locus for the origin of language. For speech depends on the unique capability of the human mouth to produce a limitless number of subtly differentiated utterances, any one of which may take on symbolic value and thereafter be used to designate any item or aspect of human experience. Lest these points should appear too obvious to mention, it must be stated that many language theorists have held that language could have originated independently of speech, in gesture for instance. They not only fail to grasp the essential role of *hearing* in the genesis of human language but also misapprehend the complex *symbolic* nature and function of language, which, as we shall see, could emerge only by way of vocal signalling and speech.

The origin of language, then, far from being a matter for speculation about the brain or the genes, is a quite unproblematic matter of anatomy and behaviour. Seen in this light, even the evolutionary problem of dating the origin of language comes close to solution. Language could not have originated before the distinctive development of the human mouth, and we may be fairly sure that it emerged at more or less the same time. The mouth provides the indispensable mechanism of speech. The other—behavioural and perceptual—prerequisites for the origin of language are equally unproblematic, being easily located among more general forms of behaviour and perception, both animal and human.

Infants, Darwin noted, quickly learn the efficacy of vocal utterance and soon turn it to their own advantage. If screaming is found to attract attention and solace, this is a bonus which initially the infant could not have foreseen but soon learns to obtain by the same device.[2] Animals also, he observed, soon learn to get rewards by similar means. Among his many achievements, Darwin laid the foundation of modern ethology, the study of the natural behaviour of animals, which until lately has been overshadowed by behaviourism, the study of animal and, alas, human behaviour as manipulated and misinterpreted by man. It was one of Darwin's profoundest insights that communication of meaning by expressive gesture is the spin-off of prior and quite independent forms of natural behaviour. He clarified what we may call the principle of *semantic efficacy* or *semantic behaviour*. Animals readily learn which of their natural forms of behaviour have beneficial semantic effects. The spreading of wings is a precondition of flight, but may come to signal aggression or threat in the face of danger. If this suffices to ward off danger, then actual flight may be substituted by semantic gesture. Such gestures become habitual and reinforced by success, or are eliminated as result of failure.

Semantic efficacy must not be confused with causal efficacy in the physical sense, as Canute pointed out to his sycophantic courtiers: neither gestures nor words suffice to stop the tide. Much primitive magic rests on belief in the causal efficacy of word and gesture. However, using wings to fly (causal efficacy) is quite distinct from using wings to threaten (semantic efficacy). The essential difference is quite simply the difference between physics and psychology—a distinction which many modern theorists fail to acknowledge. This is bad enough. But failure to distinguish between *causal* and *semantic* efficacy has a disastrous consequence: it precludes any understanding of the distinctive *symbolic* efficacy which emerges with language, and which alone makes intelligible the unique development of the mental faculties of man.

Confusion of these three quite distinct factors is fatal to any theory of knowledge. Initially, however, such confusion is inevitable, since all three factors contribute to what we ourselves confusedly refer to as knowledge. Hence, to establish how these three sources of knowledge are related, how they differ, and the order of their emergence, is the fundamental problem of epistemology. It can be solved only within an evolutionary context. After Darwin, the man who most contributed to the solution of this problem was Pavlov.

All but the most primitive animal organisms are born with an assortment of sense organs, a repertoire of instincts and reflexes, and the ability to move and inhibit movement, all of which, integrated by a nervous system of wondrous complexity, ensures some measure of orientation and control sufficient for the preservation of life. All behaviour, all knowledge, and all higher mental faculties of thought and reason build on and presuppose this physiological basis, and—although we may be unaware of this—would not exist without it. The idealist notion of pure, absolute, disembodied knowledge, of knowledge without a knowing subject, is a fallacy based on ignorance of the role of language in theoretical understanding, and of the dependence of language on more basic forms of knowledge. Idealism is essentially a counter-evolutionary doctrine. The true *basis* of epistemology was laid not by Plato but by Aristotle. True, Plato saw the need for objective norms in all higher forms of knowledge, and came close to realizing that such norms originate in language. But Aristotle grasped that all higher forms of knowledge build on pre-existent knowledge, the origin of which is to be sought not in 'pure reason' but in animal perception, experience, memory, and the ability to learn.[3] The truth is that long before we arrive at human consciousness, or even animal awareness, living creatures are in possession of quite a lot of knowledge already. Knowledge is ability to act long before it becomes ability to theorize. As noted earlier, *can* and *know* are cognate terms. Causal efficacy, then, implies a pre-existent form of knowledge, even at the animal level. But it is also an important source of new knowledge. For apart from external effects, every activity, including vocal utterance, has feedback effects on the agent. Though largely unconscious, this feedback information is the most basic source of all new knowledge, of all learning. This is most obvious in the acquisition of practical skills such as learning to walk or ride a bicycle. The importance of this feedback principle was noted in antiquity by Democritus, and in modern times by Condillac, who had keen insight into the way such unconscious knowledge regulates much of our behaviour.[4] At this stage we learn many things, including how to speak, without the slightest awareness of what processes are involved. In the wake of Darwin, this principle became Lloyd Morgan's 'method of trial and error' and Thorndike's 'law of effect'. Thereafter it became a central tenet of behaviourism. Unfortunately, the behaviourists never learnt to make two vital distinctions: that between stimulus and sign; and that between animal psychology in general and the specifically human kind. They thus led academic psychology into a dead end from which the only escape has seemed, to many, the rival mythologies of Freud and Jung, or those of other gurus of the modern age.

The errors of behaviourism however were anachronistic, since even before it established its academic hegemony, Pavlov had clarified the two issues which behaviourists still fudge: the principle of perceptual learning as distinct from reflex action; and the role of language in all distinctively human learning. This brings us to two further principles of knowledge, and to the genuine originality of Pavlov, which is quite other than is commonly thought. Pavlov cannot be credited with the principle of 'conditioning' or associative learning, since it had been made fully explicit by many theorists going as far back as Aristotle. What Pavlov achieved was to set this Aristotelian insight in a larger theoretical framework. Following Darwin, who also grasped the continuity between instinctive reflex behaviour and the higher mental faculties, as well as the distinctive novelty that emerges at each stage of advance, Pavlov clarified two important theoretical principles. First, the distinction between behaviour triggered by *natural reflexes* and *sign-mediated* behaviour. Second, the distinction between the sign-mediated behaviour of animal life at large and *language-dependent* behaviour, which is uniquely human. With his insight into what he called this 'second semantic system', Pavlov highlighted the importance of language in all that distinguishes human intelligence from animal intelligence in general. There can be no doubt that Pavlov grasped these principles as a result of the actual course his research took. He first attained celebrity for his work on the physiology of natural reflex action, then moved to the study of animal behaviour, and only later turned to the study of human psychology. These three stages of his career followed the evolutionary path. If Darwin clarified the principle of *semantic behaviour*, Pavlov clarified its complement, the principle of *semantic perception*. Indeed, insofar as perception differs from mere sensation, he may be said to have established the essentially semantic, mediated character of perception itself. While many had stated the *principle* of learning by association, in which one thing may come to signify something utterly different, Pavlov first clarified the *origin* of this process of signification or meaning. The most primitive form of behavioural response is natural reflex action. Briefly stated, what Pavlov showed was that anything confusedly connected with the physical *stimulus* of a natural reflex action is liable to become a *sign* which triggers the same reflex response. There is an amusing asymmetry in the way these two basic principles of semantics—Darwin's and Pavlov's—came to light. Darwin's infant discovered the utility of screaming by its unexpected success. Pavlov discovered that the sign-mediated response was *conditional* or dependent on a natural reflex (e.g. salivation) by observing that his frustrated dogs salivated at what, quite unaided, they had come to take as a sign of food. His famous experiments simply confirmed this.

It should here be stated that the phrase 'conditioned reflex' is a ritual mistranslation which quite obscures the true significance of Pavlov's principle, although it reflects the behaviourist obsession with conditioning as manipulation. The theoretical importance of conditioning does not lie in the obvious fact that it can be induced, as in the training of animals. It can be induced only because it occurs naturally. What Pavlov clarified was nothing less than the evolutionary transition from primitive reflex action to behaviour based on sign interpretation, itself the basis of animal intelligence, and ultimately of human intellect.[5] Pavlov also demonstrated that the meaning of signs may be transferable: that a sign may become associated, not only with an *object* of interest, but with another *sign* not previously related with that object. Signs may signify not only objects but other signs. He thus clarified what had confusedly been called the 'association of ideas', a term used previously to cover all kinds of association. Pavlov distinguished between what may be called *radical association* (that between sign and thing) and *secondary association* (that between sign and sign). He also demonstrated that the latter occurs even at the animal level. With the advent of language, such secondary associations are potentially limitless, and become what Hobbes called the Trayne of Thoughts, what James spoke of as the stream of consciousness, and what at the highest level, when logically regulated, we call rational discourse or theory.

Between them Darwin and Pavlov solved two of the most basic problems of epistemology and laid the foundation for an evolutionary theory of learning and animal intelligence. They bridged the gap between behavioural *instinct* or reflex action and animal *learning*, by showing how the latter emerges quite intelligibly from the former under natural circumstances.

Animal intelligence is most briefly defined in terms of behavioural adaptability, and the latter in terms of the ability to learn new strategies, or perceive new possibilities, which is also a form of learning. The evolutionary importance of perceptual learning is that it permits the transfer of animal interest from objects of immediate need and survival value to new and apparently unrelated objects, once these become in any way associated with the satisfaction of some animal need. Such new objects thus become signs, that is, they acquire a semantic value quite independent of their real nature. Signification and meaning enter the evolutionary scheme at this point. Sign perception vastly augments the amount of sensory information available and clearly had incalculable evolutionary consequences. Direct contact, taste, and smell—a sort of half-way house between sensation and perception—are now supplemented by visual and auditory signs which convey information at a safe distance, give advance warning and make possible anticipatory action. As Pavlov made clear, such sign responses are learnt quite naturally through association with the stimuli of natural reflexes, and like the latter become quite automatic. However, their number is infinitely greater than the relatively small number of natural reflexes, since any item of experience may take on sign-value by mere association. As Berkeley noted, two things by their mere co-existence or merely by being perceived together may suggest or signify one the other. A sign is simply anything that reminds any creature of anything else, irrespective of the degree of awareness involved.

All learning is initially associative learning, whether the association be established by behavioural feedback or by perception, or as commonly occurs by both at once. In all higher forms of life perceptual orientation is an essential ingredient of effective action; but equally some degree of behavioural alertness and concentration is the prelude to any clear perception. Likewise, all *recognition* of objects or situations depends on the recurrence of a number of previously related signs which reinforce one another's semantic effect and thus, for the perceiver, 'constitute' that object or situation, that is, form its recognizable pattern.

Clearly the shift from purely instinctive behaviour to sign-dependent behaviour put a high premium on animal intelligence —acuteness of perception and ability to learn. Signs, which naturally become confused with purely physical stimuli, vastly increase the number of things an animal may react to, thus conferring great evolutionary importance on sensory discrimination. Aristotle shrewdly made this 'inborn faculty' the basic principle of his epistemology, the source of all higher forms of judgment and knowledge.[6] But in a constantly changing world, signs which once led to success may another time lead to disaster. With sign perception not only meaning but also *error* makes its evolutionary entrance. An organism guided solely by instinct and external stimuli cannot strictly be right or wrong, whatever it does. One that can learn, and even learn to correct error, clearly opens a new chapter in the history of life.

We have so far dealt only with the behavioural and perceptual antecedents of language. We must now turn to the thing itself. Here again Pavlov showed keen insight. Just as many had seen the psychological importance of association and conditioning but failed to grasp the mechanism on which they are initially based, so also many had dimly intuited the prime importance of language in the development of human intelligence without any inkling of how the transformation from animal to human intelligence had come about. The result, we have seen, was either a crass reductionism which failed to see any difference, or a naive idealism which denied any connection. Here also Pavlov helped bridge the gap. He saw that just as conditional reflexes develop out of natural reflex action to produce novel forms of behaviour based on sign perception, so also language builds on this new potential, to produce a distinctively human form of intelligence. How language emerged, or how it functions, he did not explain, but like Darwin he saw that it was of paramount importance in the mental development of man. Above all, he grasped that language was *sui generis*, not to be explained in terms of more primitive forms of conditioning or association. He saw that 'speech provides stimuli which exceed in richness and many-sidedness any of the others, allowing comparison neither qualitatively nor quantitatively with any conditioned stimuli which are possible in animals'.[7]

Darwin and Pavlov first clarified the behavioural and semantic antecedents of language, and set the problem of the origin of language in proper evolutionary perspective. However, if in its early stages language is scarcely distinguishable from other behaviour associated with the utterance of vocal signals and response to signs, certain distinctive features of immense importance must immediately be noted.

First, the distinctive anatomy of the human mouth and speech organs. The most obvious proof that language is a distinctively human faculty, and an evolutionary development to be explained only in evolutionary terms, is that it depends on the co-ordination of various anatomical and physiological factors, each of which has an independent primary function quite unrelated with language, but with obvious analogues in related species which lack the faculty of speech. Here we are concerned not merely with secondary function—a principle on which Darwin laid great emphasis—but with the co-ordination of a whole range of secondary functions: of lungs, mouth, tongue, teeth, hearing and the like, to mention only the most obvious prerequisites for language. The very physiology of language and the distinctive anatomy of the human mouth permit the effortless production of a limitless variety of differential utterances. This sets man apart from all other creatures and provides him with an unlimited source of easily produced signals, which in turn become signs when interpreted. This vastly increases the amount of semantic information available to man, since these man-made 'sign-signals' are added to, and fuse with, the limitless pool of natural signs already available to animal life at large. Moreover, these man-made signs and signals, which we call *words*, are under human control. They not only have results, or perform a function, like other signs and signals: they can be made to do so in a determinate manner.

Second, the words of human language do not merely trigger animal reactions like pre-linguistic signs and signals. Their complex nature, which we must soon consider, and the multiplicity of functions which they serve, call not for stock responses, but for careful interpretation and understanding. By the same token, they admit of many forms of misinterpretation and misunderstanding. This is an obvious fact much neglected by all who see language as mere communication of unproblematic information from point A to point B. Error is a permanent possibility in all interpretation. More positively, error, awareness of perplexity, and correction of error, are major factors in the genesis of human intelligence. The signs and signals of language do not merely elicit mindless reactions: they are the basis of human thought and understanding.

Third, our very facility for producing a limitless number of different words and word combinations would militate against their utility for communication and thought unless some principle of economy or standardization restricted their number and stabilized their accepted usage. For language to exist at all there must be some order and some rules. This has led the unwary into positing all manner of mystical devices to explain how these rules come about. The history of western thought is strewn with the debris of such hypotheses. From an evolutionary standpoint, however, no problem exists. If all members of a community used any sound with any meaning at any time there could be no language, thought or understanding at all. Here again we can best grasp an important linguistic principle by seeking out pre-linguistic antecedents. Even among animals, standardization or 'ritualization' of semantic behaviour is an established principle of ethology. Linguistic rules, or rather norms, simply exemplify the same principle. Linguistic norms are not prior to, separate from, or imposed upon, language. They are constitutive elements of language: at once the condition of its existence, of its intelligibility, and of its utility. Human life is inconceivable without the normative function that is built into language. For unlike pre-linguistic conventions which regulate the social life of animals, linguistic norms need to be interpreted and understood before they acquire social utility: understanding words is quite unlike knowing one's place in the pecking order. Language, moreover, provides the basis for all post-linguistic norms and systems—legal, mathematical, scientific and the like—and of all theory whatever.

So far we have considered the symbolic and normative function of language as used by individuals living in a speech community or society. These symbolic, psychological and social factors, however, cannot be divorced from the world in which we live. The primary use of language is to refer to objects of common experience. All other uses derive from this fundamental primary use. Theoretically speaking, *objective reference* is the origin of language as such. This is why language cannot be reduced to mere expression or communication. Many forms of expression and communication are pre-linguistic or non-linguistic, and some uses of language are neither expressive nor communicative. They may be heuristic or theoretical, for example. Likewise, language cannot be understood as a purely formal system. In language theory it is not the peculiar forms and conventions of any given language that matter, but the logical and psychological purposes which are subserved by the forms and conventions of any language whatever. It is not so much the *forms* of language that matter as the human *uses* to which they are put. The originative principle of language, then, is not to be sought in expression, communication or even formal convention as such, but in objective reference: that is, the designation of some object of common experience by some commonly recognizable utterance associated with such an object. This initial bond between word and object, between language and reality, is the principle which underlies all later complications and developments of language, and the touchstone by which all later uses of language, even the most abstract and theoretical are ultimately to be judged. This is a topic to which we must later return.

Since the first objects of reference are objects of sense experience, language soon proves its psychological utility. Words, Plato noted, are 'analytic of reality'.[8] Linguistic reference and psychological awareness thus progress by mutual reinforcement. Words help us focus attention on objects and to remember and recall them in their absence; while keenness of perception suggests ever greater refinements of verbal discrimination. Since the learning of words thus becomes part of the process of learning to identify objects, words become an integral part of the speaker's consciousness and memory from an early age. Indeed, later in life, to disentangle the distinctive function of language in human thought and experience becomes, for most speakers, all but impossible. Language becomes part of us and tends to get overlooked. To rectify this state of affairs we need a comprehensive theory of the origin, nature and essential functions of this important faculty.

Even at this stage of the inquiry it should be clear that words are far removed from any pre-linguistic signs, signals or animal noises. For this reason Aristotle referred to words as *symbols*, a usage we shall be wise to follow.[9] For if language begins with the word, that is, a sound which is at once sign and signal and conventionally associated with some object of perception, the process of *symbolization* which is thus initiated immediately has the most remarkable consequences which we must now consider.

If objective reference is the primary function and ultimate criterion of language use, many other things immediately follow in its train. To identify an object by use of a word is to distinguish it from other objects, each of which may also be singled out and identified in like manner. Words thus help us to *differentiate* objects as well as to *identify* them. Furthermore, if objective reference begins by identifying single objects, it immediately, indeed automatically, leads us to *categorize* classes of objects, either because of their real similarity or because we fail to distinguish between them. Many primitive categories, such as those made by children, and indeed adults, arise from simple confusion, which may later be rectified. Categories, in any case, whether objectively based or subjectively motivated, are elastic entities, admitting both of greater generalization and of more precise refinement. Categorization, then, is as natural and automatic a function of word use as differentiation. These functions which arise out of objective reference permeate the whole of language. They also constitute essential principles of logic which, as we shall later see, is the systematic use and application of principles present in language from the start.

These three basic functions of language—referential, categorial, differential—are, then, the inseparable constituents of what we call symbolization: the nucleus from which all other uses of language develop, and thus the basis of that theoretical understanding which language alone makes possible. All this throws new light on what we mean by linguistic reference. For if these functions are inseparable, linguistic reference comes about, not by anything like pointing things out with the finger, but by symbolic categorization or classification which is at the same time symbolic differentiation. This process, once initiated, has no limit. New categories, involving new distinctions, create ever new forms of reference. If we are to avoid what

Hegel called a 'bad infinity' we must clearly learn to keep this fissiparous process under logical control. Yet it is the basis of all our intellectual faculties. Bacon affirmed that the subtlety of nature is greater many times over than the subtlety of sense and intellect. But the whole development of language, and of language-dependent thought, is an ongoing attempt to remedy this state of affairs. We gradually build up a symbolic monitoring system which helps us come to grips with the complexities of experience and the subtleties of nature.

Thus, as learning proceeds, language becomes for the speaker many things: a means of designation and reference, a device for classifying things and establishing some order in the bewildering complexity of our ever changing experience, an instrument of analysis and differentiation, a mode of communicating this newly developed symbolic thought, and of learning from that of others, a storehouse of mnemonic and heuristic aids, an all-purpose monitoring system for checking and trying things out in the imagination, and a vehicle for that connected discourse which we call rational thought or theory, and rightly consider to be the highest function of mind.

Whether we use the term 'mind' as shorthand for all the functions of this new symbolic consciousness, or merely for its higher and more creative manifestations, two things are clear. First, all uses of language are grounded in symbolic reference as outlined above. Such symbolic reference and the complex developments which grow out of it—language in general—provide man with a unique means of orientation and control that set him apart from all other living beings. Second, there is no reason to suppose that this unique faculty could have emerged otherwise than in the way described, and every evolutionary reason to believe that language did so emerge, and by easily traceable stages. Hence the need for a general theory which will explain how language underpins the entire intellectual and spiritual life of man, which will trace the complex development of this unique faculty, and expose the dangers—self-stultification, irrational thought and action—to which ignorance of our own mental faculties makes us prone.

One of the main obstacles to a general theory of language and mind is the fact that rational thought or discourse may be uttered or silent. Silent thought is the main source of that naive idealism which, along with a similarly naive realism, is part of the naive philosophy with which we all begin, and which few grow out of: things simply are as we know them to be, and we simply know them to be as they are. Among the limitations of this touching belief is that it makes no provision for human error, for the complexities either of reality or of our own thought, or for the remarkable discoveries of science, which commonly shows things to be quite otherwise than we thought them to be. In all this we see once again the folly of beginning the study of language at the wrong end. Language begins, not with rational discourse, but with common speech, that is, vocal utterance tied up with empirical facts in real-life situations. Once we learn to speak we may thereafter continue to speak aloud, as children commonly do even when alone, or we may inhibit utterance. Silent discourse naturally fuses with so many pre-linguistic associations and other psychological factors, in the amorphous totality of consciousness, that the spoken origin of language is quite lost sight of. Language comes to seem the mere instrument of certain pre-existent (but quite mysterious) mental processes, rather than the precondition of their existence.

The inhibition of overt speech, however, is no more problematic than the inhibition of any other form of behaviour. A comparison between the learning of language and the learning of mathematics may help clarify this. Since mathematics needs to be consciously learnt, we do not think of mental arithmetic as an epistemological mystery. But since the rudiments of language are picked up unawares, and become an essential part of our mental make-up at so early an age, its psychological repercussions create insoluble problems until, following the Aristotelian maxim, we trace things back to their origins and then follow them as they develop. We then discover that silent discourse or thought is no more problematic than the fact that children learn mental arithmetic. First they learn to count and calculate with real objects; then they learn to count and calculate verbally, without real objects; finally they learn to do all this mentally. What applies to counting, which is one use of language, applies to language in general.

Its use may, to use Bühler's term, be *empractic*, that is, tied up with some form of behaviour in a concrete situation; *purely verbal*, that is, uttered in isolation from that to which it refers; or *purely mental*, not uttered at all. That this order of development is the original one there can be no doubt. But once we have been through the three stages we confuse them quite unconsciously. In the process we forget that discursive thought was preceded by verbal discourse, and purely verbal discourse by the 'empractic' use of language in real-life situations.[10]

We see, then, that the metaphysical notion of mind, which is also the popular one, according to which mind is a mysterious entity which thinks thoughts and then deigns to express them in language, which has been invented for the purpose, is the reverse of the truth. We must learn to speak before we can learn to think. Until then we merely behave or react like other creatures. Language, Russell once said, comes first and thought follows in its footsteps. And Frege had come around to the same way of thinking about the same time.[11] Once we learn to speak, language provides us with a new psychological dimension, quite distinct from animal reaction to stimulus or sign. We do indeed react to speech, our own as well as that of others, no less than we react to anything else. The difference is that language is quite unlike anything else. So that now we have the possibility of reacting to two quite different types of thing at once: the ordinary objects of sense experience; and our own symbolic devices, essentially different from the objects of sense experience, and yet intimately related to them in a bewildering variety of ways. Sense experience of the here and now thus becomes integrated into the larger, more complex, but purely notional realm of consciousness or mind. We henceforth live not only in the real world, but also in what Herder once called 'a world which we ourselves create'. This brings obvious advantages and less obvious dangers. All depends on the subtlety and skill with which each individual is able to correlate the symbolic devices of language with the deliverances of sense.

If, then, we would understand the profundities of human

thought, and more importantly its vagaries, pitfalls and absurdities, we must first understand the origin, function and development of human language. For what takes place as the individual learns to speak is quite remarkable. Sensory awareness, the common inheritance of animal and man, becomes imperceptibly transformed into symbolic consciousness. Sensory awareness is of course retained as the basic source of knowledge and its ultimate criterion. But the indispensable basis of all higher, distinctively human knowledge is the new symbolic faculty which emerges with the learning of language. The first effects of this symbolic consciousness, this new language-mediated awareness, are to expand and refine previous knowledge, to stabilize and systematize it, to increase its range, precision and degree of control over human behaviour. This remarkable transformation comes about through learning how to use and interpret a relatively small number of words and a potentially infinite number of word combinations.

So much for the advantages. There are also dangers. This new symbolic knowledge, especially in its more abstract forms, tends to distance us from the very sense experience from which it sprang. Language, knowledge, mind, each seems to acquire an independent existence of its own, cut off from biological and physical reality. The invention of writing greatly promotes this illusion of reified language, knowledge, and mind, independent of any speaker, writer or knowing subject. The illusion is further promoted by the fact that so much of our knowledge seems to come to us ready-made from other people. The fact that only language makes this possible tends to escape attention. The reification of language, and of the knowledge and intelligence it makes possible, is illustrated by the common view that language just 'exists' in a speech community and is passively acquired by each speaker. This view utterly falsifies the true nature of language, of learning, and of intelligence. The essence of language consists not in the word forms that are used and imitated, and which vary from one language to another, but in the *uses* to which they are put and the *skill* with which they are used. These also differ, not so much from language to language, or from society to society, but more radically, from individual to individual. Each individual must learn for himself, irrespective of language or race, with whatever faculties he has and whatever aid he receives from others. All forms of linguistic and cultural relativism, which seek to classify people by their linguistic or cultural background, founder on the reef of this more fundamental difference: between individuals. Human intelligence is not determined by this or that language or culture. It may however, as Darwin saw, transcend these man-made barriers, which divide nations and races.

Learning can never be a passive affair, least of all the learning of language. The extent to which each individual learns to use and understand language, to exploit its potential, is the greatest differentiating factor in human psychology. For through language—any language—each person not only refines his knowledge and control of practical matters, but through language also he comes to formulate and know his own thought; and by use of a common language he acquires insight into the thought and experience of others. This dual function of language, as source both of self-awareness and of social consciousness, was an important theme in Hegel's study of the 'phenomenology' or stages of development of mind.[12]

Language, in truth, is at the heart of all knowledge which is distinctively human. For in its ever expanding symbolic function, language progressively integrates all our knowledge into the familiar world of consciousness, in which objective fact, subjective thought, and the linguistic symbols which mediate between the two, all merge in a fluid continuum of associations. Paradoxically, the original effectiveness of language—what in fact enables infants to learn it— depends on this very confusion of objective, subjective, and symbolic factors. At the level of common experience not only is little harm done by such confusion: without it language could not come into existence. But when we move from ordinary speech and common experience, where ambiguity and error are easily detected and rectified, into the more abstract and complex areas of theoretical discourse and explanation, then these constituent elements of common speech must be carefully distinguished and separated, if we are to avoid absurdity. In physical science this is achieved by the systematic exclusion of all subjective psychological irrelevancies, by concentrating on empirical evidence and experiment, and by careful attention to theoretical hygiene, formal definition, and logical consistency.

When we come to psychology itself, however, and to the humanities at large, where human intelligence, behaviour, motivation, meaning and purpose cease to be mere adjuncts and become the very subject matter of inquiry, then the empirical method of physical science is no longer adequate. Mind, meaning, purpose, intelligence and the like are not amenable to empirical scrutiny. They are themselves theoretical constructs. At this level of inquiry, therefore, theoretical hygiene and logical safeguards become even more important. Indeed, theory and logic must themselves become part of the subject matter of the inquiry. Once we realize that theory is nothing other than the rational use of language for explanatory purposes, and that logic is primarily concerned with the regulation of this theoretical use of language, and more generally with the nature and function of language as such, then it becomes evident that any valid explanatory theory in the humanities must have as its basis a general theory of human language and mind.

In the humanities today we have the worst of both worlds: abuse of empirical methodology where it does not apply, and general disregard for valid theory, soundly based on the principles proper to human psychology in general, and to each distinctive area of inquiry in particular. In this chapter little more has been done than to indicate the complexity and importance of our subject, to suggest that its problems will remain permanently insoluble unless they are solved together within a unified theory of language and mind, and that such a theory can only be an evolutionary theory: one which, as Aristotle suggested long ago, traces things back to their origins and then follows them in their development. Until this is done the humanities will lack any rational foundation and the theoretical chaos which at present obtains will continue.

4

Stimulus, sign, signal, symbol

> With the concept of mediation we make the transition from 'simple' behaviour to the more complex 'symbolic' processes.
> O. H. MOWRER

> A sign need have no kind of similarity whatever with that which it signifies. HELMHOLTZ

> Epistemology now becomes semantics. QUINE

Nothing indicates better the need for clearly defined terms in linguistic and psychological theory than the common confusion, in both fields, of the terms stimulus, sign, signal, symbol. The aim of this chapter is to distinguish and define these terms, and to explain why such confusion arises. First, however, a word must be said about the notions of definition and confusion, and later about the special *theoretical* character of the four terms to be discussed.

A definition is neither a description of what something is nor an account of how something ought to be. To define is neither to describe nor to prescribe. A definition is simply an indication of how some term will be used by a theorist in a given area of inquiry. Definition is the basis of all rational theory since without it there can be no formulated principles or theory whatever. Theorists who fail to define their terms are either incompetent or up to mischief, since to theorize with undefined terms facilitates all manner of equivocation and veiled contradiction, on which all bad theory thrives.

Confusion, by contrast, is a much more pardonable and even fruitful error. We are easily misled by appearances. Many things resemble others but may differ in some crucial respect. Again, things often combine to produce some distinctive novelty, which may go unregarded while one or other of the ingredients continues to attract attention. This commonly occurs with biological and evolutionary phenomena. It is indeed a principal function of evolution theory to show how novelty emerges out of the fortuitous combination of pre-existent but previously unrelated phenomena. The emergence of language is perhaps the most complex example of such an evolutionary process.

Confusion, however is by no means a merely negative concept. Confusion of sign and thing is the basis of animal intelligence. Confusion of word and thing is the basis of human intelligence. Confusion, in short, is the basis of what used to be called *association*, and is now usually called *conditioning*. Though both terms have been much misused and misunderstood, it is clear that they have to do with the initially unconscious correlation of one thing with another, and at a later stage with the correlation of one thing with a category of others: with what we call *universals*. Confusion, then, may on occasion be no bad thing. An unfortunate confusion however was that between association and conditioning. Of the two terms, *association*, with its subjective connotation, was psychologically the more useful, and it is sad that it has been generally substituted by *conditioning*, with its overtones of experimental manipulation. As noted earlier, Pavlov was led to his famous conditioning experiments because he observed that his dogs had first conditioned themselves, that they had come to associate one thing with another quite unaided.

The truth is that association is a much misunderstood subject, for while its importance has been recognized since the time of Plato and Aristotle no adequate theory of association has ever emerged. It is curious to note, for example, that while Hobbes, Berkeley and Condillac grasped the positive function of association, Locke mainly noted its negative side, how association leads us into error: which, when unchecked by any objective norm, it very often does. As a result, reflection on the subject has always tended to move toward two opposite but equally untenable positions: the one deterministic, the other sceptical. For some, association happens like clockwork. Various mechanical and hydraulic models were suggested by the early theorists, and there developed a deterministic conception of 'psychological phenomena', viewed as not essentially different from natural phenomena at large. Positivists like Taine, for example, claimed that one could study virtue and vice very much as one studies the properties of sugar and vitriol: a whole school of fiction was based on this illusion. For other theorists, by contrast, the very subjective and haphazard nature of psychological association meant that no rational knowledge was possible at all. This was the doctrine of the ancient Sophists and later sceptics. In the modern age it was given a new lease of life by Hume, for whom reason was merely 'the slave of the passions', and human nature an insoluble enigma.[1]

The influence of Hume's confused thinking was widespread and disastrous. Bertrand Russell went so far as to describe the growth of unreason in the modern world as 'a natural sequel to Hume's destruction of empiricism'.[2] This is a strange view. Empiricism since Hume's day has in fact advanced from triumph to triumph in the form of a rationally based physical science. What Hume and his disciples did achieve, however, was the virtual extinction of moral philosophy; the systematic exclusion of rationality from the study of human affairs; and the progressive fragmentation of the humanities into allegedly autonomous disciplines, to be mis-studied as though they were branches of empirical science. This fragmentation is of course a parody of the specialisms of physical science, which may be pursued in apparent isolation only because they are intimately related and build on one another's findings. In the humanities, by contrast, bogus and quite incompatible specialisms now clutter the entire field.

A serious attempt to repair the damage done by Hume was made by Kant. If Hume sought to cure moral philosophy by an injection of what he fondly called 'the experimental method', and ended up killing the patient, Kant approached the implications of Newtonian physics more intelligently. While recognizing the subjective origin of all knowledge, he saw that the new science, even in its incipient phase, proved that human knowledge need not crumble into scepticism, that objective knowledge based on sound principles was not only a possibility but now a fact. Unfortunately, if physics at this time was still in its infancy, biology in any serious sense had not yet been born, and the biological foundations of psychology were largely unknown. To make matters worse, Kant—unlike his some-time disciple Herder—had little insight into the language problem. He therefore sought to solve the most intractable problems concerning the nature of human knowledge by purely theoretical means, without reference to certain more basic factors on which theory itself rests. It is the more remarkable, then, that he got so far in his attempt to solve the central problem of epistemology: how do we come to ascribe *objective validity* to knowledge which in its origin is, and can only be, *subjective experience*?[3]

The short answer is that this comes about thanks to the emergence of objective *norms*, which not only help the individual to organize his own experience into meaningful categories and correlations, but also become public *terms of reference*, which make possible rational discourse *between* individuals. This normative function, which has both subjective and social value, which moreover links these two areas of consciousness and activity, is the principal function of language, from its inception and at every stage of its development. It is the criterion of rational discourse, and also the criterion by which irrational discourse may be exposed. All this, however, comes only with fully developed language. Here we must return to association.

The unresolved conflict between the deterministic and sceptical interpretations of classical association theory helps explain why the study of *association* and its implications was superseded by concern with *behaviour* and the ways in which it might be conditioned. Another reason was the tendency of associationists to speak vaguely of 'the association of ideas', a phrase used indiscriminately to refer to quite different kinds of association.

In oddly contrasting ways these two facts effectively blocked all further advance in the theory of mind and in the theory of language. For to begin with association of ideas—whatever they may be—is to begin too late along the line. At the same time, to account for human behaviour purely in terms of reaction to stimuli is a grotesque form of reductionism which confuses—this time in the bad sense—four quite distinct factors: physiological, behavioural, perceptual, and linguistic, all of which are indeed *fused* in what goes to make up human psychology, but which it is the task of theory to distinguish and clarify.

This brings us to a consideration of what our four terms—stimulus, sign, signal, symbol—have in common and how they differ. The first thing they have in common is that they are all *associative* terms. Each implies some associated correlate. Whether this associated correlate be referred to as a reaction, a response, an object, a thing, a thought, a meaning, or anything else, is another matter, to be attended to separately. The second thing these terms have in common—and this applies also to terms such as norm, value, meaning—is that they are *theoretical* terms. They refer not to empirical facts as such but are themselves theoretical principles designed to clarify relations between facts. In using such terms we move from *description of fact* into the realm of *explanatory theory*. The trouble is that many theorists make the transition without the slightest awareness that anything has changed. Inability to distinguish empirical facts from theoretical principles, designed to correlate and make sense of such facts, lies at the base of most bad theory in this area. Moreover, in speaking of stimulus, sign, signal, symbol, we cross *many* theoretical frontiers which, unless they are carefully distinguished and accounted for, will be a source of confusion in all that follows. It will be well, therefore, to deal with this difficulty in its simplest form: the distinction between *perceptual familiarity* and *theoretical explanation*. The ease with which we make the transition from the one to the other often leads us astray.

When we speak of a bird call as a *signal* we have moved from perceived fact to theoretical interpretation. We have attributed to an obvious fact a less obvious function, one indeed which may not be obvious at all. We have moved from the pure physics of sound not only into biology, but into the distinct but related fields of behaviour and semantics. We have moved into animal psychology. And if we interpret a human utterance as a meaningful *word* or *sentence*, then we have passed into the related but quite distinct and unique field of human psychology. It is clear that all these fields, from physics to human language, have this in common: they can only be systematically studied and clarified by what Hobbes called 'getting a good method', and by the establishment of principles proper to each field. What is less generally accepted is that the study of semantic behaviour and language is not an empirical discipline in the sense that physics, chemistry and even physiology are empirical. This does not make this field of inquiry less rational than those others: on the contrary, its ultimate aim is the elucidation of human rationality itself. For this reason, if for no other, the mistaken belief that human psychology and language theory are empirical disciplines calls for some explanation. The place to look for one is at the borderline between physiology and psychology, and in the notion of *stimulation* which is common to both fields.

It is clear that stimulation is a two-way traffic. Physiological processes affect behaviour just as they are affected by it, and, indirectly, by environmental factors which affect behaviour itself. Behaviour and sensory stimulation are thus different but inseparable aspects of the constant interaction between organism and environment. Physiological stimulation of behaviour came to be referred to as instinct or drive, while the terms stimulus and stimuli came to be used for environmental stimulation of an organism. Leaving physiology in the capable hands of the physiologists, it is clear that environmental stimulation is a matter of impingement from without, associated rightly or wrongly with some animal reaction, often referred to—prematurely at this stage—as a response. It is obvious that all animals are permanently exposed to such sensory stimulation, which varies in intensity, discreteness, diffuseness, and in many other ways. It is obvious also that the reaction of an organism to such external stimulation must also vary enormously according to many factors: animal species, number and nature of sensory organs, degree of co-ordination between them, stage of maturity, present condition, previous experience, and so on. Doubtless, if all these factors were precisely known we would understand much more about animal and human behaviour than we do. However, to argue with the behaviourists that in default of such universal knowledge we must cling to observable behaviour and ignore all else is quite ridiculous. First, because we do know that many other factors are operative, and that they must undermine any conclusions based on observable behaviour alone. Second, because such conclusions are themselves as theory-bound as the so-called mentalism that the behaviourists claim to repudiate. Behaviourism and mentalism—materialism and idealism in an older phraseology—are equally inadequate and simplistic. Psychology cannot be accounted for in primitive terms of stimulus and reaction any more than it can be accounted for in metaphysical terms.

This brings us to *signification* and the notion of sign. The essential difference between a sign and a sensory stimulus is that a sign does not necessarily impinge: its effect is not like being prodded with a goad (Latin *stimulus*). For something to be a sign it has to be noticed, indeed *interpreted* as the sign of something else. For this to happen—and it happens quite automatically even at the animal level—the sign must have previously become associated with that of which it is now the sign.[4] Stimulation and sign perception are therefore quite distinct in that the latter implies prior experience, whereas the prod of a goad has immediate effect in the form of reflex action. To call such a reaction a 'response' is clearly a misuse of language. To confuse response to a sign with instinctive reaction to a stimulus is, however, more than a misuse of language, it is a theoretical error. For while reaction to a stimulus is immediate and automatic, as when we drop a hot plate, the relation between sign and response need be neither immediate nor automatic. While there is very little we can do with a hot plate but drop it, the possible responses to any given sign are limitless. We thus move from the area of physiology and reflex action into the infinitely more complex area of sign-dependent behaviour. It is here that the break between psychology and anything resembling empirical science comes about. Although response to a sign may become instantaneous, habitual and stereotyped, it is initially and at all times *mediated* behaviour, and quite unlike reflex action provoked by an *immediate* stimulus. Semantic mediation is the dividing line between empirical science and psychology, for here we leave the realm of natural causality and move into more complex and problematic zones: first, of animal perception and behaviour; and then, of human perception, conscious causation, thought and reason. Natural *causality* and conscious human *causation* are of course related by many links, but they are poles apart and must not be confused.

A *stimulus*, then, is essentially a physiological concept with behavioural connections. Sign, signal, symbol are essentially psychological and, more precisely, semantic concepts. These also need to be distinguished if they are to have theoretical utility. An animal *signal* is essentially a form of semantic behaviour, whereas *sign* is strictly a perceptual concept. Moreoever, while signals like all forms of behaviour are in some way motivated, anything whatever may acquire sign-value by mere association: by becoming an object of perception associated in any way with anything else, including of course signals and stimuli. As for the *symbol*, the complexity of what is involved in this concept is the subject matter of this entire treatise. The essential features of the symbol were outlined in the previous chapter, and more complex aspects of symbolization, the originative principle of all human language and thought, will be considered in later chapters. It is the very complexity of this concept which makes it astounding that theorists have so frequently confused the linguistic symbol with the relatively simple concepts of stimulus, signal, and sign. Such confusions account for the abortive nature of most language theory to date.

From the evolutionary standpoint, meaning enters the scheme of things with sign perception: the interpretation of one thing as the index of another. At this point the chain of natural determinism or causality is breached, and for the simplest of reasons: animals make mistakes. Signs may be misinterpreted, and commonly are misinterpreted, in an infinite number of ways. Thorndike mused that while much is said about animal intelligence, little is said about its complement, animal stupidity. This is strictly unfair to animals in general, but very pertinent to human behaviour. For while animals do indeed interpret and misinterpret signs, they do so in a completely unconscious way. Only humans possess the symbolic consciousness which enables them to stand back from what they are doing, take stock, and thereafter make rational or irrational choice: that is, adopt the right or wrong means to achieve the purpose in hand. Herein lies the difference between sign-dependent animal behaviour and language-dependent human behaviour. With human meaning comes human error.

The epistemological importance of error has rarely been grasped. It has no place in the subject matter of natural science—molecules do not really behave or misbehave at all—but it is central to psychology, whether at the level of perception, of purposive behaviour, or of thought and theory. Nor is error a merely negative concept. Augustine had a keen awareness of its importance since he once escaped an assassin's knife by inadvertently taking a wrong turning on his way home. Descartes saw an even more positive use of error. For along with error, he observed, comes the possibility of correcting it. Error and frustrated effort often lead to new awareness, and at the human level to understanding and conscious control. Much of our learning comes about in just this way.

We must now look more closely at the signal: in particular, the vocal signal. The psychological peculiarity of the vocal signal lies in the fact that it is, or may be, a short, distinctive, easily recognizable utterance which may be interpreted as a sign and so communicate meaning of some kind to others, but which also has distinctive feedback effects and thus acquires sign value for the signaller as well. All this is no less true of the words of human language. The vocal signal most resembles the spoken word, however, in that not only is it uttered, not only does it admit of interpretation, but it commonly has objective reference, even differential reference, and this even at the animal level. How this comes about is no mystery. Signalling, like all behaviour, takes place in, and often in response to, some particular situation. Different situations naturally elicit different forms of behaviour. Moreoever, communicative behaviour, as Darwin noted, develops naturally out of expressive behaviour which is already differential, varying with the object that elicits it. (Long before Darwin, Lucretius had dwelt on the vocal repertoire of the Molossian hound: snarling at intruders, crooning over its pups, its howls, whimperings and the like.) But the most dramatic link between animal signalling and human language is to be seen in their common socializing effect. Taking the simple case of an animal alarm signal, we see a complex interaction between signal, its objective correlate, say the presence of a predator, and its effect on other members of the species that respond to the signal much as they might have responded to the danger had they perceived it themselves. Here we have a complex of factors which foreshadow important aspects of human language: constancy of usage, objective reference, social utility, resultant social cohesion, survival value.

It was noted earlier that stimulus, sign, signal, symbol are all theoretical concepts associated with certain correlates—reactions, responses and so on—which are themselves no less the product of theoretical analysis, and not to be confused with the bare data of experience. (This point was touched on by Dewey as far back as 1896.)[5] Hence the same datum, an animal cry, may be referred to at once as a stimulus (insofar as it has aural impact and may trigger some reaction); a sign (insofar as it is interpreted by some creature); or a signal (insofar as it effects some form of communication). By contrast, an animal cry not so correlated would simply be a piece of animal behaviour. This analysis could be further refined, but it serves to show that these theoretical concepts, like the phenomena themselves, are fluid, and become progressively more interrelated and complex.

When we come to the *symbol* and *symbolization*—to the nucleus and originative principle of human language—the theoretical problems increase dramatically. One thing, however, is clear: it is chiefly through an understanding of vocal signalling and its effects—and not in terms of mere stimuli or even signs—that we must approach the language problem. For we are here dealing with increasing degrees of psychological complexity. Animal signalling, which like speech is a form of behaviour, is a more complex concept than signification, just as the latter is more complex than stimulation. A stimulus is anything which produces sensation. Of things sensed, some produce an immediate behavioural reaction, while others take on a semantic value: they become signs, which may mediate behavioural responses having no connection with the stimulus apart from mere association with it on one or more occasions. From a physiologically complex, but psychologically simple, stimulus-reaction situation we have moved into a situation which is physiologically even more complex, involving the higher nervous centres, and psychologically totally different. The fact that the conditional reflex builds on a more primitive reflex action (by mere association or confusion) must not mask the enormous difference between them. Once we move into the sign-mediated zone of behaviour, all the certainties of physical science are left far behind. The error of the primitive associationists was to think that psychology could be reduced to pure physiology (of which in any case they knew very little).

Language, however, is quite distinct from sign-mediated behaviour of any other kind. The essential difference might be described in terms of *semantic descent* (signs which lead to the satisfaction of primitive needs) and *semantic ascent* (signs which lead to more complex forms of behaviour and knowledge). Animals readily learn the utility of those signs which subserve their instinctive needs, and are generally disinterested in all others. At best, therefore, sign-mediated behaviour at the animal level simply makes for a more efficient animal. (Truth to tell, this is also the case in much human behaviour.) At worst, it may lead to disaster, since animals—and like-minded humans—tend to learn the hard way, by trial and error. By contrast, the distinctively human form of learning, which is entirely language-dependent, introduces a novel critical dimension which quite transforms this state of affairs. The symbolic faculty allows many problems to be solved not only at a safe distance, and in advance, but also theoretically: that is, in correlation with many other relevant factors which animal single-mindedness tends to overlook. It also opens up new perspectives which are not tied to immediate animal need; and it is this that we may call semantic ascent, the evolutionary importance of which is that psychologically speaking it separates man from all other animal species. This fundamental distinction, like many others, was made with admirable brevity by Plato when he distinguished two basic motives of action: the 'innate desire for pleasure', that is, satisfaction of instinct and avoidance of pain—to which he raised no puritanic objection—and 'an acquired form of judgment which aims at what is best'.[6] It is this acquired form of judgment that distinguishes human behaviour from animal behaviour in general. It thus differs from the innate kind of judgment, sensory discrimination, which Aristotle rightly saw was common to animal and man. But just how we acquire this higher form of judgment, Plato did not quite explain. The answer of course is: through the prior acquisition, or rather learning, of language. We thus return to the origins of language, and to its relation with animal signalling behaviour of the vocal kind.

A vocal signal emitted by one creature may of course be interpreted or responded to by another. But this is to look at the signal from the viewpoint of the perceiver, and we are back with the sign. What we must consider is the signal, or rather the act of signalling, as such. (Nouns such as stimulus, sign, signal tend to make us reify what are in fact theoretical abstractions from complex dynamic processes.)

In several essential respects the vocal signals of animals anticipate human words or symbols. First, they are uttered, easily imitated and reproducible. Second, they may have objective reference, inasmuch as they are elicited by some object of animal need or concern. Third, they are reinforced in their semantic efficacy by both auditory and kinaesthetic feedback. (The fact that we hear other people's utterances not only in the same circumstances but in the same way as we hear our own is an important factor in the genesis of language.) Fourth, through constant association, signal and object become as one, to the extent that fellow-creatures respond to the signal as though it were the correlated object itself. Finally, a single constant or recurrent factor, the signal, being repeatedly associated with a plurality of external objects or events of more or less the same type, becomes in effect a category index, a primitive universal. What is remarkable, then, is that all these factors which are the very basis of symbolization—confusion of subjective utterance and external object, designatory, communicative and categorial function—are already present, in a rudimentary way, in the vocal signalling behaviour of animals. The problem, therefore, is not to discover what animal signalling and human language have in common, but to discover wherein they differ.

The full answer to this question is the theme of this essay. But certain essential differences have already been discussed in the previous chapter. Symbols—the basic words of language—differ from animal signals in number, in range of differential reference, in the ease with which they combine to produce more refined and complex symbolic devices, in the growing consciousness that emerges as this complex process develops, and above all in the limitless consequences of all this as piecemeal symbolization develops into syntactic speech. Words and word combinations create consciousness of those things to which they relate in ever more complex and overlapping ways. Objects of sense experience initially become confused with our own symbolic devices, which only much later will themselves become objects of consciousness and critical scrutiny. Yet even at this preliminary stage, language enables us to focus on individual things, to categorize and recategorize them in many different ways, to relate them with other things, to imagine possible connections as yet ungiven, and to use such imagined possibilities as means of orientation, and models for future action. All this we commonly call *mind*, without the slightest awareness of what this concept implies. Only much later, if ever, do we attain critical awareness of the role of language in our mental processes, learn to perfect its mechanisms, and to avoid the traps into which it often leads us. Only then do we attain knowledge in the full sense of the word: knowledge not only of our physical environment but also of our own symbolic and theoretical means of coming to grips with it, of orienting ourselves within it, and in some measure of controlling it. Only when we understand how human thought is language-dependent, how language originates, how it develops, and how it goes wrong, can we claim to have achieved human self-knowledge, without which the amelioration of human affairs in general is plainly impossible.

Throughout the development of language, as in all evolutionary matters, novelty emerges quite naturally out of existing structures and processes, by combination and progressive complication. At no stage is there need to invoke mythical or metaphysical entities to explain how language develops. Not only are evolutionary principles adequate to explain how language actually did come about, but any departure from them makes theoretical explanation in this field impossible.

Before leaving what we may call the psychology of language origins, certain points need to be stressed. First, since language originates as a special combination of signalling behaviour and sign perception, its origin *must* be a *psychological* matter. Any attempt to account for language in terms of speculative neurology or genetics, or to neglect its evolutionary antecedents, can only lead to theoretical stultification. The second point follows from the first: being a psychological affair, language—in its origins, developments, its utility and even its aberrations—is a universal *anthropological* matter. The differences between the formal conventions of actual languages, interesting as they are, are the subject matter not of language theory but of comparative philology. Finally, this may be a convenient place to touch on the vexed question of meaning, even before we come to this topic in its own right. Indeed, we must seek the origin of linguistic meaning by tracing its prelinguistic antecedents, as in part we have already done, since meaning is an even more complex theoretical concept than sign or signal, presupposing both and much else besides. The many misconceptions of the notion of meaning result from three main errors: failure to grasp the complexity of the concept; failure to grasp the unique nature of *linguistic* meaning; and the error of approaching the problem of meaning from the wrong end, that is, beginning with the fully-fledged human mind and with adult language in all the complexity of its evolved state. If we begin with the conscious aspects of language—conscious intention to communicate and conscious interpretation of what is said—we are likely to end up understanding neither language nor consciousness; and even less, the close connection between the two.

As we have seen, the purely psychological aspects of language—behavioural and perceptual—have clear antecedents in vocal signalling and sign perception in general. For there to be meaning, however, there must be a third factor which might with equal justice be called the material or the formal element: the symbols or words as such, considered as things in themselves. But as we saw earlier, sign, signal, and symbol are theoretical terms designating not physical objects or processes—things in themselves—but determinate semantic functions, which cannot be abstracted from the total framework —at once physical and psychological—in which alone they acquire meaning. At the same time, however, a sign, signal or symbol must be a perceptible *something*, material or formal, if it is to perform a semantic function.

It has long been known—since antiquity no less—that such material or formal elements fall into three quite distinct and theoretically important categories: natural signs, fortuitous signs, and conventional or man-made signs. First there are signs which are naturally connected with or even caused by the natural phenomena of which they are signs: smoke signifies and is caused by fire; a scar is at once the sign and the remnant of a wound. In former times such physical signs were referred to as the 'language of nature' and considered the subject matter of natural science: the discovery of regular concomitances and sequences among natural phenomena.

In quite a different category are purely fortuitous signs, bearing no necessary relation whatever to that of which they are signs, but which by mere psychological association come to have semantic value, however brief or lasting. Much of animal life depends on registering and responding to just such signs. Between these two types of sign—the naturally determined and the fortuitous—lies the chasm which separates physical science from animal psychology.

Yet another chasm separates animal psychology from the human kind. For with language there eventually emerged a third kind of 'sign': one that not merely evokes a response, but is consciously made to do so with good effect; one that is not just given, but may be consciously contrived to serve human ends, and which by virtue of its social utility acquires a more or less stable, conventional, or normative value. This 'more or less' must not be interpreted as a source of weakness, but of strength, for it points to the limitless flexibility and growth potential of human language. Convention is simply human agreement, tacit or explicit; and the truth is that *everything* in language is conventional, even the degree to which the conventions may be flouted or modified, as they constantly are, to meet new needs, or satisfy new purposes. It is this open-endedness of language which ensures the open-ended nature of the distinctively human form of consciousness and intelligence which we call mind.

At each stage in the development of language there comes a new potential for understanding, accompanied as always by new possibilities of misunderstanding and error. The origin of language brings us up against the most fundamental intellectual error of all: reification, which rests on the confusion of words with things. Paradoxically, as we have seen, the origin of language not only depends on such confusion, but it does little or no harm in the early stages of language learning or in common speech. The child's initial confusion of word and thing establishes the bond between them; and no sane person thinks he can eat the word *food*. The trouble begins when we move into the realms of theory, and confuse our own theoretical terms with the phenomena which they are meant to categorize and co-ordinate. This chapter has touched on several instances of such confusion. Theorists who reify their own theoretical terms—stimulus, sign, signal, symbol—not only destroy the utility of these concepts but also fail to see how they are related. It is chastening, therefore, to end by recording that this fundamental error, the source of so many others, was clearly diagnosed long ago in a brief Hippocratic treatise on the art of medicine. The distinction between empirical fact and semantic convention was never more clearly stated: 'for words are normative conventions (*nomotethēmata*) applied to nature; the real phenomena are not superimposed norms but spring from nature itself'.[7] The ancient author not only diagnosed the ill but also prescribed the cure. He had insight into the man-made and essentially normative function of language, a problem which defeated the genius of both Plato and Kant. Words are norms by which we orient ourselves in a new and purely symbolic fashion, by which we progressively analyse, order and systematize our experience of the world in which we live. Words are not things, but our means of making sense of things, of understanding both them and ourselves. Once we learn to speak, language provides us with those (quite unmystical) normative factors which both Plato and Kant saw must exist *a priori* in all distinctively human knowledge, but for which they could provide only metaphysical explanations: that is, no explanation at all. These normative elements are not prior *ab aeterno* as metaphysical archetypes or paradigms, as Plato suggested; nor are they mysteriously embedded in the human mind prior to all experience, as Kant thought. They are simply the symbolic forms of language, which are indeed prior, in the most literal sense, to all that is language-dependent: all thought and action which is distinctively human, the bad along with the good.

5

Speech and thought

> The entire progress of the human mind depends on the skill with which we make use of language. CONDILLAC
>
> Our thinking is closely tied up with language, and through language with the external world of sense experience. FREGE
>
> But language comes first and thought follows in its footsteps. RUSSELL
>
> If man were wiped out, it is in the highest degree improbable that the step to conceptual thought would be taken again, even by his nearest kin. JULIAN HUXLEY

One might have thought that ordinary speech between human beings about matters of common interest would be the only relatively trouble-free zone of language theory. Speech is readily mastered by infants and effortlessly used by the entire human race. Yet just how speech develops out of primitive symbolization has never been clarified any better than the way in which symbolization emerges out of more primitive forms of signalling behaviour and sign perception. This is less surprising than may at first appear. The infant can have no conceptual understanding before he learns to speak, and since we learn to speak unawares, and at so early an age, the last thing we become aware of—if ever—is the role of speech in the gradual build-up of human understanding and the development of thought. Moreover, those theorists who have grasped that there is an essential link between language and thought have tended to misconstrue the nature of the relationship. Some have held that language not only enables us to think, but that what we think is determined by the language we speak. Language, however, is not a thing in itself external to ourselves: it is part of us. It is not a thing at all, but a complex of skills which we must first learn, and which we thereafter exercise, well or ill. Others have believed language to be a ready-made system, which is either embedded in the genes, or one which we con by rote from our elders very much as we learn multiplication tables. But language is not innately given: it is the product of a complex evolutionary process. Nor is it an externally given system: it is, rather, the means whereby we systematize our experience and learn to think. If we misuse it we lead ourselves astray. If we use it aright we achieve understanding. Language provides each of us with a new *symbolic* dimension which enables us to monitor, correlate, supplement and even correct information of purely sensory origin. Man differs from other creatures by this very faculty. If we are ever to understand ourselves, therefore, we need to understand how this faculty arises, how it develops, and how when we abuse it we fall into irrationality and folly.

The whole process begins, as we have seen, with symbolization. But although symbolization is the originative principle of language we do not speak of language proper until we reach the stage of syntactic speech. The transition from symbolization to speech, however, is accomplished more easily and rapidly than might be thought. Symbols, the basic words of any language, even when used singly, perform many psychological functions—designatory, categorial, differential, mnemonic, heuristic—which naturally fuse to form what we vaguely call thought. Such symbols readily become associated not only with all kinds of experience but also *with one another*. In purely psychological terms, this is a large part of what earlier theorists called the association of ideas. In language, it is the origin of syntax: the meaningful combination of words. Understanding meaningful combinations of words is not essentially different from understanding the meaningful use of single words, which often refer to quite complex objects and situations. All our perceptions rest on a plurality of sense data which conjointly take on semantic value. We must *learn* to perceive. (Initial perception of an object, unlike later recognition, is always an instance of learning.) However, we do not (as some have thought) begin by identifying discrete bits of sense data, out of which we then 'construct' patterns of experience to which we ascribe names. Quite the reverse: we vaguely apprehend things and situations which, on analysis, may prove to be quite complex. Only later, if at all, do we proceed to such analysis, and only then can we name, or even identify, the constituent parts. Visual perception begins with vague adumbration, just as language develops out of holophrastic utterance: we yell and cry before we speak. Refinement and precision, in both areas, are end-products of the fruitful interaction of perception and language, as the sensory data of vision are progressively reduced to intelligible order through association with the acoustic symbols of speech.[1]

The role of syntax is crucial to this process, for by recycling existent symbols in ever new combinations we retain their analytic function while promoting the creation of new symbolic forms with new semantic potential. In the most economic way, then, syntax furthers the business of understanding, which depends not only on the constant interplay of analysis and synthesis, but also on the symbolic devices which make this possible. Syntax, by combining existing words, extends the analytic and categorial (or synthetic) functions of the symbol, creating new categories and more precise forms of reference: 'large white house' is more specific than 'house'. Syntax is thus the first intralinguistic development of language, and also the basis of symbolic innovation, of that faculty of intellectual inventiveness which is often referred to as creativity.

Once we have learnt to classify and differentiate, to signify or *refer* to objects so classified and differentiated by means of words, there is no end to the process. New categories and distinctions call for new designations. This need is met either by inventing new words or—more commonly—by combining words already in existence. The moment words are combined we can talk of speech, of human language. At no stage in accounting for the genesis of language so far has it been necessary to posit unknown entities or processes. Nor will it be necessary to posit mysterious factors at any later stage in the theory of language. Each stage in the development of language is entirely intelligible in terms of its antecedents. If, however, we abstract any phase or aspect of language from its antecedents and concomitants, we immediately create insoluble problems. This, alas, has been the fatal error of most theory in the three areas—linguistics, psychology, philosophy—in which attempts have been made to clarify the nature and function of language. Nothing illustrates this better than the current confusion about the nature of syntax.

In contemporary linguistics there are three major misconceptions of syntax (which often overlap). Some theorists seek to separate syntax from semantics, failing to grasp that everything in language is semantic by definition. Some fuse syntax with grammar. Unfortunately, modern linguistics has now produced so many 'theoretical grammars' that grammar has been rendered more incomprehensible than syntax itself. In any case, syntax is not to be confused with grammar, which deals primarily with the complex relations between form and function in individual languages. (However, grammatical analysis did yield important insights into the nature of language long ago, and to these, since they are now generally neglected, we must return in a later chapter.) The third misconception of syntax is the notion that it is somehow *prior* to language, even genetically determined, allegedly providing basic 'structures' underlying all languages, known and unknown.

It is not difficult to see why syntax, which is no more than the meaningful combination of words, has given rise to more problems than the meaningful use of words as such. For as language theory progresses from simple to more complex concepts, the dangers of abstraction and reification become progressively more acute. When theoretical terms—sign, signal, symbol, meaning, syntax and the like—are abstracted from language as a whole and thought to be things in themselves, then theory collapses and absurdity supervenes. To suggest that the meaningful juxtaposition of words is prior to the words juxtaposed is indeed absurd; and to posit a special gene for the purpose of explaining syntax is pure fantasy. Such aberrations serve to illustrate the dangers of basing language theory on either syntax or grammar, conceived as ideal 'systems' allegedly prior to actual languages; or on written language, which creates the illusion that the formal element in language can be abstracted from that to which it refers, or the human ends which it serves. Even written language is usually about something other than itself, serves some human purpose, and needs to be interpreted in order to be understood. Moreover it presupposes symbolization and speech, which is where language theory must begin. To follow the current fashion, which seeks to base the general theory of language on one or other of its own developments, is quite simply to place the cart before the horse. Since only good theory can oust bad—polemics are mostly sterile—what we must do is trace the *actual* development of language, which is quite unproblematic; and more importantly, explain how this development underpins the parellel development of human thought.

We have already seen how symbolization not only relates language to more primitive forms of expression and communication out of which it develops, but also accounts for the way in which the basic functions of language—referential, categorial, differential, mnemonic, heuristic—emerge automatically and at the same time. A word may signify a particular object like any other sign, but in so doing it becomes a category index for similar objects, for *any such* object. (English *such* and German *solch* derive from words meaning 'so like'.) But it also differentiates this object or class of objects from others, which in their turn may also be signified and classified. Moreoever, the bond between word and object, or class of objects, is initially so intuitive and unconscious that each comes to signify the other. Words thus acquire both mnemonic and heuristic value, at once suggesting past experience and possible future experience of an object, event, or situation: while these in turn remind us of the words they are called by.

There is thus established, through the medium of language, a two-way traffic between our sensory experience and our conceptual knowledge which promotes the progressive refinement of both. Words designate, classify, differentiate, and suggest objects of experience. But equally the presence of an object may suggest its 'name' or designation. This in turn may suggest similar objects and many others, related not by similarity but by contrast, and by many other forms of association. With the syntactic combination of verbal symbols, this already complex network of associations becomes infinitely more complex. Syntax facilitates not only finer analyses and more precise reference, but also more subtle and innovatory forms of symbolic synthesis, suggestive of new possibilities of thought and action.

It may now be clear why any theory of language based on analysis of the formal element alone—the sounds, forms and constructions of actual languages—divorced from human psychology and the world in which we live, not only falsifies the nature of language but leaves human psychology—behaviour, perception, thought, reason—quite unintelligible, and deprived of our most distinctive faculty: the ability to *use* the forms of language, and so monitor, analyse, correlate, and ultimately understand—in varying degrees—the deliverances of sense perception; and to use this uniquely human form of understanding to further the ever-more-complex activities which set man apart from all other animal species. The forms, words and constructions of language cannot be studied like the data of empirical science. Their value resides, not in their physicality or acoustic impact, but in their symbolic function and the human ends which they serve. Language theory is not empirical science at all. It is a unique discipline which correlates fundamental principles from several others (e.g. epistemology, psychology, learning theory, ethology) which are often considered in isolation. In this respect language theory most resembles evolution theory, of which it is indeed the most important part: for without language there could be no evolution theory, nor any theory whatever. A proper theory of language, therefore, must clarify not only the antecedents, origin, and development of language, and how we learn it; but also how, once learnt, it becomes the key to all higher, distinctively human forms of knowledge, including that theoretical understanding of natural phenomena which we call empirical science.

In between these two extremes—the learning of language and the higher flights of the scientific mind—language accomplishes its most remarkable feat of all: it constitutes the subjective consciousness of each human being. Nothing distinguishes one person, mind or character from another more than the skill with which each masters, or fails to master, the symbolic potential of language. Such skill clearly depends on perceptual and behavioural refinements which are prior to language and rooted in pure physiology. Yet it is language which mediates between these pre-linguistic factors and the fully-fledged human mind. Nor is the transition—from pure physiology to symbolic consciousness or mind—in any way mechanical or automatic, since it depends not only on the *physical* make-up of each individual, but also on the nature and extent of his particular experience; his ability to 'process' such experience and so make sense of it; his grasp of information already symbolically processed by others; and the help he receives—or fails to receive—in all this. Any one of these factors would suffice to ensure that no two minds are alike. Conjointly, they make it impossible to think otherwise. This ineluctable fact of human diversity or psychological individuality, the result of factors which are at once physiological, environmental, *and educational*, is the rock on which behaviourism, IQ ideology, and all forms of psychological determinism, founder. This does not mean, however, that human understanding, agreement and co-operation are impossible. It means that we must learn to distinguish between human education and the training and testing of animals.

Sceptics of all periods have persistently stressed the relativism implicit in the subjective origins of all knowledge. What they have failed to note is that human knowledge does develop beyond its origins, beyond the subjective impressions of individuals, in the direction of knowledge which is objectively established and valid for all individuals. Aristotle drew a parallel between this development and a similar one in ethics. We all begin by thinking we know what is good for ourselves—or, rather, each for himself—and must mature to an understanding of what is good for all of us, if we are to be members of civilized society. Kant took this parallel between epistemology and ethics further. Without prior normative criteria there can be no rational knowledge at all, just as without the prior existence of law nothing can be legal or illegal.[2] It is ironic that while Aristotle and Kant grasped important principles of human reason and ethics without any clear awareness of the role of language in their development, many language theorists subscribe to a curious linguistic relativism, of deterministic hue, which would negate the possibility of reason and ethics altogether: the notion that each language imposes certain modes of thought on its speakers, that language is indeed a 'prison house' (in Nietzsche's phrase) from which there is no escape. Here we have reification not only of language as such, but of each individual language; and with implications of cultural relativism and cross-cultural incomprehension which scarcely bear contemplation. Fortunately, any such view of language or of individual languages is utterly without foundation. All theorists who dwell on the psychological diversity of individuals, or on the formal peculiarities of different languages, in order to defend such deterministic, sceptical and even solipsistic doctrines, betray ignorance of the most important facts about language, which is, as has been evident for centuries, the key factor in the genesis of a distinctively human form of intelligence. It is the *normative* function implicit in symbolization which first enables us to think at all. It is the *logical* function common to all languages which enables us to transcend the limits of any single language and so make contact with humanity at large. It is language which enables us to objectify our subjective knowledge, make it socially available, correlate it with the knowledge of others, systematize our common knowledge, make it more co-ordinated, rational, scientific. It is language which confers on us that consciousness of alternative options which we call freedom. It is language, in short, which makes us in the truest sense human.

To see how this comes about we need to return to the basic speech situation in which language is first learnt. Theoretically it matters little whether we speak here of the original language users—whenever they emerged—or of the child who begins to speak today. This much Saussure grasped.[3] Language must be learnt stage by stage, and despite all differences of idiom and epoch, the essential process is always the same. How the process begins we have already seen. Two pre-existent and often quite unrelated processes—sign perception and instinctive vocal utterance—fuse to produce a signal which is also a sign, and which is related to some object or item of experience. Instinctive vocal expression is often so related already at the animal level, where signals, interpreted as signs, and capable of objective reference, often become standardized. This is no less true of human utterance. In both cases the very utility of such utterance depends on its fixity, recognizability, and regular association with some object. Such utterance automatically takes on a categorial function, no matter how vague the area of reference. In fact initial vagueness is not only inevitable but salutary: an alarm call that attracts attention not only to *this* predator but to *any* predator has decided survival value.

Before we arrive at human symbolization, then, many of its ingredients are already in existence, and we must ask: what distinctive novelty supervenes with human symbolization, and what makes it possible? We have already seen the extreme complexity of what is involved in symbolization and how the process, once begun, facilitates the emergence of a distinctively human consciousness. We noted also the ease with which the symbols of language become associated not only with things, but syntactically with one another in ever new combinations. There can be no doubt that the countless words and word combinations that human language has already produced, and its limitless potential for further symbolic innovation, radically differentiate human language, both quantitatively and qualitatively, from any other form of animal signalling. It has been a source of wonder since antiquity that so small a collection of consonants and vowels—a few dozen—combine to produce so amazing a proliferation of different words, which in turn combine to produce ever more complex symbolic structures. Whereas other species make do with a limited repertoire of squeaks, grunts, chirps and other noises, the peculiar constitution of the human mouth permits the effortless production of an unlimited number of subtly articulated sounds, any one of which may come to be associated with some item of experience and so become a symbol, with all the functions—referential, categorial, mnemonic and so on—that this entails. It is not to be thought, however, that the peculiar anatomy of the human mouth could by itself explain the origin of language. The human mouth is a result of the evolutionary factor known as neoteny, and cannot be divorced from prior and concomitant evolutionary factors such as size of brain, behavioural skills, perceptual refinements, least of all from refinement of *hearing*: the ability to *register* differential utterance, which is as basic to the language faculty as vocal utterance itself. But while much attention has been given to brain size, to behaviour, perception and animal intelligence in general, the sheer mechanics of speech, what makes it possible at all, and how it underlies all the higher faculties of man, these matters have never been satisfactorily correlated in an overall evolutionary perspective. Hence the need to trace the emergence and development of language.

Returning to this development, a relatively small group of articulated sounds, once they become established as conventions by virtue of their social utility, form the basic symbols, the nucleus of a language. Their diverse combinations and meaningful use, or rather uses, constitute human speech. And just as speech rests on symbolization, and the latter develops out of more primitive forms of signalling and sign-response, observable in animals and human infants, all later developments of language rest on and presuppose speech. What is less obvious, but logically indisputable, is that language is the indispensable basis of all other symbolisms and activities—mathematics, scientific theory, art, and indeed the totality of human culture—which are the peculiar products of human intelligence; since these either involve or presuppose language, and would be quite impossible without it. This little-appreciated fact underscores the importance of language theory for all other theory in the humanities, not excluding the philosophy of mathematics and natural science—as distinct from the *practice* of these disciplines which have their own theoretical and empirical checks. It is an open secret that while natural science and mathematics have over the last few centuries dramatically transformed the character of human civilization, the so-called *philosophy* of science and mathematics is as chaotic as any other branch of that unhappy discipline. The greater the need, therefore, to establish language theory on a sound basis, to clarify exactly what occurs as speech emerges from primitive symbolization, the originative principle at once of linguistic meaning and of a distinctively human form of intelligence. In order to do this we need to consider certain misconceptions concerning the nature of language and what is involved in the learning of it.

It was stated earlier that syntax, the meaningful combination of words, is the first *intralinguistic* development that language theory has to consider. Before leaving contact with reality, however, and indeed to ensure that we never do, we must return again to that confusion of word and thing which we saw to be, not a defect, but an essential feature of the first stage of language learning. It is this fruitful confusion which not only forms the basis of language but also lays the foundation of human consciousness. In ordinary thought the objects of sensory experience and the words we use to refer to them become so inextricably intertwined as to coalesce. There comes a point—rational discourse and systematic theory—at which this interfusion becomes a positive danger and must be controlled. Initially, however, sensory awareness and symbolic consciousness mutually reinforce and define one another to produce our knowledge of the familiar world of common experience, on which all other more refined and scientific forms of knowledge necessarily build. This was clearly grasped by Einstein. He not only stressed the continuity between ordinary thought and scientific theory but held that the physicist cannot adequately examine the concepts of his own specific field without coming to grips with the 'much more difficult problem of analysing the nature of everyday thinking'. It should by now be clear that there can be no hope of solving this 'more difficult problem' except in the context of an evolutionary theory of language.[4]

In the development of the new symbolic orientation which comes with language, and which supplements, transforms and vastly extends the purely sensory orientation of animal life at large, the basic functions of symbolization—referential, classificatory, differential, mnemonic and heuristic—constantly interact. This in itself would suffice to explain the fluid innovatory nature of human thought. But when we bear in mind that initially the two modes of orientation, sensory and symbolic, are thoroughly intertwined; that at this stage language, thought, and reality are utterly confused; and that many natural phenomena, the objects of sense, are no less fluid than our thought: then it becomes clear that many of the innovations we often attribute to thought are in fact suggested by the data of sense experience. Human consciousness begins with our unconscious—but none the less effective—use of symbols. The innovations of thought lean heavily on the initial bond between word and thing, between language and reality. In our awareness of reality we are usually unaware of the role of language in the formulation of our categories of thought; and in our use of language we are usually unaware of the degree to which much of our thought is suggested, through such linguistically formulated categories, by external reality.[5] Without minimizing the power of human creativity, therefore, we must begin our theory of language proper not with syntax, but with this initial phase in which words and things mutually define and suggest one another. Only thus can we avoid the naive notion that language, or more paradoxically thought, is a 'free creation' of the mind, an entity which has hitherto resisted all attempts at definition. It would be more correct to say that thought and mind are emergent products of the language faculty, as it gradually develops, by perfectly obvious stages, from its humble origins. Only if we adopt an evolutionary methodology, which traces things back to their origins and then follows them as they develop, shall we be able to accommodate, in the right order, the various stages of this development. Only then shall we understand how our primitive faculties of vocal utterance and auditory perception eventually enable us to categorize, analyse, co-ordinate and somehow stabilize our fleeting experiences, to recall and theorize about them, to imagine and devise new possibilities of thought and action, to explore hypothetical alternatives and make rational choice. In a word, we shall see that what we call mind, reason, scientific intelligence, are the outgrowth, the end-products of the language faculty; and that language, properly understood, is no abstract formalism or ready-made vehicle for the conveyance of pre-existent knowledge, but is itself the outcome of a complex development of prior behavioural and perceptual faculties, which further develops to become the very foundation of human knowledge as such.

Among the chief obstacles in the path of an evolutionary theory of language are two academic fallacies. The first, already noted, is the belief that the subject matter of language theory is empirically given, like the physical objects to which (among other things) language refers, and that language may be studied by empirical methods. This doctrine is on a par with pseudo-empiricism in psychology, of the type exposed by Sherrington and Eccles. The language faculty is not empirically given, but a complex of skills which each individual must learn, well or ill, to exercise for himself. It generates, not physical objects, but meaningful speech and thought; and through these, human intelligence and civilization. The sounds and written forms of language cannot be studied like the data of empirical science, since they are human conventions, designed primarily to refer to things other than themselves.

The second fallacy confuses language, not with empirical science, but with mathematics. This aberration is the basis of the modern mystique known as 'structuralism', initiated by Saussure, but which later spread confusion in the humanities far beyond the zone of language theory. (A related confusion between mathematics and logic will be considered in a later chapter.) Either separately, or in unholy alliance, these two doctrines have dominated academic linguistics for the best part of a century. Their anachronistic character hardly needs to be stressed. Language clearly antedates both empirical science and mathematics by many millennia: and since both scientifc theory and mathematics are advanced forms of human linguistic discourse, it follows that they cannot be the paradigms of human rationality, but are in fact among its products.

The damage caused by such 'models' of language borrowed

from mathematics and empirical science is two-fold. They block any fruitful advance in the most fundamental discipline in the humanities: that which alone can clarify the distinctive nature of human psychology, of human reason and—most important of all—of human irrationality. By the same token they foster and underpin the most harmful and absurd doctrines in all areas of human concern except, ironically, mathematics and empirical science which have, as noted above, their own theoretical and empirical safeguards. Here we may consider one such erroneous doctrine: the most nefarious of all since it concerns the nature of human learning and intelligence. (These terms are very closely related. Intelligence is most briefly defined as the ability to learn, and in an ever-changing world the ability to learn from experience is the clearest index of intelligence. This ability, when mediated by language, not only distinguishes the human race from all other species, but is also the psychological factor which most distinguishes one individual from another.)

By detaching language from its physiological, psychological, and physical or environmental setting, as well as from its behavioural and perceptual antecedents, and by viewing it as a quasi-mathematical formal system, modern linguists since Saussure have ensured that the origin, nature and function of language remain to this day enveloped in mystery. The most disastrous result of this is that language, viewed almost exclusively as a vehicle of communication to the neglect of all its other functions, is seen as a ready-made code which is either genetically determined, or passively acquired by exposure to some given speech community. One weird doctrine manages to combine both these hypotheses. Such views entirely misrepresent the nature of learning, whether of language or of anything else. Learning is always something which each individual must do for himself, with varying degrees of success. Such views also obscure the fact that language is not merely a vehicle of communication—which is a universal animal faculty—but also the basis of a distinctively human form of consciousness, capable of retaining a vast amount of categorized information for further analysis, correlation, and recombination; and providing terms of reference by which to assess new experience. This symbolic consciousness is utterly distinct from mere sensory awareness of the here and now, which again is a universal animal faculty. Further, linguistic or symbolic communication is quite unlike any other kind of animal communication.

Language, then, is not a ready-made system but the means by which each individual, as he learns to speak, learns also to systematize his own experience, to analyse it, reflect on it, and so in some degree to make sense of it. Language, in short, is the basis of individual human consciousness and thought. But equally language is the basis of social consciousness and hence, as many have noted, of the most remarkable evolutionary development of all: human civilization. For while the uniqueness of each person's physical and psychological make-up remains intact, the fact that similar individuals, coming to grips with similar problems in a common environment, have a common idiom in which not only to think for themselves, but also to think *with others*, is assuredly the basis of human rationality, both of thought and action. This is true *within* a given speech community. When we come to the topics of discourse and logic, we shall see that language as such is the only basis for the non-violent solution of human problems *between* speech communities. Language in this broader sense, beyond the oddities and peculiarities of individual languages, is the true subject matter of language theory. Yet certain linguists deny the very possibility of any such theory and implicitly, therefore, of any possibility of cross-cultural understanding or concord.

It may now be clear why linguistic relativism, the notion that all language users are the victims or prisoners of language in general, or of the language they first learn to speak, is absurd. The psychological determinism implicit in this view is absurd because it is precisely language which allows us that degree of reflection, thought and theoretical foresight which distinguishes human action from any other kind, and thus affords human beings a measure of conscious choice denied to lesser breeds. It should also now be clear that the more ethereal type of language theory, which divorces language from all which is not pure form, is harmful not only because it perpetuates utterly discredited forms of metaphysical idealism, but because it allows other more harmful perversions of language theory to go unchecked.

Nothing will here be said about the grammatical and logical categories which are implicit in common speech. Grammatical analysis, the examination of form and related function, only became necessary or indeed possible after the chaotic variety of the spoken language had been 'reduced' to the written form. Grammatical categories, then, will best be left until we consider the distinctive novelty which supervenes with the invention of writing. The problems of language and logic must likewise wait until we have considered the nature of *theoretical* discourse. For most speakers—and even for entire cultures which never developed a system of writing or a tradition of critical thought—language is simply an integral part of human life which unobtrusively articulates the totality of our experience. It is for this reason that ordinary speech far exceeds all later developments of language in richness, complexity, spontaneity and inventiveness. Indeed, most later developments of language are expressly designed to prune and restrict this complexity and richness, and to stabilize usage for determinate ends. Lacking the frame of reference of direct speech between people in a real-life situation, these later developments also lack the infinite expressiveness which speech derives from tacit allusion to such situations, and also from the behavioural and psychological concomitants of speech: intonation, gesture, tone, mood, irony, wit and the like. Specialized refinements of this original form of language will later make possible marvels of precision and control, as in mathematics and empirical science. But only the greatest literature ever recaptures anything like the effortless precision and subtlety which the speech of ordinary people, even of children, naturally possesses.

There will be more to say on this topic—the difference between ordinary speech and later developments of language—when we return to the topic of meaning and consider the notions of reference and modality: more precisely, the crucial distinction between direct reference and modal reference. Before that, however, we must consider the topics of verbal discourse and of writing.

6

Discourse and theory

> We must come to an agreement as to what rational discourse really is. PLATO
>
> There is nothing more practical than theory. BOLTZMANN

As long as language remains at the level of common speech between people in real-life situations little can go wrong; or if mistakes occur they can easily be rectified. On such use of language, with natural correctives in empirical and practical realities and the intervention of other people, the whole co-operative and social life of mankind primarily and ultimately rests. Speech of this kind, however, by no means exhausts the potential of human language, and the major problems of language theory arise precisely when we leave the realm of ordinary speech, and long before we come to the written language, which is a relatively late arrival in the development of language. It must be stressed, however, that the problems referred to—the problems of discourse and of the theoretical use of language—become insoluble if we ignore the earlier stages of language development, and equally so if we commit the opposite error: if we were to think that writing was prior to the discursive use of language. Children ask questions and seek to answer them, speculate and theorize, endeavour to explain the unknown in terms of what they know as soon as they acquire linguistic fluency at all, and long before they become the beneficiaries, or victims, of the writings of others, or before they themselves learn the quite special arts of reading and writing. Many people, and indeed even entire cultures, never acquire these arts, but do not on that account refrain from seeking answers to those larger questions concerning the human condition which symbolic consciousness almost automatically leads us to ask.

When we come to the discursive and theoretical uses of language we enter the great unexplored territory of language theory, or rather a territory hitherto explored chiefly by theorists in logic and mathematics who not only seem incapable of drawing any distinction between logic and mathematics, but also seem to be utterly unaware of the relations existing between these disciplines and natural language. This curious situation—to which we must return in a later chapter—helps explain the paradox that while most people have no great difficulty with language when discussing matters of common fact or of immediate practical interest, nonsense and contradiction are rife as soon as they begin to discourse on those larger issues—ethical, political, economic, educational—which most closely concern our common welfare and survival. It also explains why language theory to date has tended to oscillate between hair-splitting analysis of the formal element in individual languages and wild speculation about the nature of language in general. Only by tracing what happens as common speech takes wing and essays more ambitious tasks shall we be able to lay bare the source of certain errors which have made modern philosophy—of language, of mind, of logic, even of mathematics and science—a new Babel of dissension.

Discourse has quite humble beginnings. Just as speech proper begins with syntax, the meaningful combination of words, so discourse begins with the meaningful combination of sentences. Since the notion of a sentence is intermediate between syntax and discourse, and since sentences have given theorists not a little trouble, from antiquity down to the present, this subject requires some attention before we proceed further. In fact, consideration of the sentence illustrates better than anything else two important theoretical points which we have met already. First, the fluidity or continuity of all developments within language. Second, the fateful consequences of any attempt to hypostatize any phase of language development, or to divorce any aspect of this development from the complexity of language as a whole. Disembodied, 'decontextualized' sentences and propositions have long been a major source of obfuscation in language theory, logic, and philosophy at large.

A sentence is simply any word or word group which intelligibly expresses the judgment, opinion, intention, desire, request, belief, doubt or any other attitude or state of mind of some individual, within the conventions of a given language, or even by some novel extension of these conventions. Individual judgments, opinions and the like, expressed in and understood through the formulation of sentences, are of course variously conjoined in common speech about matters of everyday interest. In addition, however, sentences may be more carefully connected, perhaps to give an account of certain more complex areas of experience, or to correlate the findings of some form of inquiry. This process passes through many stages and may culminate in the formulation of systematic theory, both in empirical science and in the humanities.

In everyday speech, the meaning of a sentence is often intelligible simply in terms of that to which it refers. But where a sentence forms part of a sequence of interconnected sentences its meaning must depend also on the meaning and coherence of those other sentences with which it is linked. We thus enter the realm of *continuous discourse*, the next stage of language development which we must consider. Throughout this development, which stretches all the way from the behavioural and perceptual antecedents of language to general theory in natural science and the humanities, there is no break of continuity. Signs, signals, symbols, syntax, sentences, and scientific discourse form an unbroken chain. As Russell once put it: 'There is a gradual development between what I call animal expectation up to the most refined laws of quantum mechanics. The whole process starts from experiencing A and expecting B.'[1]

As with all else in language, discourse has relatively unproblematic beginnings: in narrative, and in description. Problems will arise only if we neglect these beginnings and plunge in at the deep end, beginning our inquiry with more complex forms of explanatory and theoretical discourse which depend on the prior elaboration of causal and logical principles. The elaboration of such principles occurs very late in the history of human thought, is peculiar to very few cultural traditions, and is by no means complete. Narrative and description, by contrast, are universal uses of human language. Moreover the almost imperceptible transition from narrative and descriptive discourse to explanatory and theoretical discourse, brings new hazards, new potential for error, in the form of mythical and metaphysical discourse. Indeed, how we get from relatively unproblematic narrative and description to valid explanatory and theoretical discourse is one of the most important problems which language theory must solve. And the problem must be solved, not by side-stepping myth and metaphysics, but by showing how initially they were essential stages in man's first gropings in the direction of systematic theory: and how, having outlived their utility in this respect, they are now serious obstacles to progress in the rational solution of human problems. For positive and negative reasons, then, myth and metaphysics are too important to be ignored. They must not be by-passed but defused.

As speech develops, and with it the wider consciousness and understanding which it makes possible, its functions naturally go beyond the more basic, obvious and constant forms of language use: designation, categorization, ordinary conversation and the like. Language, once instituted, creates a momentum of its own. Each new development not only brings a new awareness but opens up new horizons, suggests new areas of interest and stimulates new inquiry. Moreover, as man comes to feel more at home in his familiar world, as he more efficiently and confidently controls the conditions of material existence, there naturally arises the desire, and often the need, to understand more systematically the world of nature. At the same time, as social life becomes more complex, there comes increasing awareness of the various notions and beliefs about the nature of human life itself which are implicit in the diverse forms of social organization and behaviour which historically develop. Such social factors differentiate one society from another, affect the quality of life which each permits, and through increasing inter-cultural contacts provide yet another source of reflection. It was doubtless this mixture of half-conscious beliefs and dawning awareness of problems that stimulated man's first moves in the direction of what, much later, was to become rational theory.

Rational theory, however, was not born in a day. It did not come of age in natural science until quite recently, and in the humanities can hardly be said to have come of age at all. Rational discourse had to emerge slowly out of more lowly but valid forms: narrative and description. But it also had to extricate itself from two historically important but invalid forms—myth and metaphysics—in which primitive attempts at theoretical discourse of any complexity inevitably become entangled. Myth and metaphysics must later be considered, each in its proper place. Here it may suffice to say that broadly speaking mythical thought is the first attempt of the primitive mind—which of course is still very much in our midst—to make sense of the more general problems of human existence, but without adequate principles or objective norms; while metaphysics is a more sophisticated but no more reliable way of doing the same thing, hampered moreover by illusions of logical grandeur to which mythical thought, in its innocence, makes no pretension. If, therefore, we seek to clarify theoretical and rational discourse without prior consideration of these antecedents—narrative and description, myth and metaphysics—we shall be saddled with two quite distinct types of problem. For even narrative and descriptive discourse are not without their snares and difficulties, while mythical and metaphysical forms of discourse will remain a permanent obstacle to rational progress, especially in the humanities, until we understand their origins, their initial utility, and their fatal weaknesses.

Narrative discourse seems innocent enough at first sight. It occurs in colloquial speech, as when we recount a sequence of related actions or events. But even here there are traps. No such account can be exhaustive. There are necessarily gaps in our knowledge, which we often unconsciously fill with imagination, supposition, and prejudice. Then, we necessarily select, consciously or otherwise, even from the data we possess, according to the purpose in hand and many other factors. Moreover we may erroneously think we see relatedness where none exists, and likewise fail to see it where it does exist. Again, human actions naturally become associated with their many effects and repercussions, whether contrived or accidental. As a result, narrative discourse slips almost imperceptibly into explanatory discourse, with all the attendant dangers of misconception and error that such uncontrolled transitions involve. Subjective factors—sensory acuity, degree of psychological maturity, previous experience or the lack of it—obviously colour even the most innocent narrative account: all this quite apart from any conscious bias, guile, or mendacity. Naturally, in any discipline such as history, where narrative discourse takes on an explicit explanatory function, difficulties concerning interpretation, reliability of information, assessment of evidence and causal connection become central problems of that discipline, and must be squarely faced. What is less obvious is that such problems are implicit in the accounts and explanations which we give of even the most commonplace actions and events.

What applies to narrative discourse, the correlation of actions and events in time, applies in large measure also to descriptive discourse, which seeks to correlate co-existent phenomena in a theoretical framework which may make their relationships and interactions more intelligible. Description also slips almost imperceptibly into explanation; and problems of selection, emphasis, relative importance, interpretation and misinterpretation, arise here as before. More precisely, the problems of selection, interpretation, correlation and so on arise *before* we begin to narrate or describe. It is only because we tend to 'solve' such problems unawares that we think narrative and description to be trivial matters, and fail to see that they are the incipient stages of theoretical discourse. Everything we refer to as factual has been verbally categorized as such in advance, and categories and their interconnections are the basis of all theory. There are, however, many ways of categorizing things. The greater the need therefore to ensure that theory is consciously based on explicit categories and principles, and that it be logically coherent. These are topics to which we must return in later chapters.

The essential difference between the narrative and descriptive forms of discourse needs to be clarified if we are to understand their complementarity. Narrative discourse deals primarily with human behaviour, and leads not only to an understanding of human history but also to an understanding of the conditions and consequences of human behaviour in general. Human action, unlike animal behaviour, is not only causative but may be consciously so. We thus possess a measure of freedom and conscious choice which sets us apart from all other species. By tracing sequences of causative actions and their effects we come, with practice, to understand them. The criterion of true understanding is the ability to explain, and the intelligent explanation of recurrent forms of human action is the only guide we possess for any higher theory—ethical, legal, political, economic, educational—which is designed to make provision for the future. There is, then, clearly more to narrative discourse than telling tales about the past. As it develops into explanatory discourse it leads ultimately to moral philosophy, known in former times as moral science and nowadays—with scant justification so far—as human or social science.

If narrative discourse leads, at no matter how many removes, to *moral philosophy*, descriptive discourse in turn develops into that form of theoretical explanation which in Newton's day was called *natural philosophy*, but is now referred to as natural science or, more properly, as empirical science. As they develop, then, these two apparently simple forms of discourse provide—when properly grounded and logically controlled—the basis of all rational theory, be it in the study of human affairs, or in the study of nature at large.

Initially, this distinction between narrative and descriptive discourse, with emphasis on the divergence of their respective developments into two radically different forms of explanatory theory, may seem artificial and invalid. Narrative is itself a form of description; and given that all things are in a state of flux, description of natural phenomena necessarily involves the correlation of events in time. Moreover, the study of life embraces not only natural science but also the study of man, and must therefore somehow bring moral philosophy within its purview. Here, once again, we shall find that evolution theory alone can accommodate these apparently unrelated areas of inquiry, vindicate the above distinction, and so help eradicate all reductionist and determinist preconceptions which currently plague the academic study of the humanities.

This brings us back to the problem of misplaced empiricism, on which all such errors rest. The source of this aberration is none other than the old problem of *causality*, usually regarded as one of the more intractable problems in all philosophy. The problem, however, has a simple solution, since it rests on a simple muddle: the confusion between human causation (the intentional achievement of human purpose through appropriate action) and natural causality (the impersonal interplay of natural processes as studied in empirical science). Since both personal action and impersonal processes may have similar effects—I may close the door or the wind may blow it shut—the primitive mind is tempted to posit similar kinds of cause or agent. It is amusing to note that this confusion, which takes two forms, accounts at once for the errors of primitive mythical thought, and also for the absurdities of modern pseudo-science. While the early primitive mind erroneously but understandably read something like human causation into nature—the pathetic fallacy—and peopled the universe with spirits and demons to 'explain' natural phenomena, the no-less-primitive pseudo-scientific academic mind reads impersonal empirical causality into intelligent human action, and even—more mystically—into human thought. But as we have seen, intelligence, thought, consciousness, and all behaviour that these make possible, are mediated by a multiplicity of non-empirical factors—signs, signals and symbolic forms of ever greater complexity—which must be interpreted, and are liable to be misinterpreted, in a limitless number of ways. Any notion of an unbroken chain of empirical cause and effect is here utterly out of the question. This does not mean however that we have left the realm of rational discourse. Quite the contrary: we are here concerned with the origins of the very rationality that made empirical science possible in the first place. Interpretation, error, correction of error, the devising of means—objective norms and systematic theory—to prevent error, all these form part of the intelligent behaviour of the scientist, but *not* of the phenomena he studies. The fatal error of pseudo-empiricism is that it fails to distinguish between the *phenomena* studied and the psychological, symbolic, theoretical *means* by which they are studied, and which make them intelligible. Any attempt to convert the study of human psychology, language theory, or epistemology into subdivisions of empirical science is quite simply to put the cart before the horse.

It becomes clear, then, that while narrative and descriptive discourse of the colloquial type contains in germ what will later become explanatory theory, both in the humanities and in empirical science, the transition is by no means an easy one. It took empirical science many centuries to come of age, and theory in the humanities still seems to be in a state of irremediable chaos. These two facts are not unrelated. As empirical science gradually freed itself from myth and metaphysics, moving from triumph to triumph in the process, it came to seem not so much the *product* of human intelligence, but its very source and paradigm. This error in no way affected further advance in empirical science itself, but it had disastrous consequences in the humanities, in which theorists came to appear academically respectable only insofar as they aped the techniques of empirical science. The result has been not only theoretical stultification in the humanities, but worse, moral determinism: the negation of human freedom to affect human destiny in any way. If the primitive mind read human causation into the workings of nature, the modern academic mind has all but excluded intelligent causation from human behaviour altogether. Taken to its logical conclusion, such determinism makes no distinction between an act of murder and death by disease. To one who accepts this doctrine, awareness of choice, conscious design, deliberation, the fulfilment of purpose by co-ordinated action, all become meaningless terms: we are invited to believe that the

Parthenon rose from the ground by the same causal processes as Etna or Vesuvius. Alas, the patent absurdity of moral determinism has been no obstacle to its wide acceptance. To many, its attraction has been too strong to resist: for like its mythical forerunner—Fate—it relieves its devotees of the inconvenient burden of moral responsibility.

The misconceptions noted above must not blind us to the *historical* and, initially, even the *theoretical* importance of myth, and later of metaphysics. They were the earliest attempts to develop simple explanatory discourse in the direction of more comprehensive forms of explanatory theory, concerned with such larger issues as the workings of nature and the organization of human society. As such, both played a positive role in the development of human thought. Inevitably, however, they soon became serious obstacles to the development of more rational theory, are so still, and until properly understood will so remain. The theory of language, even at this point, enables us to get rid of one very common error which hinders such understanding: the notion that myth is the most primitive stage in the development of human thought. Man's first attempt at systematic discourse—however inept and erroneous—is anything but primitive: it presupposes all previous stages of language and thought that we have traced so far. The very complexity of mythical thinking, the multiplicity of its functions, its role in the social life of organized communities, all indicate an advanced stage in the development of human thought. Metaphysical thinking, of which the doctrine of moral determinism is an example, is a more abstract form of discourse with philosophical pretensions, and clearly developed even later. Metaphysics is indeed the distinctive aberration of purely theoretical discourse and further consideration of it must wait until we come to the subject of logic. Myth, by contrast, is a more homely aberration. But both exemplify the semantic confusion which, as we have seen, tends to accompany each new development in language and thought.

Leaving aside the more numinous aspects of myth, along with fetishism, magic and other kinds of non-explanation, the chief explanatory device of mythical thought is the analogical leap from one situation, already understood, to another, doubtless similar in some respects, but which may be essentially different in others. Such analogical leaps—association on the grand scale—are not only natural, automatic and inevitable; they are sometimes valid or at least helpful. But often of course they are completely wrong and lead inquiry to a dead end. The most famous example of a successful analogical leap is Archimedes' legendary discovery of how to measure the volume of irregular solids. The most famous example of the other sort is the so-called pathetic fallacy or animism: the attempt to explain natural phenomena by projecting something like human causation into nature. But even where such explanations are wrong, they may, if the subject matter is empirical, be proved wrong and so lead to their own correction. Where, however, they deal with matters which are not amenable to empirical testing—and this includes the entire field of the humanities—then mythical thinking engenders ever more extravagant forms of speculation and we move into the world of pure fantasy, or worse, into the realm of conflicting ideologies, in which myth, metaphysics and half-baked fact make common cause in kaleidoscopic profusion.

Yet even the more gratuitous inventions of the mythical imagination may have their utility: in the creation of *ordering principles* and the notion of conformity to *objective norms*. Such factors, no matter how irrational their origins, form the essential basis of all later rational procedures. Polybius noted how the Romans—one of the most superstitious peoples in recorded history—had forged the main bonds of their social order out of mythical beliefs, and their behavioural counterpart, ritual practices.[2] Even the remarkable skills of the Romans as administrators and engineers may not be unrelated to their habit of fastidious observance of rules of a less rational kind. At a certain stage of human development there can be no doubt of the socializing effect of mythical thought in binding an individual community together in a common system of beliefs, behaviour, and explanations, which commonly includes a moral code, ritual practices, a cosmology of sorts, and much else. We thus come to see both the strength and the weakness of mythical forms of discourse. The fluidity of mythical conceptions leads to limitless associative extensions, which may come to embrace the totality of human activities and concerns in any given community. But such monolithic systems tend to become exclusive and dogmatic. What unites one community separates it from others and often becomes a source of strife. What began as open-ended speculation aiming at a wider understanding of life and the world tends to become fossilized orthodoxy, or rather a multiplicity of conflicting orthodoxies. The supreme virtue of rational theory over all mythical and metaphysical systems and ideologies is that reason alone is universally human and may be subscribed to, without loss of face, by all.

Up to now only natural science offers any convincing example of how to advance, beyond such primitive attempts at co-ordinating human knowledge and experience, to a form of explanation which commands the rational assent of any informed person. This situation is fraught with danger, for it has placed ever more powerful instruments of destruction in the hands of moral primitives. Scientific intelligence has vastly outstripped general human understanding and self-knowledge, which it is the task of the humanities to promote but which our educational system seems designed to prevent.

If modern physics and cosmology are no longer an appendage of primitive creation myths, certain other disciplines also have at least partly detached themselves from the matrix of mythical thought. History gradually extricated itself from fabulous accounts of remote origins to become, to some extent, a guide to how human populations tend to behave in similar and in dissimilar circumstances. (As any serious historian knows, the patterns of human history and human folly are repeated *mutatis mutandis* with depressing regularity. While natural science develops by building on knowledge already established it seems that in the humanities each generation must begin from scratch, only to learn how to make the same mistakes as its predecessors. This indicates a serious breakdown in education, in all areas except physical science and technology.) Even earlier, literature also had begun to transcend the limitations of localized myth and ritual, to provide insight into what Aristotle called the more universal or philosophical aspects of human life: what people have in common rather than what separates them.[3]

And yet, though these developments have brought a genuine advance in human understanding, something also has been lost. The all-embracing unity of the mythical world-view, which undoubtedly 'solved' too many problems too quickly and too confidently, has given way to a vapid relativism, to scepticism and uncertainty about matters not only of common sense but even of common interest and common survival. Where there was once a bogus consensus and certainty about the rightness and inevitability of all things, we now have a multiplicity of bogus disciplines, each committed either to the unique rightness of its own orthodoxy or to the thesis that all problems of general human concern must remain permanently insoluble. Added to which we have an ever-increasing number of shady 'interdisciplinary' alliances which largely consist in the interchange of jargon between one dubious discipline and another. Such latter-day aberrations are not too difficult to explain. It is clear that if mythical thought was man's first attempt at systematic theory, a naively ambitious attempt to correlate the most diverse areas of human experience, its eventual collapse was bound to lead to many crises. For such premature syntheses provided not only a co-ordinated system of beliefs for the individual but also became the very basis of social stability and cohesion in any given community. To tamper with any detail was to undermine the whole structure, not only of personal belief but of the fabric of society. This helps explain the eternal conflict between genuine innovators and those who see themselves as the guardians of established values.

Such a crisis occurred in ancient Athens when the scepticism of the Sophists threatened to undermine all traditional beliefs and values. To meet this challenge Plato and Aristotle managed to consolidate a metaphysical tradition of thought which—in various guises and alliances—was to last until the eighteenth century. Then a new crisis arose. By this time empirical science had begun to come of age, and idealist metaphysics along with its *a priori* natural science began to decline. Empiricism now became the order of the day. This transition produced perhaps the most bizarre misconception in the history of human thought, and one that haunts us still. Idealist metaphysics was an incipient but sadly defective theory of mind, which also contained a completely fictitious *a priori* theory of nature. Empiricism, by contrast, was an incipient but far from complete theory of physics, which soon claimed, quite implausibly, to be a theory of everything else as well, not excluding human psychology. The notion that either idealism or empiricism could provide the basis for a complete theory of human thought and of the phenomena of nature at the same time was quite absurd. Yet what happened—without anyone, it seems, being aware of the fact—was that the totalitarian claims of classical metaphysics were simply transferred to the new empirical science. One absurdity was thus substituted for another.

The fatal error in this attempt to introduce the 'experimental method' into non-experimental areas, to leap straightway from physics and mechanics into psychology and moral philosophy, was that it sought to by-pass the intermediate zone of biology. The error was perhaps pardonable since at that time biology could hardly be said to exist. What is less pardonable and quite anachronistic is that the ancient quarrel between metaphysics and empiricism should continue to rage more than a century after Darwin laid the foundations of a comprehensive theory, capable of articulating what we know of *all* aspects of life within a yet larger framework, in which there is complete harmony and coherence between what we know of nature at large, of life in general, and of the distinctive intellectual faculties of man. The naive systematizations of primitive myth and the more sophisticated ones of classical metaphysics foreshadow the possibility of a more rational synthesis which modern evolution theory alone makes possible. Only when we grasp this may we appreciate the historical importance of these premature systems, without falling victim to their alluring offer of universal knowledge on the cheap.

The virtue of mythical thought in primitive societies was that it provided a co-ordinated set of beliefs and imperatives which all accepted. When, with the slow and uneven advance of more rational forms of explanation, mythical thought ceases to be a source of social cohesion, it becomes a source of tension and conflict, within societies and between societies. We live in such a world. We need, therefore, to examine how those who first became aware of the conflict between rationality and myth sought to safeguard more rational forms of discourse and thought, and how logic emerged in the process. Before that, however, we must consider an earlier development in the history of language—the emergence of written language—and some of the complexities of linguistic meaning which it will be the task of logical analysis to clarify..

7

Written language

> It is wondrous that so great a diversity of humanly uttered sounds can be reduced to so small a number of letters. VIVES
>
> The invention of *printing*, though ingenious, compared with the invention of *letters* is no great matter. HOBBES
>
> Written discourse seems to speak to you as if it were an intelligent being, but if you cross-question it to learn more it just repeats the same thing over and over again. PLATO

After the emergence of speech no single development in the history of man is comparable in importance to the emergence of writing. If speech allowed man to develop a distinctive new faculty, without analogue in any other species, writing and all that it made possible conferred on humanity further distinctions and skills without which modern civilization would—for better or for worse—not exist. Boons and burdens such as mathematics, scientific technology and modern bureaucracy would be inconceivable without the prior existence of the written word. We must therefore consider writing as a major advance in the development of language, and not as the mere 'reduction' of the spoken language to visual form, which it neither is, nor in the nature of things can be. At most, the written word is either a cue or a mnemonic for the spoken word. In fact, apart from literary dialogue, legal depositions and chatty epistles to absent friends, it usually serves quite different purposes altogether. We rarely write what we say, and only on special occasions do we say what we write. The marked contrast between the ease with which infants learn to speak and the difficulty with which older children learn to read and write, and the fact that many who speak fluently never learn these skills at all, indicate how unautomatic is the transition from speech to writing. It is not living speech and thought, but only the abstracted phonological patterns of individual languages, that can be reduced to written form. This allows a degree of permanence, and brings a quite novel potential for the diffusion of linguistic records in time and space. But all this is bought at a price. The advent of writing is a critical turning-point in the development of language, and like all others it brings new advantages and new problems.

Theoretical discourse, as we have seen, often deals with remote events, causal explanation, deliberation about future action and the like. Yet even when the check of immediate fact has been left behind, spoken discourse is still uttered by someone to other people about some matter of common interest at a given place and time. Given all this, it soon becomes apparent if and when matters get out of hand. When we come to written discourse, however, all must be taken on trust or may even be completely unknown: authorship, place and time of composition, the nature of the matter discussed, the purpose and motive of the writer, even the meaning of the language used. The peculiar disembodied character of written (or otherwise recorded) theoretical discourse so impressed Popper that he fell into the temptation of creating a 'third world' to accommodate it. In his somewhat eclectic epistemology, this 'third world' complements two other 'worlds': that of physical reality, and that of subjective experience or mind. He thus came to believe in a 'world of objective contents of thought' and adopted a form of objective idealism inspired by Frege and Plato.[1] This extreme form of reification well illustrates the special prestige which the written language has always enjoyed in priestly and academic circles. Clearly, we need to integrate writing into a comprehensive theory of language before it does more mischief than it has done already. For it is the written language, rather than language as such, which is the main source of metaphysical idealism: either of the kind which hypostatizes our own thoughts and concepts; or of the Platonic kind which suggests that concepts or ideas have an original *substantive* existence of their own. Theoretical neglect of the written language, of its distinctive nature and function, leads at once to these misconceptions (which vitiate all further theory in the humanities), and to a falsification of language theory itself (which alone could set matters aright). This apparent impasse only disappears when we realize that most language theorists have tacitly and erroneously taken the written language—neat and tidy, with its visible forms already analysed and categorized in grammar books—as the subject matter of language theory as such. This is the inevitable consequence of their refusal, or inability, to trace language back to its origins in living speech, and further still, in symbolization and its pre-linguistic antecedents.

There is, however, a genuine similarity between writing and speech which—once we accept the obvious primacy of the spoken word—is most illuminating. In its own way, writing does for the phonetic complexity of speech what speech itself does for the complexity of raw experience: it offers norms, it helps us stabilize the flux. It helps us orientate ourselves amid complexity. But the complexity is now of our own making. The natural spontaneity and inventiveness of subjective utterance, along with many other factors, constantly undermines the unity of a common idiom. Certain norms are of course implicit in all social behaviour and therefore inherent in all social use of language. This applies not only to the actual words used, and their pronunciation, but also to their syntax and grammar. In speech the maintenance of a common idiom comes about by tacit convention. Even so, fragmentation takes place. There is abundant evidence that what originally were branches of a common language have developed into mutually unintelligible dialects or new languages. (The comparison with speciation in biology is here something more than a fanciful analogy. The ability of its members to interbreed defines a species just as people's ability to intercommunicate by purely linguistic means indicates that they speak a common language. In both fields there are border-line cases and zones of indeterminacy.)

In certain cultures—but by no means in all—the advent of some form of writing has been a potent factor in arresting the centrifugal, disintegrating tendency which is a constant threat to the unity of the spoken language, and which is often aggravated by geographical, cultural and other factors. This fact however in no way explains the *origin* of writing, which is to be sought in the pictorial image; much less the origin of *alphabetic* writing which was to emerge later. Even so, this later function of the written language indicates once again the essentially *normative* function of language, from its origin in the vocal symbol and at every stage of its development. The written word does not copy or duplicate the spoken word—a visual pattern cannot copy a vocal sound—but it may help stabilize it. The written symbol is a distinctive new development in the history of language. It can no more copy or reflect the vocal symbol than the latter can copy or reflect some object or item of experience. The common misunderstanding of writing—that it merely copies speech—is therefore not so remote in character from the general misunderstanding of speech and language in general. Just as the spoken symbol is not the copy of a particular thing but the categorial sign of a whole range of similar things, so also the written symbol does not copy a vocal utterance but is the categorial sign of a multiplicity of vocal utterances which may sound very different but which fulfil a similar function or have, as we say, a similar meaning. One need only think of the many possible pronunciations of a written word in English. (In the extreme case of the ideogram, a form of writing which may be common to several speech communities, the written symbol is the categorial sign for vocal utterances which may have no phonetic connection whatever.)

How then, we must now ask, did our modern system of alphabetical writing emerge from pictorial representation, from the visual image? The evolution was clearly a slow and tortuous affair, involving the interaction of several different cultures and traditions, but the main stages of the transition seem not to be in doubt. Primitive depiction, even sophisticated depiction, is often more or less schematic and generic, rather than realistically precise. In this respect the incipient written symbol coincides with the spoken symbol, which is generic by definition. The more schematic and general the image of, say, a bird, the better it suggests this kind of *animal* as distinct from others, rather than this kind of *bird* as distinct from others. (Initial categorization, we may recall, develops out of the confusion of similars. It calls for no 'creative act of mind' or ability to 'perceive similarities' but is accounted for—less dramatically—by the common animal and human failure to perceive differences. At a later stage of consciousness, of course, we do indeed categorize with intent.) The more schematic the visual image, then, the more readily it takes on the categorial function which is implicit in the pre-existent *verbal* symbol, with which of course it is associated from the start. The origin of writing is therefore much less problematic than the origin of speech, since writing presupposes speech and the rich stock of categories which the spoken language first creates. Writing is thus quite unlike speech in that it is a conscious product of the intelligence which speech first makes possible. Writing also presupposes, indeed develops out of, the distinctively human activity of pictorial representation or depiction, which is widespread even in non-literate cultures. This fact provides the final *reductio ad absurdum* of any theory of language which takes the written language as its basis; but it also has a wider epistemological significance which calls for attention.

The graphic representation of an object—whether by depiction or, much later, by the written word—is what first gives the fleeting concepts of thought a certain fixity, a visible reality, indeed an objectivity which we rarely associate with the volatile spoken word. Quite apart from more mystical associations which readily cluster around the graven image, we have here a common source of reification and philosophical idealism: that fatal tendency to hypostatize our own symbolic creations, placing them on the same footing as the things to which they refer; or, in more extreme versions, on a higher footing. Two opposed but complementary insights into this problem—the relation between real things and the symbolic forms which we use for categorization and reference—gave rise to the most famous misunderstanding in the history of thought: Plato's insistence on the epistemological priority of generic ideas (*eidē*, *genē*) and the derisory repudiation of this doctrine by Aristotle, who emphasized concrete substances as the primary objects of knowledge. The notion that only a theory of language could reconcile these seemingly antithetical positions eluded both these thinkers. Plato, however, also had his laugh, at the expense of 'those who think nothing real unless they can seize hold of it with both hands, excluding from reality such things as actions, processes, and all things not visible'.[2] Among those things which are not visible are, of course, the original acoustic symbols of speech, which not only *express* our generic ideas, but in association with experience actually *constitute* them. This brings us to two distinct but closely related problems: how did *visual* forms come to represent *non-visual* objects, and how did they come to represent the *sounds* of speech?

Whatever the initial functions of pictorial representation—ritualistic, magical, instructional, ornamental, even perhaps narrative or communicative—it has one serious drawback: it is limited to the representation of that which is visible. Of course, the interpretation of a pictorial representation may be eked out with the aid of verbal commentary. But this would not be an advance on common speech, which from an early stage accommodates and finds expression for the whole gamut of common human experience, visual and non-visual alike, taking in a considerable degree of abstraction, syntactic complexity and logical sophistication along the way. As the more schematic forms of graphic representation gradually moved in the direction of something like a written form of discourse—a process doubtless accelerated by the advantages of discursive thought which ordinary speech confers at an early stage—this restriction to the purely visual must have become more and more irksome. A series of visual symbols without prepositions, conjunctions or other syntactic aids would be no better than a cartoon strip without captions. And yet the virtues of an alternative mode of language, especially the advantages of possessing visual records of relative permanence, must at a certain stage of social development have appeared very great. Appreciation of the subtlety of human speech, and of its constitutive role in the development of human intelligence, comes very late, if at all. The utility of written scriptures, laws, economic accounts and administrative records, clearly impressed itself on the human mind at a much earlier stage, as history shows. These are the very roots of the modern bureaucratic state.

The theoretical question, however, remains: how did writing develop and establish itself as an alternative mode of language, one indeed which has been widely mistaken for the thing itself? How did visual forms come to represent and symbolize the non-visual concepts which ordinary speech accommodates without trouble? Historically, two main solutions emerged, one of extreme complexity, the other of breath-taking simplicity. Either one could extend the pictographic principle with which writing began, devising an ever-greater number of visual symbols to meet all needs. Or one could turn to the words of speech, with which language itself begins, and seek to analyse them into their phonological components. While in any given language the number of *sound* components is as limitless as analytic finesse may care to determine, it so happens that the system of significant components, the sounds which can effect change of meaning in standard speech, is relatively small: on average a few dozen or so. A knowledge of these components, once isolated and designated by distinctive marks, permits the phonological analysis and synthesis, and thus the writing and reading, of any word in that language.

It is not to be thought, of course, that this momentous development was consciously planned or came about quickly. It was the slow growth of time and many cultural interactions, approaching alphabetic perfection for the first time in archaic Greek. The development of writing as we know it was by no means inevitable or necessary. It was, however, a further manifestation of that potentiality, at once analytic and synthetic, which first emerged with the uttered sounds of spoken language.

Even in the transition from speech to writing, the primacy of the spoken language is once again established. Alphabetic writing came about when selected hieroglyphs or pictograms were made to take on a purely *phonological* function as letters, which enable us to analyse verbal sounds into their essential elements, and later enable us—as well as others—to resynthesize the words so analysed, either aloud, or in silent reading and thought. Speech is evanescent, and writing affords some degree of permanence. But we must not forget that writing was invented to give more permanent formulation to concepts and discourse first symbolized by speech. The correlation of these two distinct but intimately related forms of language ought to have laid the basis of a sound theory of language already. With their respective strengths and weaknesses, each illuminates the other, as well as the general phenomenon of language overall. Unfortunately, what has most commonly happened is that familiarity with the multiple virtues of speech has blurred awareness of its fundamental importance; while the visible, almost tangible objectivity of the written language has been mistaken for language itself. The very advantages which writing makes possible—its effect on cultural continuity, the recording of information, the provision of documented evidence which may be consulted tomorrow or in two thousand years, its role in the development of subjects as diverse as literature and higher mathematics—all this has led many theorists to view language as a thing in itself on a par with the reality to which it refers: quite detached from its human origin, from human purpose, judgment, and fallibility. As a result, language has been made a source of endless mystery and mystification. This will become apparent when we come to later developments in the theory of language, and consider certain confusions between logic, mathematics, and metaphysics. But even at the more humdrum level of *grammar*, the disembodied written language has been a constant source of confusion, not least in linguistic theory itself.

It is possible that no subject has been more studied and less understood than grammar. From antiquity onwards it has held a central place in formal education, yet to this day there is little agreement as to what grammar is. There is, rather, vast disagreement concerning its origin, nature, function and utility. To many, grammar has never been more than a matter of etiquette concerning which linguistic forms to adopt and which to avoid. At the other extreme, grammar has been presented as the very essence of a universal, genetically determined language faculty, of mysterious origin and even more mysterious function. Against this, some maintain that each language has its own distinctive grammar along with its distinctive lexicon, and that this radically determines the way its speakers actually think. (The first of these forms of linguistic determinism would make intercultural communication inevitable, the second would make it impossible.) In addition to the grammars of existent languages, modern linguists have created *ex nihilo* a plethora of 'theoretical grammars'. (The purpose of each of these, however, seems to elude all but the initiates of the school in question.) For some theorists, the function of grammar is normative, designed to regulate and stabilize usage; while others maintain that grammar is merely descriptive of whatever forms and constructions are in use in a given language or dialect. Some would argue that it is the task of grammar to correlate linguistic form and function, but while this is plausible in certain highly inflected languages it becomes more problematic in languages where one word can perform many functions. Moreover the very mention of function raises many problems—logical, semantic, psychological—which are themselves unresolved, and will remain so until we possess an overall theory of language. Much modern linguistic theory is sustained by the illusion that it has to do with purely *formal* analysis. This simply means that all other aspects of language are taken for granted, with their problems not only unresolved but not even consciously acknowledged. It is impossible to theorize about *any* element of language or grammatical form without reference to *function* and *meaning*.

What then is grammar, what is its origin, and why has it caused so much trouble and produced so little understanding? Confusion in this field is chiefly due to the fact that the same word designates (i) substantive grammars of actual languages, and (ii) the theoretical study of grammar in general. What we have here is a special case of a more general confusion: that between actual languages, effortlessly used by the entire human race, and theoretical understanding of human language as such, which has so far eluded most members of the human race, including professional linguists.

Grammar in the first sense is the set of conventions

governing the meaningful connection and modification (for number, tense, mood, and so on) of the conventionally accepted words of a given language. Such lexical and grammatical conventions are not only inseparable from that language, they constitute its distinctive forms. Learning how to use these, and how to adapt them to new uses, is tantamount to learning that language. Such conventions or norms are not designed to be conformed to. Quite the contrary: they are not designed at all. They are the growth of time and custom, surviving by their utility, falling into disuse when they no longer serve any purpose. They are, however, the preconditions of any linguistic communication or intelligibility whatever. Yet in the spoken language such conventions are flexible, not to say elastic: they admit of all manner of innovation, of deviation from the norm, and it is a matter of historical record that they change. As noted earlier, everything in language is conventional, even the extent to which the conventions themselves may be flouted or modified, intelligibility alone deciding between what is language and what is not. In a completely oral culture, language developments are accommodated and problems solved as they occur, linguistic change, or incipient change, being either assimilated or repudiated. There is a natural integrity in the speech of monolingual illiterates in a closely knit society. Such speakers have intuitive knowledge of grammar in the first sense: the system of conventions which is implicit in any language whatever. What they do not have, nor indeed need to have, is knowledge of grammar in the second sense: theoretical understanding of those conventions and the functions they perform.

Grammar in this second sense originates only at an advanced stage of literacy and is consciously designed to solve a number of problems which the written language brings in its train. With the accumulation of written records and the passage of time, sacred, legal and literary texts, fixed in a given form, become progressively more remote in idiom as linguistic change of various kinds affects the spoken language. An earlier stage of one's own language in which such texts are preserved may appear more and more like a foreign language, in need of exegesis and commentary. Meanwhile, intercultural contacts raise problems of understanding and translating *genuinely* foreign languages. These naturally observe not only different grammatical conventions, but often totally different *kinds* of convention. This fact—the source of many ill-conceived notions of linguistic relativism and determinism—certainly places many obstacles in the way of comprehension and creates problems which only a more theoretical understanding of language can solve. Finally, the first attempts to grapple with the even more formidable problems of logical discourse soon led to critical analysis of the linguistic forms in which such discourse is not only expressed but on which it depends. Although all human discourse is language-dependent, this fact first becomes fully apparent and inescapable only at the level of the more systematic and rational forms of discourse, which depend on purely linguistic *connectives*, without which no discourse would be possible at all. It is at this level of logically correlated discourse also that the possibility of cross-cultural communication, and the absurdity of linguistic relativism and determinism, become apparent: rational discourse on matter of common interest, such as survival, translates with admirable precision.

These various factors—hermeneutic, didactic, logical—doubtless contributed to the gradual emergence of the first rudimentary grammars of individual languages. It was at this stage that the first step was taken from concern with problems of form and related function in *particular languages* towards analysis and theory of the functions of *language in general*. For to produce what may appear a purely descriptive grammar calls not only for familiarity with the language in question, but also for logical analysis of the basic functions of any language. There thus emerged some of the first but also most penetrating examples of logical analysis: the analysis of the so-called *parts of speech*. This analysis, which has remained the basis of all sane grammatical theory since Greek antiquity, admirably confirms Darwin's statement that 'language still bears the stamp of its gradual evolution'.[3]

With only slight modifications, these early analyses of the parts of speech are no bad guide to the development of language as such, from its pre-linguistic origins, by way of reference to external fact, through various kinds and degrees of abstraction, up to the purely logical level of theoretical discourse. This is best illustrated by beginning with the two extreme parts of speech: the exclamation, and the conjunction. The *exclamation* is scarely distinguishable from instinctive animal utterance. It thus relates language to its pre-linguistic antecedents. It has no referential or symbolic value but is nevertheless a fully integrated and highly expressive part of language: it may on occasion affect linguistic meaning with greater immediacy and pointedness than any other. The *conjunction*, at the other extreme, is likewise devoid of referential or categorial value. Conjunctions—and, or, also, but, if, then, therefore, and so on—are purely logical connectives: they indicate the emphasis and direction of the thought expressed by other more substantive words. Between these two extremes lie the other principal grammatical categories traditionally recognized: name, noun, pronoun, adjective, verb, adverb, preposition.

The distinction between a name and a noun is simple enough once stated, but has often been neglected, with unfortunate consequences in language theory and logic. Failure to distinguish a name from a noun is failure to distinguish a mere sign from a categorial symbol. A *name* is no more than a verbal sign associated with some individual. The *noun*, by contrast, is the categorial symbol *par excellence*. Classes of discrete individuals linked by some common factor and categorized by a common word are the most basic categories both of language and of human thought. For this reason they were for Aristotle the starting point of all further logical and epistemological analysis. His psychological acumen in this matter has rarely been appreciated, for all 'higher' grammatical, logical and epistemological categories do indeed presuppose these primary categories which coincide with the primary symbols of common speech: those which at once designate and categorize common objects of visual perception.

The *pronoun* may be simply 'deictic', indicating some real person, thing or situation. But it also has intralinguistic uses which betoken an advanced stage of syntactic sophistication, as when it substitutes a word or words already uttered—its so-called anaphoric use—or conjoins a noun with a relative clause, and so on. The *adjective*, by contrast, reflects a certain analytic refinement, being a second-order category word which presupposes and qualifies, or more closely defines, some more substantive category symbolized by a noun. On the debit side, when adjectival qualifications are reified, that is, placed on the same categorial level as the things they qualify, they then become a potent source of error. While, *true*, *good*, *just* are relatively easy to use and understand, *truth*, *goodness*, *justice*—which are both linguistically and logically derivative—have long been a rich source of metaphysical confusion. The *verb*, on the other hand, which is abstract by nature, rarely seems to cause such trouble, even when it takes on the grammatical function of a noun.[4] The verb characteristically categorizes an action, a process, or the beginning, end, or result of an action or a process. And just as the adjective qualifies the meaning of a noun, the *adverb* proper qualifies or modifies the meaning of a verb. However, the so-called adverbs of place and time—here, now, there, then and so on—have special functions, deictic and anaphoric, not unlike those of the pronoun.

Actions and processes are abstract, but they may at least be visible or otherwise perceived. The *preposition*, which signifies pure relationship, is more abstract still. Yet language easily accommodates such prepositional abstractions. They present problems only when we ourselves abstract relations from the situations and contexts in which objects are related. (Many 'philosophical' problems can be traced back to the reification either of qualities or of relations.) Even relations, however, may be perceived. We all know what it means to say that one thing lies between two others. The *conjunction* or logical connective, by contrast, has no referential or perceptual content whatever. The conjunction has a purely intralinguistic function, linking word with word, phrase with phrase, sentence with sentence. It is the *sine qua non* of any logical discourse. In the words of an ancient grammarian, conjunctions 'fix the train of thought in a definite order and fill the gaps in its interpretation'.

Further analysis of the written language reveals many more complexities and subtleties: how, for example, one word may serve many functions, and how these functions often develop one from another. Yet even the cursory account above enables us to see how the emergence of writing provided a powerful stimulus to the development of analytical thought, which in turn created awareness of that analytic and synthetic potential which we have seen to be implicit even in the spoken language from the start. This awareness, however, came about as a side-effect of alphabetical writing, which by making language 'visible' in analytic form, first made its logical analysis possible. The original effect of writing as such was the creation of a more formalized standard language: one that transcends personal idiosyncrasy, local variation, and constant change, which may be no great disadvantage in speech, but which militate against that wider diffusion in time and space which is the distinctive utility of written texts. This development was not without its danger. The visible 'objectivity' of the written language, detached from its original human, local, and temporal setting, created the illusion that this was language itself. As a result the written language was erroneously made the basis of language theory in general, and largely remains so to this day.

This persistent error has not only prevented the emergence of a systematic theory of language: given the fundamental importance of language in all thought and behaviour which is distinctively human, it may be said to have stultified all general theory in the humanities at large, from antiquity down to the present.

Misconception or ignorance of the role of language in human psychology soon led the early thinkers into metaphysical tangles from which they sought to extricate themselves by various attempts to elaborate a system of logic. The initial error was thus compounded. For to create a system of logic without a theory of language and verbal discourse, which it is the purpose of logic to regulate, was to court disaster. The result was not a system of logic but a multiplicity of systems of metaphysics. We must soon turn to the important topic of logic and its problems. Before that, however, we must consider certain other problems concerning meaning, the different ways in which we refer to things, and the different kinds of things to which we refer.

8

Meaning, reference, categorization, modality

> To have meaning, it seems to me, is a notion confusedly compounded of logical and psychological elements. RUSSELL

> There is a group of terms, including 'refer' . . . which somehow seem to connect language with objects in the widest sense. A. R. LACEY

> There are many senses in which things are said to 'be' but all refer back to a single principle. ARISTOTLE

> Modality is not an alluring theme. F. H. BRADLEY

Little has so far been said on the topic of meaning, on which others have written so much. There are two reasons for this. First, everything linguistic has meaning: in talking of language, therefore, we are talking about meaning all the time. The attempt to theorize about linguistic meaning in abstraction from other aspects of language is as futile as the attempt to theorize about these other aspects—phonology, syntax, grammar and so on—in abstraction from meaning. Second, the topic of meaning covers a much wider area than purely linguistic meaning. We have already had occasion to consider *pre-linguistic* meaning when dealing with the origin of language. Pre-linguistic semantic factors such as signs and signals play an important role in the genesis of language. But there is also a vast field of *post-linguistic* meaning, comprising many departments: mathematics, visual art, music, scientific theory, indeed any activity or symbolism which presupposes human language and intelligence, and would thus be impossible without them, but which deals with matters other than those dealt with in common language or discourse. We shall later have to consider two areas of post-linguistic meaning—mathematics and scientific theory—because of the havoc caused by the age-old fallacy that they are logically prior or somehow superior to language. In fact, without language neither would exist. And as we must also consider the nature of logic and philosophy, this may be a convenient place to mention another fallacy: that logic and philosophy concern matters remote from common experience and discourse. Logic, as we shall see, is concerned with the very nature and regulation of linguistic discourse; and philosophy has for its subject matter nothing other than the most general problems with which common humanity must contend at all times, and with which it can contend only through the medium of linguistic discourse logically regulated.

These two extremes—pre-linguistic meaning and post-linguistic meaning—set natural limits to what we may call ordinary linguistic meaning, which is complex enough to be treated as a subject in its own right. We thus have three distinct areas of meaning. Between them there are many overlaps and interrelations; but also there are many differences which make it imperative that we should not confuse these three areas. As a bonus, if we do make this tripartite division of semantics, most of the problems traditionally associated with the topic of meaning evaporate. Concentrating now on purely linguistic meaning, there are three or four further distinctions, obvious enough once stated, but which are commonly neglected and must therefore be theoretically established if we are to avoid confusion. In its origin, and in common speech most of the time, language embraces three quite distinct sets of factors—psychological, formal, environmental—all of which are commonly said to have meaning, and are tied up with the understanding of meaning. First, there is the meaning of the speaker, and there is also the interpretation of this meaning by the hearer. Only in the simplest speech situations is it to be expected that these two psychological kinds of meaning—intention expressed and interpretation construed—will more or less coincide. The degrees of understanding and the ways of misunderstanding other people's meaning are legion. A further point: even the speaker (or writer) himself may later re-interpret his own utterance in a sense different from its original meaning. He may see in it more than he intended; or he may find it wanting, and then modify or correct it, improve it. Such self-improvement forms a large part of our mental development. Over-emphasis on social communication by means of language often obscures the way in which language enables each individual to educate himself, to allow his thought to mature.

It is to be noted that the two main *psychological* uses of the word 'meaning'—meaning intended and meaning interpreted—are common parlance, and are plausibly applied, beyond language, to the emission of, and response to, signals in general, be they animal or human. This is a salutary reminder that meaning in the purely *formal* sense—the meaning of the words we use—is a late arrival and presupposes more primitive semantic processes, which do of course form part of language, but to which it cannot be reduced. This helps us keep linguistic meaning and all language-dependent meaning and thought in evolutionary perspective. It also helps us avoid the main source of metaphysical idealism. For idealism also is language-dependent, but in a bad sense. Idealism takes language for granted, without inquiring into its nature and origin, and then treats language-dependent ideas and thought as insoluble problems, or—what comes to the same—presents a plethora of conflicting solutions which ensure that controversy will be permanent. If we abstract the *formal element* from language as a whole we create insoluble problems. If we place it in context it is quite unproblematic. The meaning of the words we use is determined primarily by their conventional associations, many of which we assimilate intuitively, and which—with varying degrees of precision—are registered in dictionaries and grammar books; and secondarily by the circumstances—psychological and environmental—of their utterance. Such circumstances, which are always unique, modify and render more specific the generic associations which the words in isolation vaguely suggest.

In addition to meaning in the formal or verbal sense and the two kinds of meaning in the psychological sense, there is a third common use of the word 'meaning': the meaning of the things we speak about, of what concerns, interests, or puzzles us. What, we commonly ask, is the meaning of some novel situation or unforeseen event? How are we to interpret, extract meaning from, or read meaning into, some new state of affairs? It is clear that the search of meaning in this sense is the search for understanding and explanation, and that it is not restricted to human language and behaviour but extends to the world at large. Yet, paradoxically, while language alone enables us to understand and explain our experience of the world, it is easy to forget that linguistic reference originates with the categorization of objects of external experience, of things in the world. This is because language, once instituted, enables us to refer also to many other kinds of objects, and since these are referred to in the same way—by means of words—we tend to lose our sense of priorities. Here again only an evolutionary approach can set matters in the right order.

We thus come to the topic of *reference*, which, if simple enough in its origins, becomes decidedly more complex as the linguistic plot thickens. For it is clear that we make reference by means of words not only to mice and men and other substantive particulars, which Aristotle rightly saw to be the primary objects of categorization, but also to such things as truth and falsity, feeling and thought, belief and doubt, hopes and fears, necessity, impossibility, the nature of reality, the projected constitution of a well-ordered republic, and even to such oddities as the square root of minus one. Clearly, if meaning is a complex concept, reference is by no means a simple one either. As with meaning, however, problems only arise when we fudge matters, neglect distinctions, and ignore complexity. It is not complexity which breeds problems but our neglect of it: especially our neglect of categorial complexity, and our consequent reduction of all categories—and thus all objects of reference—to the same logical status. One cannot lay hands on truth or necessity in the way a cat catches a mouse or an angler catches a fish. Language, however, which is a great leveller, creates the illusion that we can, and thus becomes a major source of logical reductionism. Since all objects of linguistic reference have similar word status, it is natural to think that they have—or to be unaware that they do not have—the same logical status, function, or categorial level. When errors of this kind occur we stand in need of logical theory.

As noted in the last chapter, logical analysis is implicit in grammatical analysis of the various functions which words may perform in linguistic discourse, and of the different levels of abstraction which—unbeknown to most speakers—even common speech contains. Linguistic analysis is indeed the first stage of logic. Any attempt to approach logic by any other route is doomed to failure, since the inbuilt logical complexity of language is at once the subject matter and the *raison d'être* of logical inquiry. The very word *logos*, cognate with the Greek verb 'to speak', means rational (i.e. logical) linguistic discourse, whether spoken, written, or silently thought; and in order to be rational or logical, discourse must be grammatically articulated, not a mere jumble of words. However, before we come to logic proper, it will be well to have some idea of how the problems which it is designed to solve first arise. To do this we must examine the complexity that lies beneath the surface of even the most ordinary forms of common speech. Otherwise, logic will remain what to most people it has always been: arid, useless, and quite incomprehensible. There is little hope of solving problems before they are clearly seen to exist.

Logical analysis of the elements of discourse—the so-called parts of speech—reveals the complexity of language when fully developed. But when considering the nature of symbolization we noted that language was quite complex from the start. The starting point of language is objective reference, which as we saw earlier has rudimentary antecedents in animal signalling. In language, however, such reference comes about by the use of words, which are associated with objects of external experience by social convention. Empirical reference of this kind is the sheet-anchor of language, the bond between language and reality on which all other uses of language ultimately depend, and to which—at no matter how many removes—all refer back. This point was clearly grasped by Aristotle.[1] But the way in which language refers or relates to reality is anything but simple. Linguistic reference is not like pointing at something with the finger. Moreover, the function of the symbol is not only referential, but also categorial and differential at the same time. In using a word to refer to an object we implicitly class this object with others similarly categorized, and obliquely differentiate it from others differently categorized. In addition, the symbol has mnemonic and heuristic functions, which link the object to others previously experienced, and facilitate the identification of others yet to be encountered. Linguistic reference, then, is a highly complex and open-ended affair from the start, and becomes progressively more so as each speaker develops his own linguistic skills. Linguistic reference does not remain fixed at the stage of recognition and joyful designation of objects which so elates the infant as it learns to speak. (Latin *infans* means 'non-speaker', and like *logos* draws attention to early awareness of the importance of language in the development of human intelligence.) Linguistic reference is not restricted to mere designation—cat, dog, and so on—but soon essays more ambitious tasks: the cat is on the mat, the dog walks on its hind legs. This form of *secondary reference*, saying something more about an object referred to, is traditionally known as predication, and though it gives the infant little trouble it has always given the logicians a great deal. The main reasons for this are the extreme range and diversity of characterizations which can be described as predication, and the vast number of persons, things, events and situations—real, imaginary, or even non-existent—which (in grammatical terminology) are said to be the *subjects* of such predication.

Subject and predicate make a sentence. By the time we reach the sentence, then, linguistic reference, already complex at the stage of primitive symbolization, becomes immeasurably more complex. And when later the attempt is made to concatenate sentences into rational discourse on matters of any theoretical difficulty, the inbuilt logical complexities of language create almost insuperable problems for even the most judicious theorists in all fields outside physical science. Even to begin to understand why this should be, we need to make a distinction which is one of the most fundamental in the entire theory of language. It is the distinction between *empirical reference* and *modal reference*. By empirical reference is here meant linguistic reference to the immediate perceptual experience of the speaker. By modal reference is meant any other use of language whatsoever. While empirical statement, whether true or false, is a relatively simple matter which may be verified by observation, or (in the case of recurrent phenomena with which physical science is commonly concerned) by experimental means, modal reference is an area of immense complexity. It covers a vast semantic field, indeed the greater part of language, and constitutes the chief problem area in language theory. Modality, as the term implies, comprises many different modes of reference. Yet the differences between different types of modal reference are as nothing compared with this more fundamental difference: between direct reference to objects of immediate experience (with which language begins) and modal reference (which includes all modifications of this primitive function, and hence the entire development of language beyond that point).

The reason for stressing the fundamental importance of this division is two-fold. First, to emphasise that all other uses of language do indeed develop out of its primitive use: empirical reference. This ensures that these later developments do not lose contact with their roots, since they are—no matter how indirectly and at no matter how many removes—dependent on empirical reference. Second, to draw attention to the twin absurdities which ensue if we neglect this distinction. For then we will either consider all reference to be like empirical reference, inventing quasi-empirical 'realms' and 'worlds' to which modal statements supposedly refer; or modal reference will lose contact with reality altogether. Both errors—which are not all that far apart—are matters of historical record, and underlie many of the verbal wrangles which are politely referred to as philosophical controversy. These two errors exemplify two of the most persistent forms of metaphysics: one which maintains that we have knowledge of worlds other than that in which we live; and the other which seeks to divorce the world in which we live from the knowledge we have of it, and then claims that the relation between external reality and human understanding is an insoluble problem. One of the major utilities of a critical theory of language is that it enables us to isolate and expose these fallacies, and at the same time understand how they came about. Moreover, once it becomes clear that such errors spring from misconceptions about the nature of language, it becomes equally apparent that only a valid theory of language can eradicate them.

Modal reference, like semantic mediation, has proved to be one of the most problematic topics in both language theory and epistemology. This is hardly surprising since mediation and modality permeate the whole of human language and thought, both of which develop, from quite simple beginnings, through ever greater degrees of complexity. Yet neither concept is difficult to understand if—following our evolutionary precept—we trace these processes back to their origins and then trace their progressive complications. This evolutionary method, which seeks to explain *actual developments*, is to be preferred to the approach of 'structuralist' metaphysicians who remain permanently mesmerized by complexity, in a world of unchanging, timeless abstractions.

Semantic mediation is the process by which one thing comes to be associated with, and thus signify, another. This occurs quite automatically in both animal and human life, and explains the origin and development of all forms of meaning: pre-linguistic, linguistic, and even post-linguistic. (Semantic relations and substitutions underlie the entire fabric of mathematics, for example; and the whole of art likewise draws on various kinds of semantic association: for no other reason is it, or could it be, meaningful.) If semantic mediation explains the origin and progressive extension of *all* kinds of meaning, the notion of modality accounts for the major distinction within the field of purely linguistic meaning: that between empirical reference and modal reference.

The characteristics of modal reference are semantic and logical complexity. Semantic complexity we take in our stride at an early age. It is indeed already present in empirical reference, which depends for its meaning not only on the words or *forms* of speech, but on the total situation—psychological and physical—in which they are uttered. Hence the absurdity of any purely formal or 'structuralist' approach to language theory which takes as its starting point, not human speech in real-life situations, but the written forms of a particular language, abstracted from any situation whatever. Logical difficulties and problems of interpretation occur precisely when language is so abstracted from a concrete speech situation. For then all the semantic complexities which in speech we take in our stride, and many others which may be implicit in the subject matter of discourse so abstracted, call for special interpretative skills if we are to understand those uses of language which are valid, or unmask error in those which are not. All this quite apart from the fact that modal reference creates ambiguities and problems of interpretation even in colloquial speech. Modality is a minefield of hidden implications, which it is the task of logical analysis to detect. Modal expressions always mean more than they formally state.

Given the priority of *empirical* reference to objects of external experience, *modal* reference must be based on it and yet be different from it. The key to understanding at once this link and this difference is to be sought in the *universal* or *categorial* function implicit in all symbolization, and so present in language from the outset. Not only is categorization an important subject in its own right, but it affords the simplest and most obvious examples of how empirical reference turns into modal reference. Briefly stated, there is a world of logical difference between using a category word to refer to an *object* of sensory perception—say, this fish—and using the same word to refer to the *category* of all such objects: fish in general, all fish, present, past, and yet unspawned. Categories, even categories of empirical objects, are not themselves objects of empirical experience, of sensory perception. All categories, and not merely the more abstract ones, are purely notional entities. They are, however, none the less important for that. Of such stuff are our notions made. What is less easy to grasp is that our initial notions, concepts, categories of thought, are not only post-perceptual—experience being prior to thought

—but also language-dependent. More difficult still is to understand that the distinctively human kind of perception, which involves the identification and differentiation of a vast number of categorized objects of experience, would be impossible but for the mnemonic function of words. Perception is not mere sensation. Nor do we simply perceive things, think about them, and then assign names to them. Or rather, by the time we can do that sort of thing, we have come a long way. That is not how human perception and thought begin. It is by learning to associate words and things that each individual must create human perception and thought for himself. This comes about through the complex function—at once referential, categorial, differential, mnemonic, and heuristic—of our first words or symbols. After our first halting steps, the process knows no limits. But it also creates many problems.

We noted earlier that both *meaning* and *reference* are complex topics, but also that they engender problems only when we disregard their complexity. The same is true of *categorization*. Before turning to the complexity of modal reference, therefore, we must consider some of the complexities involved in our many modes of categorizing things: for the complexities of modal reference are inseparable from the complex nature of our categories, and from the much neglected fact that the same object or individual may be categorized in many different ways. The same man, for example, may be categorized as tall, rich, son, father, brother, musician, amateur photographer, football enthusiast, and in many other ways. Likewise, a given material object may be a complex of wood, canvas and pigment, of no great value; a priceless work of art; or a commercial item worth one million pounds. For human knowledge, to *be* is to be categorized. And clearly, there are not only many categories but many *kinds* of category: substantive, adjectival, relational, functional, aesthetic, and commercial, to name but a few. Yet all are the product of linguistic symbolization, without which neither human intelligence nor the countless categories which subserve the multifarious needs, interests, and whims of humankind could exist. Without linguistic symbols we could neither remember, utilize, nor extend the potentially limitless number and variety of human categories, by which we not only *refer* to things known, but without which we could not even *know* them in any human sense of the word. For in a curious way, which has intrigued many thinkers, linguistic symbols *constitute* the very categories of the things which they categorize. This fact, alas, has often led idealist metaphysicians into the trap of thinking that our notional categories constitute also the things categorized. We shall shortly see that this curious belief comes about through failure to make two essential distinctions: that between empirical and non-empirical categories; and the related distinction between empirical and modal reference. Until these distinctions are understood, we shall constantly confuse our own awareness with the things of which we are aware; and also with the symbolic devices which mediate between the two areas: human consciousness, and the amazing diversity of things which are referred to as its objects. We have noted before that it is out of such confusions that both language and human consciousness are born. Also that at the level of common sense the confusion does little harm. The trouble begins when our thought takes wing and we begin to speculate about higher things. When our theorizing is cut off from immediate empirical reference it tends to run amok, unless the strictest safeguards are introduced to prevent this.

It is salutary to recall, therefore, that even our most primitive empirical categories—on which all other categories are modelled and ultimately depend—have a normative function, the importance of which it would be impossible to exaggerate. First, because until understood, we are constantly liable to hypostatize this normative function of the categorial symbol in the form of *concepts* and *ideas* mysteriously lodged 'in the mind', but without any explanation of how they got there. This is a fruitful source of metaphysical idealism. Second, because when rightly understood, this normative function is seen to be not only constitutive of our categorial concepts, but constitutes thereby the first principle of logic: the principle of logical identity (which is, of course, quite distinct from the notions of either physical or personal identity). Since all other logical principles presuppose logical identity, we shall find that logic is not a discipline superimposed on language, but permeates its entire development. (Neglect of this fact explains why we have not so far had either an adequate theory of language or a proper understanding of logic.) Finally, this same principle is also a basic principle of epistemology: the antique 'problem of universals' disappears when we grasp that universal concepts are simply the categorial symbols of ordinary language. Previous nominalist arguments to this effect, however, always foundered through ignorance of the complex nature of linguistic symbolization, of its origins, and of its essentially normative function. The problems to which classical philosophy rightly drew attention but could not solve—the central problems of human psychology or mind, of logic and the nature of rational discourse, of epistemology or the study of the distinctive nature of human knowledge—can be solved only in the context of a systematic theory of language, which alone can clarify and co-ordinate these other disciplines that have so long and so fruitlessly been pursued in isolation.

The normative function of the categorial symbol manifests itself in two ways. First, no matter how tentative and vague our initial categories may be—indeed inevitably are—not just anything can qualify for membership of an empirical category: there must be objective factors which constitute criteria for such membership. Second, as our categorizing finesse develops, the categories established reciprocally define and delimit one another. These points are simply illustrated by the apparent errors of infantile categorization. Having learnt to recognize what a dog is, the infant may then extend the word 'dog' to cover all other quadrupeds newly encountered. This does not indicate precocious insight into zoology, but neither does it indicate a mistake. It indicates the ability to categorize. Some dogs look not unlike cats, and a horse seen from afar may plausibly be mistaken for a dog. All primitive categories are of this kind: visual objects having certain features in common are associated by use of a single word, at once uttered and heard. Vision, hearing, and vocal utterance are thus equally indispensable factors in the genesis of language and human psychology. (Neglect of this fact is the more surprising in that the same three facts are correlated even at the level of animal signalling.) All later categories build on these primitive ones by progressive refinement, and may eventually leave visual perception far behind, as in the upper reaches of mathematics and physics, or even in abstract discourse in ordinary language. We cannot, however, kick away the ladder, as Wittgenstein thought, since it is our only contact with the ground, with reality.[2] What we must do, rather, is explain how we climbed up it: how we derived more complex and more abstract categories from these more primitive ones. To this end we must consider more closely the notion of category, and later the topic of modality.

In dwelling on the categorial function of the linguistic symbol we must not forget that this function cannot be separated from the others: least of all from its mnemonic and heuristic functions. To understand the use of the word 'fish' means that you can refer not only to fish now swimming but also to their remote ancestors, and even identify fish in the future. You may later have trouble with eels and seals, but nothing that a little common sense and categorial refinement will not remedy. Such categories are the basis of that 'large discourse looking before and after' that Hamlet speaks of. We must, therefore, get rid of a common misconception. Not even a primitive, empirical category, such as 'fish' stands for, is a class, a set, or a plurality of existent objects, since it refers to these along with others not yet in existence and yet others already extinct. This complexity present in our primary empirical categories draws attention to two points which help us avoid two further misapprehensions. First, our empirical categories, on which all others are modelled, must indeed be rooted in empirical fact, but are not restricted to it. Categories are not classes of given objects. Second, while any category whatever must be constituted by a linguistic symbol, this does not mean that categories are therefore 'free creations' of the human mind, as modern idealism frequently claims. Our basic categories are compounded of both psychological *and* empirical factors, and all 'higher', more abstract categories presuppose and rest on these more basic ones. The whole process of symbolic categorization is much more complex, but also far less mysterious, than is commonly supposed.

Before it became clear—if indeed it is yet clear—that all categories are language-dependent, they were usually referred to as *universals* or universal concepts. Ignorance of their origin led to many centuries of speculation as to their nature and function. Did universals have their being in things, in the mind, or somewhere else, as Plato notoriously claimed? If in the mind, were they prior to experience, or did they result from it, and in what way? How do moral concepts—those which refer to human thought and action—differ from all others? Any piecemeal solution to these problems proved to be quite impossible, and no more systematic approach has yet appeared. By placing such questions in an evolutionary perspective, however, we are in a position to understand their validity and importance, to see their interconnection, and even to answer them. For if human knowledge (based on such universal concepts) begins with identification and categorization of the empirically given, it certainly does not end there. And as we have seen, even such primary categories have complex functions other than the purely referential. We must therefore consider the above problems in sequence and see how they tie up.

Clearly, if empirical categories did not have some basis in empirical fact—in things—they would not exist. Likewise, if we did not somehow have such categories in our minds they would not form part of our knowledge. Why then did Plato refuse to locate his generic ideas—which cannot be essentially different from anybody else's—either in nature or in the mind? A full answer to this would call for an entire book. The brief answer, therefore, is that Plato was the first and to this day one of the very few who have grasped the essentially *normative* function of our categories and general ideas: that they are the norms by which other more variable things and thoughts are known and judged. As such, they could not be placed on the same logical level as the changing phenomena of nature. But even less could they be located in the volatile minds of giddy men, who constantly defend the most contradictory theses, convinced that they are in possession of the truth. Plato never fell into the error—so common today—of believing 'the human mind' to be an invariant entity, identical copies of which are lodged in the heads of all human beings, or more absurdly, in their genes. He grasped two obvious truths which seem to have eluded most other labourers in the philosophical vineyard: that men differ psychologically just as they differ physically; and that civilized life depends on the establishment of objective norms by which the thought and action of different individuals may be co-ordinated, in the interest of social harmony; and judged, when discrepancy or conflict occurs. This being so, if generic ideas, which enable us to correlate empirical data and co-ordinate human thought and action, are to perform their normative function, they must be sought for 'somewhere else' or, as we should say, on a different logical plane. Plato's theory of ideas did in fact begin as an inquiry into the logical status of universals. And in the *Republic* he explicitly correlates his generic ideas with the category words of ordinary language.[3] Whatever we may care to think of Plato's metaphysics, his logic is here impeccable.

There is, then, a hint of the truth in each one of our first three questions concerning the nature and logical status of universals. But the whole truth emerges only when we correlate all three factors hinted at: *empirical data*, indispensable ingredients in our primitive categories, and indirectly therefore in all others; complex *psychological processes* (vaguely referred to as 'the mind'), the genesis of which we examined earlier; and the normative function of our *linguistic symbols*, through which each speaker progressively builds up what Plato called a 'network of ideas', without which, he stated, there could be no rational discourse or thought at all.[4] Whatever he may have meant by this, it is quite in order for us to extract the logical kernel from the metaphysical husk. The guarantee of objective knowledge, which Plato sought to vindicate, is not to be found ready-made in nature. But neither is it to be found, equally ready-made, laid up in some Platonic heaven. It is a by-product of language, which not only makes possible the subjective thought of each individual, but is the basis of social cohesion, and of the means of ensuring its continuance: by the provision of objective norms, public terms of reference, to which all can reasonably be called on to conform.

The remaining questions concerning universals and concepts are also interconnected, and are best considered together. The first—are universals prior to experience or do they result from it?—we have already partly answered. The universal, or unifying concept, is simply the categorial function of the complex linguistic symbol, which also has heuristic and other functions. Symbolization is an ongoing process of thought. It is not merely a way of labelling categories of things we know but an aid to discovery of more things of the same kind, as well as a means of establishing new categories on the basis of differences. Even empirical categories, therefore, which are initially *a posteriori* acquire in the course of experience an *a priori* character. It is noteworthy that the Epicurean term for 'concept' was *prolepsis*, 'prior grasp', 'anticipation', which registers this heuristic aspect of the symbol. Latin *conceptus*, by contrast, implies a (logical) 'holding together', reflecting the categorial aspect. Anticipation, of course, is implicit in the notion of conditional reflex: in response to a sign, the dog salivates in anticipation of food, even if there be none. Indeed, all pre-linguistic signification—and a great part of linguistic meaning also—conforms to this simple pattern of experiencing one thing and expecting another.

Recognition of this heuristic *a priori* function, present in even our most primitive categories, is the first step towards understanding the innovatory or creative potential of human language and thought. It is also of paramount importance for understanding the difference between *empirical* and *moral* concepts. The term 'moral' is here used as in 'moral philosophy' in the broad sense: not restricted to ethics alone but meant to cover the entire field of the humanities, all areas of inquiry in which human consciousness and action determine the very nature of the subject matter; in short, all areas of knowledge which are not the subject matter of empirical science. (We shall later see that empirical science, being a distinctively human pursuit, must itself become a topic of philosophy so conceived, and that when certain misapprehensions are removed, it greatly clarifies the nature of symbolic discourse and human thought in general.) Moral concepts, then, are those which refer to all things distinctively human. Habits and customs (*mores*) are naturally included. Obsession with social inertia, however, has always had a stultifying effect on anthropology, sociology, and psychology. Here we are more concerned with the products and effects of *conscious* thought and action: institutions, artifacts, laws, money, education, civilization, warfare, to name but a few.

We thus come to the last of the questions noted above. What distinguishes moral concepts from all others is not only this obvious human dimension, but also a feature which, from a logical point of view, it would be difficult to overestimate. It is that unlike empirical categories, which may indeed acquire an *a priori* function, many moral concepts are prior (to that which they categorize) from the start. Put another way, what they categorize would not exist without them. This is not to say that all things human are consciously premeditated, but rather, for example, that while nothing can be legal or illegal until so categorized and laid down by law, fish would continue to swim whether we categorized them or not.

It is at this point that language theory can make its greatest contribution to human self-understanding. For if we fail to note this distinction, which is relatively simple, we shall certainly fail to understand what is at issue in the main problem areas in human affairs, where these different types of concept merge and are commonly confused. In particular, we shall fail to understand those problems which arise as a direct *result* of human behaviour, but not of conscious human *design*. The most obvious of such problems is, perhaps, over-population, with such resultant problems as food-shortage and starvation, or unemployment and civil strife, that may come in its wake. But the most fundamental problem of this sort is the problem of language itself, which also comes about as a result of human behaviour, but could not possibly have come about as a result of human design. This fact was stated, with unusual clarity, by Schelling, who noted that since without language no human consciousness is conceivable at all, the foundations of language could not have been consciously laid.[5] Rousseau and Herder also puzzled over this problem but were unable to solve it. When approached in an evolutionary perspective, however, the natural history of language, and of language-dependent thought, ceases to be an enigma.

In making the above distinction between empirical and moral concepts we reach, as it were, logical and epistemological rock-bottom, and begin to understand that while our primitive categories do indeed have a basis in nature, language and thought gradually take on a new dynamic or creative character of their own. Precisely because language underlies all distinctively human thought, it constitutes all our concepts and categories, empirical and moral alike. But whereas empirical categories take the given as their starting point, moral concepts may themselves be starting points, helping us create or bring about that to which they refer. And what applies to simple concepts and categories applies of course to more complex symbolic structures—statements, discourse, theory—in which they occur. They thus become paradigmatic in at least one of the senses which Plato claimed for his famous Ideas. (It is noteworthy that Plato was primarily a moral philosopher and that his doctrine becomes absurd only when applied to empirical concepts: when it is suggested that empirical concepts underlie not only *our knowledge*, but also *the reality* of that which they categorize.)

Moral concepts are thus quite different from empirical concepts, being more in the nature of originative principles. They are, as it were, categories in action, which not only refer to given objects and forms of behaviour but suggest new possibilities, guide and prescribe future behaviour. This is most obviously true of all procedural, legal and ethical categories, and more so of the rules, regulations and laws which embody them. These are, by definition, oriented towards the future, designed not to describe the given, but to determine what is to be.

Such innovatory, future-oriented concepts necessarily build on and extend existent knowledge and forms of behaviour. The wheel, we may assume, was suggested by natural objects such as logs and rolling stones, even though someone must have invented the axle in a flash of insight. Metallurgy doubtless emerged with the discovery of metal deposits in ovens designed for more domestic purposes. But whatever the course of events, new techniques and artifacts gradually emerge—steam engines, motor cars, machine guns, washing machines, atom bombs and so on—which were not originally 'given' in nature but had to be humanly *conceived* before they could exist at all. Similarly, habit, custom and natural hierarchies of power automatically regulate the social life of animals and humans alike; but human beings alone consciously create laws for themselves, in order to regulate social life in a rational and humane manner, and devise new laws, when necessary, to meet ever-changing conditions. All this would be unthinkable without the innovatory function of the categories of language-dependent thought, which enables us to conceive not only that which is, but also that which is not, but which may be, or which ought to be.

Although this fundamental distinction—between things and processes which come about by nature and those which, while presupposing the latter, depend on the special contrivance of human beings—was explicitly made by Plato, it is one which we constantly overlook. It is, therefore, important to understand why this should be so. This is not too difficult. For just as our empirical categories take on a heuristic or exploratory function, so also do our more creative categories come to take on an empirical function. Once in existence, the products, effects, and results of human contrivance—artifacts like chairs and tables, patterns of behaviour such as driving on the right, mathematical entities such as squares, circles, and numbers, not to mention language itself—appear to us to be not so very different from any other objects of experience. This illusion is promoted by the levelling influence of language, which lulls us into the belief that all things verbally categorized are on the same logical level, and hence on the same ontological plane also. This is to ignore the one unequivocal lesson of both Plato and Aristotle: that there are different *kinds* of category, corresponding to the different aspects of what we call reality. The illusion is also promoted by the fact that two very different kinds of category—empirical and moral—are commonly fused. We make bricks (artifacts designed to serve human purpose) out of clay (a natural material). We enclose plots of land in geometrical patterns. There are man-made lakes. In many cases perception is the leveller. We see squares and circles in the same way as we see the outlines of natural objects. A washing machine is just as visible an object as the cat sitting beside it, although millennia of evolution separate the two. People performing rituals, or even conforming to more rational patterns of behaviour, exhibit certain regularities not unlike those observable in other animal species, or even in purely physical phenomena.

These facts easily suggest misleading analogies. Such analogies indeed provide the shaky foundations of various schools of psychology and sociology, for whose practitioners the study of human beings is not significantly different from birdwatching, or more absurdly still, from physical science. The quite different principles proper to ethology, physics, and human psychology have thus become utterly confused. All such confusions can be eliminated only when we possess an adequate theory of language. For without language we could not create the multiplicity of concepts of different kinds which we all too often confuse; and without a theory of language we shall lack proper understanding of how, and in how many different ways, our language relates to what we vaguely refer to as reality. Yet even as we comment on all this we become aware of the extreme complexity of the knowledge which, all unawares, we take in our stride in our use of common language in everyday life. Language, or the symbolic consciousness which it underpins, provides, as it were, the unconscious theory of our common experience. For everyday purposes, as long as it works, it suffices. Formal theory is only needed when things go wrong. If all people were always healthy, there would be no need for medical science.

In the previous chapter we saw how even a brief analysis of the 'parts of speech' reveals the semantic and logical gamut of ordinary language, all the way from exclamations, scarcely distinguishable from the expression of animal emotion, up to purely abstract connectives or conjunctions, which are indispensable features of logical discourse. In this chapter so far we have touched on the great range and variety of objective reference which linguistic symbols make possible. In the process we have seen how complex are both the reality to which we refer, and the linguistic means by which we refer to it. We must now return to the thorny problems of *modality* and *modal reference*, which constitute the most complex and least understood part of language theory, and as such are the prime breeding ground of logical error. In particular, we must consider how modal reference differs from empirical reference, which is, we may say, the sheet-anchor of language, the original bond between language and reality on which all distinctively human knowledge ultimately rests. Initially, it must be said that these problems, like most others, become distinctly less thorny once we know they exist and face them squarely. Hitherto the topic of modality has been explicitly treated only by logicians and grammarians, in ways which are quite inadequate to the importance of the subject. It is a sad fact that logic has never quite weaned itself from theology.[6] So-called 'modal logicians' exhibit an obsession with propositions which are 'necessarily true' in a plurality of different 'worlds', specially created for the purpose. Many logicians are further afflicted by the belief that logic is a mathematical discipline and thus capable of 'generating' statements which are indeed necessarily true. Alas, the necessary truths of mathematics are simply equations, and hence tautologous. (They are none the worse for that: therein lies their utility.) More to the point, mathematics is a post-linguistic symbolism and activity, of immense importance, but quite remote from the type of semantic complexity which is the main subject matter of language theory and logic. (The two, as we shall see, are inseparable: logic, unless based on language theory, is vacuous; and language theory without logic is, in the most literal sense, nonsensical.)

The treatment of modality by grammarians was scarcely avoidable, since in Greek and Latin grammar the moods of the verb—infinitive, imperative, subjunctive, optative and so on—were elaborately distinguished in a multiplicity of forms. It is possible to interpret the notion of verbal modality in the sense that the *normal* use of the verb is indicative or empirically referential, and that all other uses are developments or *modifications* of this use. If we take the word 'normal' in the most literal sense this is both true and theoretically important, since objective reference is indeed the most primitive use of language, and is presupposed by all later uses. There is here an important parallel with Aristotle's scheme of the most general categories, in which substantive particulars take precedence over all other categories: quality, quantity, relation and so on. If we speak of six green bottles, clearly bottles are the substantive things which are then quantified and qualified. We may say that the indicative verb does for the predicate what the substantive noun does for the subject of the sentence. Together they produce an empirical statement. There are however many other kinds of subject and many other kinds of predicate, and these constitute the realm of modality, which embraces all other kinds of statement and language use in general. Language *begins* with empirical reference—first simple designation, later categorical statement—but it certainly does not end there. (The notion that language begins with, or only consists of, 'well-formed sentences' is a modish piece of academic obscurantism which not only obscures the origins of language, but even the origin of well-formed sentences.)

If modal reference is any use of language other than empirical reference based on the immediate perceptual experience of the speaker, it follows that modality cannot be restricted to metaphysical speculation—which is what 'modal logic' amounts to—or even to the grammar of the verb. In truth, modality is built into language from the very start. For all linguistic reference, even empirical reference, comes about not by pointing at objects, but by symbolic categorization. (The still widely held belief that language could have originated in gesture rather than vocal utterance and speech betrays a total misconception of how language works. This view also betrays ignorance of the essential role of *hearing* in the genesis of language and human thought. It is, therefore, salutary to note that Aristotle had already grasped this fact more than two thousand years ago.)[7]

But not only is modality built into the first words of language, thanks to their categorial function. As noted earlier, this very function illustrates the simplest form of modal reference possible: the use of a category word to refer, not to an object of external experience, but to the category itself. The fact that the same word—say, dog—is used to refer to an individual creature and to the category of all such creatures makes the transition from empirical reference to modal reference almost imperceptible. The example is trivial, but neglect of the logical difference involved accounts for many 'philosophical' problems. Higher categories—mammal, vertebrate, animal—are more modal and logically complex: they refer to more complex categories, and implicitly to more numerous and complex correlations. Modality is a labyrinth of hidden meanings.

Another simple case of modal reference—almost certainly the first which we consciously use—is exemplified by *negation*. We are tempted to consider positive and negative concepts as being on an equal logical footing, and the same may be said of positive and negative statements. It is not possible, however, to make empirical reference to a non-existent object or state of affairs, but only modal reference. Negative concepts and statements always *imply* at least the possibility of positive ones. Modal reference always implies more than it states. We do not say 'There are no chairs in this room' unless we know what chairs are, need chairs or expected to find chairs, or when someone has wrongly led us to believe the contrary, or made a statement to that effect. This last calls for a special form of negation—denial—which implicitly refers not only to a real situation, but also to a statement already made about it; possibly also to human error, mendacity, misunderstanding or the like. It may here be said that although negation has caused the logicians not a few headaches, the psychological origin of linguistic negation presents no problem whatever: it is to be found in human need, desire, and expectation, especially frustrated desire and expectation. The infant soon learns which things satisfy his needs and whims, and once he learns how to refer to such things he soon learns also how to refer to their absence, usually with much greater emphasis. Hence when Russell wrote, disapprovingly, that meaning is 'a notion confusedly compounded of logical and psychological elements', he was closer to the truth than he thought.[8] The remedy, however, is not—as he first believed—to get rid of the tiresome psychological (i.e. human) element in order to attain pure logical truth and timeless metaphysical certitude, for no such things exist. The remedy is to show how the logical element is inseparable from, indeed grows out of, human psychology, experience and, above all, language; and to clarify the process by showing how language, once learnt, enables each individual to order and take stock of his complex experience by means of normative, that is logical, categories.

For it is words, in their categorial function, which establish our first logical categories: vague and elastic at first, but capable of whatever degree of refinement and precision we choose or need to give them. The origin of language is also the origin of logic. The development of logic is concerned with demonstrating just how complex our own logico-linguistic categories can be, and guarding against the error into which our ignorance of this fact inevitably leads us. As noted earlier, we here touch on fundamental principles not only of language and logic but also of epistemology: of any knowledge which rises above the level of animal awareness, memory, and cunning. Perhaps the chief reason why this important area is still one of mystery and confusion is our failure to grasp the distinction between the relatively simple nature of empirical reference and the immensely complex nature of modal reference.

Generality and negation are undoubtedly the most basic forms of modal reference and may be said to engender all the rest. Generalization, reference not to this particular categorized object but to categories as such—for example, to the category of any such objects, real, imaginary, past, present, future—implicitly contains all possible objects of reference, since without categorization, no matter how vague or how precise, linguistic reference does not exist. The essence of categorization is the registering of similarities and continuities: correlation. The essence of negation, by contrast, is the registering of dissimilarities, discontinuities, distinctions: differentiation. For in addition to calling attention to the absence of things, and to denying erroneous statements, negation has a third and logically more important function: that of delimiting or determining an area of reference, of making finer categorial distinctions, and thus of creating new categories. These two functions, categorization and differentiation, constantly interact in all our thinking. Categorial correlation and categorial differentiation are, as it were, the warp and woof of the entire fabric of human thought.

The hallmark of modality is implication. Modal reference is an area of immense complexity and endless ambiguities, for not only does it vastly extend the semantic range of language beyond reference to the here and now, but any instance of modal usage may admit of several interpretations, which often shade into one another, may even all be intended. Even where circumstance and linguistic context suggest an interpretation, vagueness may remain. Expression of vague impression or opinion may be the purpose of utterance. 'He is here now' is quite clear. 'He may come later' could mean that I am unsure, that he is undecided, that circumstances may not permit, or all of these things. Statements involving modal verbs such as *could*, *ought*, *must* may be even more complex or polysemic. The naive view of language as a code in which unequivocal messages pass from point A to point B is quite erroneous. The complexity of modal reference—by far the greater part of all uses of language—exposes once again the fallacy that the meaning of language resides only in its words or formal structures, or that meaning can be divorced from the purpose and circumstances of utterance, or from the constant need for intelligent interpretation.

There are other oddities. If, referring to the same person, place, and time, I say: 'He is here now and he is not here now', I contradict myself. But if I say: 'Maybe he will come and maybe he will not come', there is no contradiction. This is a salutary reminder that there can be no empirical reference to the future, but only prophecy, prediction, or conjecture, which commonly turn out to be wrong.[9] Despite this, we are constantly tempted to refer to future events as if they were empirical facts (even though 'fact' comes from Latin *factum*: something done, achieved). The future *tense* is not in the indicative *mood*. Nor, strictly speaking, is the past tense. Strictly indicative or empirical reference is always about the here and now. Reference to the 'not yet' or the 'no longer' stands in need of special kinds of validation. In English, even the simple present is a modal form. To say of someone that he swims does not usually mean that he is swimming, but that he is known to swim. A vast amount of our information comes to us indirectly by such verbal devices, is often taken on trust, and we are often deceived. We can of course be 'deceived' even by the testimony of our senses and our own faulty judgment, but this is quite different from being deceived by other people's report.

Modal reference is not dependent on special forms of the verb only, or on the use of modal auxiliary verbs. Different languages effect modal reference in a great variety of ways. It may be effected by use of modal adverbs (e.g. perhaps, probably, conceivably); of modal adjectives (e.g. possible, visible, breakable); of modal conjunctions (e.g. if, until, unless); by syntactical inversion (e.g. Do you sing? Had I known . . .); and in many other ways. English, for example, distinguishes the generic (modal) statement 'Snow is white' from the empirical statement 'The snow is melting' by simple omission of the definite article. Spanish registers many distinctions between generic and empirical statement by having two different verbs meaning 'to be'. In other languages, very often the logical difference is not formally registered at all. It is this lack of any systematic correspondence between logical function and grammatical form that differentiates one language from another more radically than differences of phonetics and lexicon, and which creates major problems in translation from one language into another.

Nevertheless, the verb plays a highly important role in modal reference. All verbs which lend a subjective colouring to any statement render that statement modal, and separate it from all statements (whether true or false) which lay claim to stating empirical fact. Hence all verbs used to affirm or indicate what are alleged to be facts are themselves modal: verbs such as say, state, know, believe, think, claim, and so on. Just as the modal auxiliaries—may, can, must, and the like—need to be complemented by verbs which are semantically more specific, so verbs of affirmation and belief need to be complemented by a statement of exactly what is said, known, believed or claimed to be true. Likewise, all verbs expressing supposition, doubt, or denial need to be complemented by a statement of what is supposed, doubted, or denied. Ignorance of this simple principle, and of the nature of modal reference as such, has caused much philosophical time to be wasted on certain absurd paradoxes of the type: 'What I am saying is false'. Bewildered logicians believe themselves to be here on the horns of a dilemma: that the sentence, if true, is false; and if false, is true. Since however the sentence contains no substantive statement whatever, it is neither true nor false, but a piece of logical nonsense. Its sole utility would be to help us see that logic cannot be divorced from language theory, but is in fact an integral part of it.[10]

We are now in a better position to see more clearly the nature of the distinction between empirical and modal reference, and to dispel some possible misapprehensions at the same time. The distinction is not like certain others: true or false, useful or useless, informative or uninformative, objective or subjective, meaningful or meaningless. Nor is it like the distinction between a statement and other kinds of sentence (interrogative, imperative, desiderative, dubitative and the like). The modal sentence 'He can swim' is perfectly objective, may be true and useful to know, is certainly meaningful and informative, and it is a statement. Least of all is the distinction between empirical and modal reference to be equated with the distinction between empirical science and the humanities. All theoretical discourse, in the humanities no less than in empirical science, ultimately rests on empirical reference, which alone ensures that our theory does not lose contact with reality. (If there seems to be any difference between the two fields in this respect, it is because theory in empirical science not only begins with the world of empirical fact but takes the trouble to refer back to it. Much theory in the humanities, by contrast, tends to create a fantasy world of its own.)

All rational discourse necessarily builds on empirical reference, and all theoretical discourse—indeed, even the greater part of common speech—is necessarily modal: that is, logically complex and indirect. By *logical complexity* is meant, for example, the multiple implications and heterogeneous semantic correlations which may lurk behind some apparently simple statement. Modal reference always implies more than it states. The term *logical indirectness* reminds us of the degrees of remoteness which may separate any theoretical formulation from the field (or fields) of empirical reference on which ultimately it rests. For theory to be valid, this logical chain must at no point be broken. These two factors—logical complexity and logical concatenation—are intimately related, since logical complexity is largely determined by the varying degrees of remoteness between formulation and fact. The higher the level of generality, the greater the amount of implicit reference which needs spelling out. As Hegel once noted, to say that zoology is all about animals can hardly be said to exhaust the subject.

The essential difference between empirical and modal reference is, then, the difference between logical simplicity and this doubly complex form of logical complexity. Reference is the characteristic use of language. We use language to refer to things, and refer to them further by saying other things about them. But the number of things to which we make reference is legion: persons, animals, objects, actions, situations, processes, qualities, quantities, relations, things past, present, and yet to come, or not to come, things real, imaginary, possible and impossible, and many more, including language itself. And the things we say about them are even more various. Language, as it gradually develops, matches this complexity with a hidden complexity of its own: logical complexity, or the complexity of linguistic function. It is the hidden nature of this complexity which creates most of our theoretical problems. For behind the apparent simplicity and homogeneity of the spoken or written language, in which one arrangement of words seems to be not so very different in kind from another, lies the whole multiplicity of quite different objects of reference we have noted, and the whole range of logical functions bunched together under the term 'modal reference'. To confuse matters further, different languages commonly express the same logical function in a great variety of ways, or may express quite different logical functions by the same formal device, leaving circumstance, context, tone of voice or some other factor to determine meaning and interpretation.

Compared with empirical reference which is, relatively speaking, logically simple, there is no doubt that modal reference is the main source of logical complexity, confusion, and error. Given the immense semantic range of modal reference, such confusion and error is unavoidable until we grasp the nature of both modality and logic. Here, as throughout the entire theory of language, we must begin at the beginning, and if we do so we shall be richly rewarded. For only then shall we understand how both modality and logic are built into language from the start. Modality is implicit in the categorial function of the linguistic symbol which is the precondition even of empirical reference, and thus of all use of language whatever. Logic is implicit in the normative function of the linguistic symbol which serves at once to identify and to differentiate our categories of thought. These enable us to reduce the infinite number of objects and aspects of possible experience to some sort of order, to refer to them, and to correlate and reflect on them. Neither language nor thought could exist if we had to name each item of experience with a separate sign. The belief that words are merely the names or signs of things, or that language copies or mirrors reality, is based on total ignorance of the logical complexity of language and thought. Words do not copy reality, they draw attention to those aspects of it which are of human concern in any given situation. Both language and thought come about through a subtle and flexible process of symbolic selectivity, and through ceaseless recombinations of a relatively small number of words, which yet create possibilities of reference of indescribable complexity. Even to attempt to *describe* this complexity would be to fall again into the copy-theory fallacy. What is needed is to lay bare the *principles* which explain how this semantic complexity comes about. For this complexity, approached from the wrong end of the process, has always defied the comprehension of even the keenest logical minds. With a simple change of perspective, however, it can be traced back to a single principle. The first principle of language is also the first principle of logic. Symbolic identity—not to be confused with either physical or psychological identity—is logical identity, the basic principle not only of common speech but also of rational thought. The main *subject matter of logic* is made up of the progressively more complex semantic functions which develop out of the linguistic symbol. But when the complexities of our own language begin to lead us astray, language ceases to be a source of rational thought and becomes a major source of irrationality. Linguistic discourse itself then stands in need of regulation and rational control. Such regulation and control is the principal function of the *discipline of logic*, the subject to which we must now turn.

9

Logic

Logic is entirely conversant about language. RICHARD WHATELY

The forms of thought first manifest and establish themselves in human language. In our day it cannot be sufficiently stressed that what distinguishes man from beast is thought. Language permeates all inner experience or thought which man makes peculiarly his own, and whatever he expresses in linguistic form—be it obscure and confused or clear and explicit—has categorial content. So natural is logical thought to man; or rather, we may say, it constitutes his distinctive nature. HEGEL

Admit one absurdity and the rest will follow. ARISTOTLE

The modern logician may, in time to come, be regarded as the true mystic, when the basis of the world in which he believes is scientifically examined. C. K. OGDEN and I. A. RICHARDS

The word 'logic', observed Russell in 1914,is never used in the same sense by two different philosophers. His own view of logic, also, was to change dramatically more than once. In 1964 another logician, Benson Mates, found it 'necessary to acknowledge that logicians do not agree among themselves on how to answer the seemingly fundamental questions' to be treated in his *Elementary Logic*. Such admissions are almost routine in manuals of logic, the authors even congratulating one another that they are not likely to run out of problems.[1] This alarming state of affairs in a discipline well over 2000 years old creates the impression that either the subject is one of fearsome complexity, or that its practitioners are quite inadequate to their chosen task. The profusion of alternative and even 'deviant' logics at present on offer to the public hardly inspires confidence. Indeed, a strong case could be made that logic is currently the most illogical discipline in the modern university, having by now been equated with virtually everything—from empirical fact to metaphysical fantasy—but only very rarely with the logical nature and function of language, with which alone it is concerned.

True, there has always been a persistent belief that logic has to do with rational argument and valid inference, but this is too restrictive a view, and often involves misconception of the nature of logical inference. True, also, there have recently been brave attempts to examine the logic of ordinary language, but being ungrounded in any systematic theory of language such attempts have remained fragmentary and tentative, enmeshed in the minutiae of colloquial speech. However, the most ancient and persistent misconception of logic is due to its confusion with mathematical reasoning and the type of deductive argument which occurs in mathematics. Since this is based on a misconception of the nature of mathematics no less than of logic, consideration of it must wait until later. Both mathematical reasoning and scientific theory are indeed logical uses of language for highly specialized purposes. Logic, however, permeates the whole of language, being inseparable from the normative function operative in language from the start, and present at every stage of its development and use. Logic concerns the difference between linguistic sense and nonsense.

The unhappy history of logic, the countless polemics even as to what it is, and the notorious bickerings of logicians down the ages have always convinced most people that this is a subject best left alone. Not, it must be said, without a certain sense of relief. The prime utility of the study of logic is to prevent people from talking nonsense and—worse still—from acting on it.[2] And if the logicians cannot agree on what logic is about, this seems to leave others—economists, politicians, journalists, academics and indeed everybody else—free to talk whatever nonsense they please. To tamper with so convenient a belief must surely be a hazardous undertaking. If logic ever became prevalent among humankind it would prove lethal to many orthodoxies and ideologies which, in an ever-changing world, can sustain their increasingly irrelevant myths and dogmas only by subterfuge and contradiction. The subject however cannot be shirked. Nonsense may often be harmless, but when converted into conflicting ideologies, harnessed to political power, and armed with modern weaponry, it can bring about irreparable harm. That we have reached such a danger point in world history is a commonplace of journalism, a source of vague concern among the elderly, and of despair among the young. Paradoxically, it is only in the field of empirical science and technology, which have now created the possibility of human self-destruction, that logical methods are doggedly adhered to. In the humanities, which should be concerned to ameliorate this doom-laden state of affairs, we find only acrimonious dissension and theoretical chaos. We see here the dangers inherent in a situation where man's technical intelligence has outstripped his moral intelligence, or even his awareness of common self-interest: in survival.

Yet the belief that man is a rational animal, that rationality—which manifests itself chiefly in purposive action—is grounded in intelligent thought, which in turn is dependent on the logical use of language, this doctrine was accepted by thinkers of the most diverse schools for many centuries. On this view, logic would be the very core of both language theory and human rationality: language, thought, psychology, epistemology and human reason comprising one single, if complex, zone of inquiry. Before asking why this doctrine is no longer widely accepted we might first ask: is it valid? Can so irrational and self-destructive a species as ours be considered rational? How can so many absurd, conflicting and contradictory ideologies pass as products of logical thought? The question is important and the answer has already been hinted at, since it concerns the modal nature of negative reference. All negative concepts presuppose positive ones. Hence all that is irrational is strictly post-rational: a perversion of human reason yet, for that very reason, dependent on it. The best exemplification of this is that the ultimate products of scientific intelligence are now the potential means of human self-destruction. In less obvious ways, however, the same fact—that irrationality is a by-product of reason—accounts for all distinctively human forms of error, just as reason accounts for all distinctively human forms of success. Without language, which underpins all human understanding, we would indeed lack reason: but equally we would lack the distinctive forms of madness which characterize our species no less than the many marvels of human ingenuity. For the same reason it is quite incorrect to describe as *irrational* the pre-rational behaviour of animals and infants. Pre-linguistic, pre-logical, and pre-rational are almost synonymous terms.

The close bond between reason and irrationality exemplifies a principle which Aristotle refers to more than once: that the same discipline often deals with opposites (medicine with sickness and health, politics with good government and bad, and so on). In many fields it is the 'pathology' of the subject, rather than any disinterested search for knowledge, which is the main stimulus to inquiry and theory. Such was the case with logic. In our tradition, it grew out of the verbal muddles and contradictions in which early thinkers soon landed themselves once they had become critical of primitive theory and sought to theorize about knowledge itself. It soon became clear that abstract discourse—about problems of knowledge, ethics, statecraft, and other general problems—needs special checks and norms if it is not to lead to absurdity. The search for stabilizing and regulative principles of theoretical discourse, initiated by Socrates, Plato, and Aristotle, was explicitly undertaken to counter the sceptical arguments of the ancient Sophists, who seemed to be undermining the very bases of human knowledge and social order. This historical fact had three unfortunate consequences from which logic has not so far recovered. First, logic was associated from the start with contentious argumentation, its positive critical and regulative functions often being subordinated to the scoring of polemical points. Second, the attempt was made to establish a theory of logic before there was any adequate theory of language. Since logic is concerned with nothing but the critical regulation and use of language, this placed logic at a serious disability from the start. It is difficult to regulate something unless you know what you are regulating. Third, the belief arose that logical discourse gave access to superior forms of knowledge which conveniently dispensed with experience altogether.

Thus was born metaphysics, a mode of thought which, although generally discarded in physical science, still plagues the humanities, and thus requires our attention. If logicians disagree as to the nature of logic, metaphysicians have notoriously disagreed even more as to the nature of metaphysics. This makes good sense, since metaphysics is the distinctive aberration which supervenes at the level of logical discourse. for where the homely fantasies of mythical discourse are tolerant of contradiction, vague analogy and imaginative leaps in the dark, metaphysical doctrines, by contrast, usually lay claim to rigorous validation on strictly logical grounds. In fact, however, metaphysics makes no advance on myth, since the premisses which it seeks to concatenate into logical discourse either derive from myth or are equally gratuitous. To illustrate this we need only consider the origin of the term itself. The term 'metaphysics' was invented by an editor to designate a famous treatise by Aristotle. From this and related works we learn that nature—the realm of transient phenomena —is a mere fraction of the universe. Nature stops at the moon. Beyond lies a vast realm of eternal, imperishable reality, about which Aristotle claims to know a great deal. The whole system, which is geocentric, consists of some 55 concentric spheres and culminates in a bizarre (albeit ingenious) theology, of Aristotle's own invention. (All this is the more remarkable in that much of the time Aristotle was an admirable naturalist. His pioneer work in zoology was highly praised by Darwin, and his psychology is positively evolutionary in conception. At the end of his *Analytics* he traces all higher forms of knowledge back to sense perception, an 'innate critical faculty' common to animal and man. How so distinguished a logician got from here to theology is only one of the many mysteries of metaphysics.)[3]

This brief conspectus of the early development of the subject helps us set logical matters in perspective. First came primitive theory, immature attempts to correlate and understand complex and heterogeneous factors in some area of inquiry such as the study of natural phenomena, or how best to organize human society. Primitive theory construction of this sort, no matter how naive, mythical, or irrational, draws attention to the origin, purpose and positive function of what we vaguely call logic. Logical criticism of the inadequacy of primitive theory clearly presupposes the existence of such theory, and is thus a second-order activity. But primitive criticism, although an advance in logical sophistication, is liable to be as imperfect as primitive theory, and when it disturbs traditional systems of belief, with nothing better to put in their place, may be socially disruptive. At this stage more serious theorists sought to counter such purely negative criticism by the discovery of objective principles which might clarify the nature of valid theory, and help refute bad theory. In this, initially, they had much success, to be marred later by their failure to relate logical theory to language theory in general, and by the lure of metaphysics.

Logic, then, has three main aspects, constructive, critical, and theoretical: being concerned with the *construction* of rational discourse and theory; with the *critical analysis* and regulation of discourse and theory; and with the *principles* on which all rational discourse and theory ultimately rest. When we discover that the most fundamental of these principles—that of logical identity—is also the fundamental principle of language in general, we may begin to see why it is an error to view logic as restricted to theoretical discourse, formal argument, inference and deduction. Logic is concerned with *all* forms of symbolic reference, with the semantic function of language as such: potentiality, with the analysis of any meaningful utterance in any language, but more especially with the basic semantic functions common to all languages. Moreover, the main problem area of logic is not rational discourse, which is largely a matter of having something to say, good reason and evidence for saying it, and avoiding equivocation, contradiction, and inconsequentiality in the process of saying it. The main problem area of logic is modal reference. This, as we saw in the last chapter, is an area of immense semantic complexity and tacit implications, which incessantly calls for conscious or unconscious logical analysis. Such analysis in fact is a large part of what we call human understanding. (Modal reference, we may recall, accounts for the greater part of all uses of language.)

There are other reasons for not restricting the notion of logic to rational discourse, deductive argument and the like. No argument can be evaluated and judged rational without logical scrutiny of the statements and terms which compose it. In short, all valid uses of language are logical, and all invalid uses can be shown to be such only by logical analysis. Then, there are forms of rational discourse—descriptive, explanatory, exploratory or heuristic, literary and so on—which are not logical in the narrow sense which equates logic with inference and deductive argument. Contrariwise, arguments may be 'logical' in this special sense and yet be completely irrational: when, for example, the premisses are gratuitous or absurd. (Examples of such arguments abound in manuals of logic.)

It is clear, then, that logic concerns all uses of language and not merely discourse and argument. It should also be clear that logic is an integral part of human thought and understanding. Attempts to separate logic from epistemology on the one hand, from the use and interpretation of language on the other, or to make logic a self-contained quasi-mathematical system cut off from the world of human experience and human concern: all such attempts lead straight to metaphysics and intellectual stultification. Logic is not an academic amusement, nor is it a subdivision of mathematics. If, for example, we believe (with most academic logicians) in the myth of a 'propositional calculus' which deals with various relations between unanalysed propositions, usually dubbed *p* and *q*, then we end up with all manner of paradoxes. In such a system it can be 'proved' that a false proposition 'implies' any proposition whatever, and that any proposition whatever 'implies' a true proposition. If this grotesque scheme were accepted as a means of discovering truth, or as a means of regulating logical discourse, then any hope of solving the most pressing problems affecting the welfare of the human species would clearly be impossible.[4] All attempts to formalize or mechanize logic, in order to save people the trouble of thinking, ultimately rest on the misconception that language resembles a mathematical or a physical system. But the confusion of logic, or any aspect of language, with mathematics —whether pure or applied to physical systems or electronic circuits—is a gross anachronism. Mathematics is a post-linguistic symbolism subserving highly specialized activities which could only have emerged at an advanced stage of human culture. Both the existence and the many uses of mathematics presuppose not only human intelligence but also the theoretical use of language, which is one of the higher manifestations of human intelligence.

Logic, then, is not an arcane discipline. Nor is it a set of rules imposed on language from without. Logic is intrinsic to language at every stage of its development—from primitive symbolization to the most elaborate forms of theoretical discourse—since it concerns the very function of language: the *uses* we make of language and the way we regulate those uses, as distinct from the spoken and written *forms* of actual languages. This is not to deny the importance of the formal element in language: without formal conventions there could be no language at all. Nor is it to deny the limitless potential for semantic inventiveness and expressivity which the skilful exploitation of the resources of a given language makes possible. But the study of the formal conventions of actual languages, their phonology, lexicon and grammar, belongs not to the theory of language as such, but to philology. Likewise, the study of the innovatory uses made of the resources of a particular language by individual speakers and writers belongs to stylistic and literary criticism. Philology and criticism of this kind not only may but must take as given the *standard* functions of language: symbolization, empirical and modal reference, statement, and the like. Language theory and logic, which are inseparable, may not. They have as their task the elucidation of the origin, nature, and development of language, and of the basic principles, functions, and uses which are common to all languages (and on which all more idiosyncratic uses of language rest). It is these common or universal principles which alone enable us to speak of *human language*, as distinct from the countless different *languages* which exist or have existed.

In identifying logic, in the broad sense of the term, with the theory of language in general, we come full circle. For whatever misconceptions of the nature of logic there may be, no one would contest that logic must be involved in the most rigorous kind of theoretical discourse, which needs to be regulated by explicit norms. And what pre-eminently characterizes all uses of language, at all stages of its development, is precisely its normative function. Without relatively stable and recognizable norms there could be no language, and without language there could be no other kind of normative or rational behaviour: that is, behaviour under conscious human control. Words are our first norms and the source of all others. For long before we consciously contrive norms—what is to be a unit measure, what is a right procedure to attain some end, what is or should be a law of social conduct, and the like—we have unconsciously assimilated normative behaviour in learning the use of language. Language is one great complex of normative factors. Without a set of recurrent sound patterns there could be no words. Without relatively constant word use there could be no categories or linguistic meaning. Without standard ways of modifying word meaning and combining words to form new meanings there could be no speech or theoretical discourse. Without logical principles to regulate discourse there could be no rational theory. This same normative principle is the condition of any intelligible use of language whatever. For this very reason we hardly take note of the normative or logical function of language in common speech, any more than we think of the importance of the ground on which we walk. But when we pass from the combination of words into sentences to the combination of sentences into theoretical discourse, this same normative or logical function of language is forced on our attention by the multiplicity of errors and disputes which this more complicated use of language brings in its wake. At this stage the logical or normative function cannot be ignored if language is to retain its intelligibility and usefulness. Hence the common misconception that this is where logic begins. Logic does not begin here, but it is here that we are obliged to take note of it: to acquire a theoretical understanding of logic.

To this end, the subject is best viewed at three different

levels: the subject matter of logic, logical practice, and logical theory. In all matters biological and psychological, the order of emergence is always the best guide to theoretical understanding. The *subject matter of logic* is, as we have seen, the function—the various functions and uses—of human language, which necessarily emerged long before there could be any conscious practice of logic in the form of theory construction and theoretical criticism, or any awareness of the principles underlying language and logic. The essential function of language lies in the normative function of words. Words, used and responded to, meant and understood, create *linguistic meaning*. This differs from *pre-linguistic signification* in that the semantic efficacy of pre-linguistic signs comes about by mere association or conditional reflex. Their utility may be durable or short-lived. One need only think of Russell's parable of the chicken: the hand it had come to associate with feeding one day wrings its neck. The durability of linguistic meaning, by contrast, in ensured by the fact that words are not haphazard associations of one thing with another, but norms or conventions which establish regular categories of meaning. These guarantee not only stability of linguistic reference but are norms in relation to which even differences and changes of meaning become intelligible. Without a norm there can be no deviation from the norm. This is obvious in the case of a yardstick or a pint measure. Here the norm is a clearly defined quantitative limit. It is obvious also in the case of a clearly stated regulation or law. It is no less true, however, of the categories established by linguistic symbols. Although initially more elastic and accommodating, such categories may, by precise definition, be made as exact as any special requirement demands. Mathematical norms and carefully defined regulations and laws are not, because of their precision, superior to linguistic norms, but merely special extensions of the normative function present in human language from the start. Moving to the other end of the semantic spectrum, however, it is quite absurd to extend the concept of norm or law *beyond* the human field, except metaphorically. The 'law' of the jungle, meaning the hegemony of brute force, is a grotesque metaphor indicating precisely the absence of any human law or norm.

The *practice of logic* has two closely related parts: *theory construction*, the correlation of the basic principles in some area of inquiry into a coherent system, designed to aid understanding and further inquiry in that area; and *theoretical criticism* designed to ensure the logical coherence of such theory, and of course to expose the inadequacies of bad theory. Implicit in these two forms of theoretical discourse—constructive and critical—are certain *logical principles*. All theoretical discourse is, or aspires to be, logically coherent: only thus can it make sense of its subject matter. What then are the logical principles which ensure such coherence? With this question we move from logical practice to *logical theory*. We also come up against some of the most troublesome questions in the history of logic and the theory of language. Such questions are unlikely to concern the ordinary speaker, who commonly uses language to good effect without the aid of theory. Nor do they usually concern theorists in natural science, where the empirical nature of the subject matter often acts as a corrective when theory goes astray, and where there is a healthy tradition of rejecting, modifying, and extending theory in the light of new information. Where logical insight is most desperately needed is in the much more problematic field of the humanities, where a vast amount of uncritical theory, interfused with pure myth, has accumulated over the centuries, and is uncritically passed on with depressing regularity from one generation to the next. Moreover, theory in the humanities is primarily concerned with the difficult task of making provision for the future, and thus stands in special need of rigorous logical safeguards. This is most evident in such matters as politics, economics, education; and, not least, in deciding which purposes, or whose purposes, the findings of natural science are made to serve. To entrust the future of civilization to a witch's brew of primitive myth and half-baked conflicting ideologies, in a technological age which has thrown humanity together cheek by jowl and armed to the teeth, can only portend disaster.

Why logic has proved so unpopular with the human race, whose continued existence may well depend on it, is a matter we have already touched on, and to which we must return when we come to consider certain curious doctrines of the modern breed of 'mathematical logicians'. So far, it has been argued that if logic embraces all functions and uses of language, which are essentially normative, then logic in the broadest sense can be nothing other than the critical theory of language. Traditionally, however, logic has been construed in a more restricted sense, being chiefly associated with theoretical argumentation; and in former times—before logic was taken over by mathematics—with three principles considered peculiar to this level of discourse: the principles of logical identity, logical contradiction, and logical implication (logical inclusion and exclusion). These principles are, as we shall see, of fundamental importance for any theory. It is also true that theoretical discourse is the basis of all systematic understanding and explanation (as distinct from mere description) in both empirical science and the humanities. As such, it certainly merits special attention. Moreover, being the most general and abstract form of discourse, it stands in greater need of logical control than any other use of language, and more so in the humanities than in empirical science. Given all this, it was unfortunate that the continuity between theoretical discourse and its logical antecedents in ordinary language was never properly understood. As a result, logic came to be thought of as a source of knowledge in its own right; then, after various metaphysical misadventures, it was eventually swallowed up by mathematics, declared redundant, and has now virtually ceased to exist as a serious subject. The main effect of this little-noted intellectual catastrophe has been to obstruct rational progress in the study of the humanities.

Let us then consider logic in this more restricted sense, viewed as the study of the principles of theoretical discourse, traditionally referred to as 'the laws of thought'. These principles have had a strange history. They were discovered in antiquity, yet they remain largely unknown to the present day. There has never been any consensus as to which principles are canonical, or even what some of them mean. The most fundamental of them—the principle of logical identity—has rarely been understood at all, and the dependence of the others upon it seems never to have been noticed. The so-called principle of excluded third (or middle), which is usually included in the list, is not strictly an independent principle at all. It spells out what is involved in the principle of contradiction: between two *strictly* contradictory statements there is no third possibility. If one is right the other must be wrong. This distinguishes strictly contradictory statements from those which are merely *contrary* or *incompatible*, but which may both be wrong, and often are. Failure to make this distinction is one of the commonest sources of logical error: when there is a dispute between persons holding equally absurd opinions, the confusion encourages each to think (wrongly) that he is right, the moment he sees (rightly) that the other is wrong. Of such stuff are human polemics commonly made.

Strangely enough, the principle of logical implication (which concerns both logical inclusion and logical exclusion) was often omitted from the list of fundamental logical principles. According to this principle, whatever is affirmed or denied generally commits the speaker to affirm or deny the same of any case or cases implied by such a general statement. Failure to conform to this principle leads straight to self-contradiction, which by common consent is the most heinous of logical crimes. The omission is the more strange in that the Aristotelian syllogism, which dominated logic for so many centuries, is concerned with nothing else but logical inclusion and exclusion of this kind. Stranger still, this logical principle, like others, has even been called into question. It was formerly referred to as the principle *dictum de omni et nullo*. Yet a modern logician, Lukasiewicz, insists that 'Aristotle is by no means responsible for this obscure principle' (*sic*). It comes as no surprise to learn from the same author that 'logic has no more to do with thinking than mathematics has'. This is characteristic of the views of many modern logicians, for whom mathematics and logic are quite independent of the human mind, not to mention human language.[5]

What is most remarkable about our three basic principles of logic is that many people, when made aware of them, tend to dismiss them as self-evident or trivial: yet the same principles are constantly flouted, and their infringement constantly goes undetected. As noted above, they have never been related to any general theory of language, in the context of which their true importance can alone be grasped. Finally, modern logicians—tenaciously clinging to Russell's belief that logic was a branch of mathematics long after the master had abandoned this illusion—have called the validity of the principles of logic into question, and have even recommended their abrogation.

Clearly, we have here many problems on our plate. Briefly anticipating, what we need to show is that these three principles are indeed valid and adequate to their purpose: to ensure the coherence and consequentiality of theoretical discourse, especially in areas where the generality or the complexity of the subject matter may be a source of error. While recognizing this special *regulative* function, we must establish also the continuity between these principles and the other principles of language we have discussed earlier. We must also note certain differences and sources of possible confusion: for example, the difference between modal implication and strictly logical (or syllogistic) implication. We need also to consider why the principles of contradiction and syllogistic implication historically received so much attention while the principle of logical identity, on which they rest, received so little. We must, in fact, show that all three principles are intimately connected. We must also examine the historical and theoretical basis of the age-old confusion between logic and mathematics. Above all, we must stress that neither logic, nor indeed language, is itself a source of knowledge independent of experience. The principles we are concerned with are the *preconditions* of valid theoretical discourse. This, with one notable exception—the theory of language—always has a subject matter *other* than itself, which must be established by diligent inquiry, not by 'pure reason'. (This was the great lesson of Kant which, if properly driven home, would have put an end to metaphysics once and for all.) Even the theory of language, as we have seen, must be grounded in something other than itself: in facts of anatomy, pre-linguistic behaviour and perception, reference to objects, and so on. Finally, the principles of logic are normative principles of discourse, which is primarily *positive* argument, and only secondarily contentious debate. While these principles are useful for refuting the nonsense of others, their prime function is to ensure that we ourselves talk sense. The only kind of contradiction in logic is self-contradiction.

As for the validity of our three principles—logical identity, logical contradiction, logical implication—we shall shortly see that they are impregnable, since the first is reducible to a tautology, and tautologies cannot be impugned without contradiction; the second draws attention to this fact; and the third exposes more indirect forms of contradiction by spelling out what is implied by a general statement: namely many specific statements. The adequacy of these principles to their theoretical function is based on the fact that theory is principally a matter of general statements, and of their interconnections and implications; and also on the fact that all theoretical error and fallacious argument can be shown to be an infringement of one or other of these principles.

We need to stress yet again the special *logical* character of these principles, since there are other quite valid uses of the key terms—identity, contradiction, implication—which we must shortly consider in order to obviate confusion. There are also other kinds of error than that with which we are here concerned. There is factual error, which needs to be eradicated by empirical investigation. There is error based on ignorance, misinformation, gratuitous assumption, and so on. All these may be built into an argument and need to be eliminated by careful scrutiny, better information, critical analysis, but are not strictly infringements of the principles of logical discourse as such. Logical principles are concerned exclusively with the consistency or inconsistency of theoretical argument: not with questions of objective truth or falsity, but with the purely subjective issue of whether the speaker (or writer) is talking (or writing) sense or nonsense. We may talk sense and still be wrong. If we talk nonsense we cannot be other than wrong. It is a gross error to confuse true or false *statements* with consistent or inconsistent *arguments*. Only statements can be true or false. Logical consistency (or the lack of it) has to do with the combination of statements. Although both logical consistency and correspondence to fact are necessary conditions of valid theory, we must not confuse them. Error can occur at either level and commonly does. Many theorists even manage to have the worst of both worlds. As Aristotle said of certain predecessors: their premisses are false, and their conclusions do not follow. But the truth or falsity of premisses is not the immediate concern of logic.

Another confusion to be guarded against is that between these *logical* principles and other kinds of identity, contradiction and implication. For example, we speak of physical identity: the same object encountered on different occasions; of personal identity: Socrates young, middle-aged, and old; of mathematical identity or equation, as when the same quantity is represented by different symbols. The unlimited transformability of mathematical entities is what constitutes mathematics as a unique deductive system, and has lured many into the belief that language also constitutes such a system; but it does not. In any case, logical identity is quite distinct from these other kinds, being rooted in the universal or categorial function of the linguistic symbol.

The need for the principle of logical identity is easily explained. In common speech the greatest flexibility in the use of terms is permissible, provided intelligibility is maintained. When we move into the more complex and problematic field of theoretical discourse, however, a simple requirement must be imposed: it is that the same person must not use the same term with different meanings in the same theoretical context. More positively, where understanding hinges on grasping the *ambiguity* of some commonly used term, as often happens in the humanities, it is the task of the theorist to introduce a formal distinction where ordinary language makes none. A relevant example is the use of the term 'logic' to refer to the theory of language function in general, and the use of the same term in connection with the principles of theoretical discourse in particular. Provided this distinction is made, the retention of the term in both senses—general and particular—enables us to grasp the essentially normative or logical function which characterizes *all* uses of language, and to see the continuity which exists between the principles of formal logic and those of language in general.

The sole purpose of the principle of logical identity, then, is to eliminate equivocation, whether intentional or inadvertent;

and indirectly, those forms of contradiction which feed on equivocation. Another point: the principle requires not only consistency in the use of terms, but also consistency in what is affirmed or denied. In any discussion, observed Plato, it is always useful to know exactly what the discussion is about. Much logical analysis and refutation is concerned to detect infringements of this principle, which might with equal justice be called the principle of logical consistency. Trivial as it may seem, infringement of this principle is an extremely common source of logical error. Tacitly changing one's position in mid-argument is one of the chief expedients of sophistry. Failure to detect subterfuge of this kind was in former times referred to as *ignoratio elenchi*.

It is generally agreed that the supreme logical inconsistency is contradiction, which is doubtless why it has received so much attention. For Aristotle it was the most secure logical principle of all. Certain points, however, need to be stressed. First, being an infringment of the principle of identity or logical consistency, the principle of contradiction clearly presupposes this more fundamental principle, already implicit in the categorial function of ordinary language. Second, there are two distinct forms of contradiction: loose contradiction, the assertion of incompatible statements which cannot both be right but *may* very well both be wrong; and strict contradiction, the assertion of statements that establish an exhaustive dichotomy such that if one is right the other *must* be wrong.[6] Confusion of these two forms of contradiction vies with equivocation as the main source of logical error. It leads people to think they are in the right when they perceive the falsity of a statement which is incompatible with their own counter-statement, even when the latter is equally false. Third, contradiction is often delayed or concealed, and its detection often involves the principle of logical implication. Few people are foolish enough to affirm and deny something in the same breath. They commonly allow several sentences, paragraphs or pages to elapse, by which time they may have forgotten what they earlier said, or may hope that others will have lost the thread. There is contradiction in good faith as well as bad. In his treatment of the subject, Plato recommends the bringing together of separated parts of a discourse so that such implicit, concealed or delayed contradictions may become apparent, and then eliminated.[7] Finally, as noted earlier, contradicting what another says is not *logical contradiction*, which is always *self-contradiction*. Disagreement with others is not a logical sin: only disagreement with oneself in a given theoretical context.

Logical implication must likewise be carefully distinguished from other kinds of implication. When treating the topic of modality we noted that all manner of implication is built into all but the simplest forms of language use. In colloquial discourse, moreover, the hidden implications of modal reference fuse with the limitless number of implicit meanings latent in the physical and psychological speech situation itself. But nods, winks, sly looks, the state of the weather and other attendant circumstances have nothing whatever to do with the principle of logical implication. Here we are concerned only with the principles necessary for the regulation of abstract theoretical discourse. In such discourse, whatever is universally affirmed or denied commits the theorist to affirm or deny any other statement which the more general statement implies. The importance of this principle is evident if the theorist happens to be a legislator, politician, educator, or any other concerned with making provision for the future of human society. (The superstition that empirical science alone admits of valid theory helps obscure the fact that it is in the humanities that theory stands in the greatest need of logical safeguards.) Logical implication, in fact, is simply an extension of the principle of logical identity, just as logical contradiction is the negation or infringement of the principle of logical identity. The latter, therefore, is the fundamental principle of logic, being presupposed by the other two. It is also continuous with ordinary language, being simply a more explicit and strict formulation of the normative function of the linguistic symbol, imposed, for reasons of theoretical hygiene, in abstract discourse which lacks the natural checks and safeguards of person-to-person discussion in and about a real-life situation; or the empirical findings which alone validate theory in natural science.

Incomprehension of the principle of logical identity amounts, quite simply, to incomprehension of logic and rational theory in general. It is also the principal reason why we need an adequate theory of language, since language and logic are inseparable concepts. Historically, such incomprehension has been the rule rather than the exception. Even Aristotle thought the principle of contradiction the 'most secure' of all principles, although the number of times he uses words for 'same' or 'identical' in its formulation should have led him to think otherwise;[8] as also his own inquiry—in the wake of Socrates and Plato—into the nature of universal concepts. The principle of logical identity was first formulated, though scarcely understood, by medieval logicians in the form of a tautology: *ens est ens*. This later became A = A. Such formulations moved Locke to mirth at their apparent vacuity. In his *Essay concerning Human Understanding* he invites us to consider 'a monkey shifting his oyster from one hand to the other' and, had he but words, saying: 'oyster is oyster'. Earlier in the same essay, however, Locke had stumbled upon the true importance of the principle of logical identity, noting the errors which ensue when people apply words 'very unsteadily, making them stand now for one, and by and by for another idea'.[9] It is greatly to Locke's credit that half-way through the same work he also stumbled upon the importance of language, and decided to dedicate a special section to its 'nature, use, and signification'. With similar candour Russell informs us that it was not until 1918, after the completion of *Principia Mathematica*, that he realized that the relation between language and non-linguistic fact might be in any way problematic.[10] (It may be added that neither Locke nor Russell achieved any great illumination in their belated inquires into the language problem.)

Incomprehension of the nature of language and of logic, and the confusion of both with mathematics, go hand in hand. The consequences of this can be quite dramatic. In his *Methods of Logic*, for example, Quine informs us that logical laws have been 'protected from revision by the force of conservatism'; that they are laws 'an apt revision of which might offer the most sweeping simplification of our whole system of knowledge'; and even that the laws of mathematics and logic may be abrogated altogether. Some fifty pages later, however, and rather like Locke, he correctly states the principle of logical identity as the very precondition of sound reasoning in general: 'the trustworthiness of logical analysis and inference depends on our not giving one and the same expression different interpretations in the course of the reasoning. Violation of this principle was known traditionally as the *fallacy of equivocation*.' Yet, later in the same work, he defines logical identity in the completely opposite mathematical sense: the use of *different* expressions to indicate *one and the same* object or value.[11]

Principles which, while being the very conditions of logical discourse, can be so easily confused, so lightly abrogated, and so casually reinstated by so distinguished a logician, can hardly be said to be well understood. Such principles were formerly referred to as the 'laws of thought'. It is no surprise, therefore, to learn from S. Körner, writing in a modern encyclopaedia of philosophy, that 'the results of modern mathematical logic have deprived the laws of thought of their privileged status as the supreme principles of all logical truths'.[12] This view—which, as the place of its publication indicates, is now common in philosophical circles—conveniently sanctions all manner of equivocation, contradiction, and disregard for logical implication, by anyone who sets up shop as philosopher or logician. This particular *trahison des clercs* is the least-publicized scandal of the modern university.

The confusion between mathematics and logic we must return to shortly. First a few words need to be said about tautology, and about the laws of thought. Tautological statements may appear to be vacuous and therefore useless. Yet tautologies are, in the last analysis, what contradictions contradict. One use of tautology therefore is to draw attention to the absurdity of contradiction, which undermines any rational theory whatever. Without explanation of this point, however, it was indeed misleading to represent the principle of logical identity as a mere tautology, in the manner ridiculed by Locke. Tautology also has more positive uses. Mathematical equations are tautologies. To say the sum of two and two is four may seem trivial: but if we thought otherwise mathematics would collapse. Curiously it was Russell's metaphysics which collapsed when Wittgenstein drew his attention to the tautologous character of mathematics. Theoretical definitions—not to be confused with descriptions—are also tautologous. Without clearly defined terms, however, there could be no rational theory. We must conclude that tautology is not without its uses.

The word 'law' is much misused, but two uses of the term are widely accepted. One is the proper use of the term to mean a norm of human conduct, consciously laid down and intended to be conformed to, in the furtherance of some human purpose: pre-eminently the harmonious co-existence of individuals in society, or of societies in a world community. (For less important purposes we usually speak of regulations and rules.) The other accepted use of the word is strictly metaphorical and quite different. It refers to some empirical regularity or theoretical principle, not invented or laid down, but discovered as the result of inquiry, as when we speak of the 'laws of nature', which are certainly not man-made edicts. The notion of 'laws of thought' happily combines both uses of the term. For as we have seen, the fundamental principle or law of logical discourse is implicit in all meaningful use of language from the start. Neither the principle of identity nor the other logical principles were consciously invented. They were gradually discovered, as and when logical analysis came to be focused on the problem of the nature of logic itself. Once it was discovered, however, that these principles are the preconditions of rational discourse, it was natural they they should be invoked and imposed as the norms or laws of any future discourse that claimed to be rational. Since all this happened long before modern mathematics existed, and since mathematics itself is a specialized form of logical discourse, it is absurd to claim that 'the results of modern mathematical logic' could lead to the abrogation or demotion of the principles of logic in general. Mathematics is a post-linguistic symbolism and hence presupposes logic. Logical thought is not, as Russell once suggested, the child of mathematics, but one of the parents: the other being the possessive urge which led men to count sheep and measure land.[13]

If the entanglement with mathematics has brought about the stultification of modern logic, a major threat to logical discourse has at all times been metaphysics, or the belief that such discourse can be a source of substantive knowledge in its own right: either empirical knowledge (arrived at by *a priori* reasoning) or some more ethereal kind. Metaphysics is an overvaluation of the power of logic, which is neither a source nor a guarantee of truth about the world, but simply a safeguard against talking nonsense. Paradoxically, the genuine fruits of the logical analysis of language—which illuminates so much about ourselves and our modes of thought and conduct—have gone largely disregarded, while the lure of knowledge on the cheap has ever been a temptation for people to argue themselves into the most fantastic—and quite incompatible—beliefs. Not to mention lesser mortals, Plato, Aristotle, Descartes and Leibniz all claimed to have privileged access to higher forms of Being by dint of pure reason, and also believed in the possibility of an *a priori* physics: having the best of both worlds, so to speak. After Newton and Kant such modes of thought ceased to be tenable. Yet even these eminent thinkers had their backslidings and inconsistencies, since until biology was placed on a sound basis there was little hope of any non-metaphysical psychology or theory of knowledge; and even less hope of insight into the role of language—with its inbuilt normative or logical function—in the mental make-up of man. What is depressing is that more than a century after Darwin provided the necessary foundation for a theory of knowledge which is at once naturalistic and rational, myth and metaphysics still dominate human thought: no longer, to be sure, in empirical science and technology, but in the humanities, that is, in all fields concerned with the welfare, education, moral progress, even the very survival, of the human race.

The failure of rational theory to establish a foothold in the humanities is due in no small measure to the withering away of logic, consequent upon its confusion with mathematics. This confusion rests on many misconceptions and one great fallacy. The whole sad tale would merit a treatise to itself: here we can deal only with essentials. The misconceptions concern the similarities and differences between language and mathematics, especially the manner in which each relates to empirical fact; the belief that logic constitutes a quasi-mathematical deductive system; the failure to grasp that mathematics derives its deductive power from its empirical origins; the refusal even to countenance such origins; and the long and fruitless search for the 'foundations' of mathematics in idealist metaphysics.

This last point may help illuminate the kind of problem we are dealing with. Since it comes in two varieties—subjective and objective—metaphysical idealism has either seen mathematics as a pure invention of the human mind; or defended it against this view, seeking to relate it to Plato's objective idealism: wrongly, as it happens, since Plato shrewdly saw mathematics as somehow *intermediate* between his transcendent ideas (which we know to be linguistic in origin) and the objects of sense experience.[14] Erroneous as they are, however, both forms of idealism are closer to the truth than the crudely empirical conception of mathematics which they oppose, and which sees mathematics as simply 'given' in nature: as though numbers grew on trees along with the apples. Subjective idealism rightly stresses the *creative* aspect of mathematics, but risks making mathematics a purely arbitrary business. Objective idealism rightly seeks to vindicate the *objectivity* of mathematics, but looks for help in the wrong place: in ancient metaphysics rather than in contact with reality.

The great fallacy which emerges from the interrelated misconceptions noted above is the belief that language, which was a necessary factor in the genesis of the more specialized symbolism of mathematics, then back-fired, as it were, turning itself into a calculus of the kind it had helped to create, and thus became a powerful *source* of knowledge with guarantee of apodeictic certainty. To eliminate this general confusion between language, logic, and mathematics, we need to clarify what language and mathematics have in common, and show how they differ.

Mathematics both resembles language and differs from it in important respects. Both begin humbly enough in correlations of one thing with another. Each symbolism grows out of itself, as it were, by progressive developments and refinement of use, without break of continuity. In their origins both have clear empirical associations: in the naming and categorization of sheep, for example; in counting sheep; or in land measurement, which is the original meaning of the word 'geometry'. Both, however, soon develop a creative dimension, eventually leaving immediate empirical reference far behind, attaining many different kinds and degrees of complexity which greatly enhance their theoretical utility, but create at the same time ever-greater problems of theoretical understanding. The 'philosophy' of mathematics is no less chaotic than the 'philosophy' of language. Yet mathematics and language need create no philosophical problems at all, if we trace each symbolism back to its original functions and then follow each in its development. Initially they have much in common. We may even say of language what Dedekind said of the so-called natural number system: that it rests on our ability 'to relate things with other things; to make one thing correspond with another; or to represent one thing by means of another'.[15] Both language and mathematics rest on these three basic factors: association or correlation of one thing with another (which occurs naturally even at the animal level); the institution of regular associations or correspondences; and the invention of semantic devices by which we refer to such regular correlations.

This said, certain differences must be noted. The latter two operations clearly presuppose the existence of language, which enables us not only to register associations as animals do, but to establish and exploit conventional *symbolic* associations. We thus create for ourselves a new theoretical orientation which enables us to refine, expand, and correct the merely sensory orientation available to animal life at large. We do not merely *have* experience, we refer to it, we talk and think about it. Mathematics clearly presupposes this stage of psychological advance, being itself a highly sophisticated form of language: referring not to physical objects as such, as the category words of ordinary language do, but to dimensions of, and relations between, physical objects. This is only possible through the invention of special norms (such as unit measures), and control systems (such as those of arithmetic, geometry, algebra), indispensable for measurement, counting, calculation and all other mathematical operations. All this presupposes not only language and human intelligence, but also an advanced stage of cultural life.

Further, while language and mathematics begin with forms of empirical reference, both in origin and later development these forms of reference are quite distinct, and serve quite different purposes. Mathematics begins with empirical reference but not with semantic reference in the linguistic sense. To correlate a given animal and others like it with the word 'sheep' is to categorize it by linguistic symbolization, the consequences of which we have traced throughout this essay. To correlate the same animal with a pebble (Latin *calculus*) and other animals with other pebbles is simply to establish a one-to-one correlation between pebbles and sheep. Implicit in this operation—which may be applied to any objects whatever —is human interest in the 'number' of sheep possessed. In other words, mathematics presupposes not only language and human intelligence but a stage of economic advance in which people not only know what sheep are, how to refer to them, and what they are worth, but have devised a special technique for knowing how many they have. Another point is that mathematics (as the etymology of the word implies) must be consciously learnt, and initially even taught, unlike language which infants assimilate without formal instruction. In this mathematics resembles writing: many fluent speakers remain both illiterate and innumerate throughout life. The post-linguistic status of mathematics is most evident, of course, in higher mathematics, which would be unthinkable without written notation. Writing, we must remember, is a late and by no means inevitable cultural development.

It is not to be thought, however, that the mere pairing of sheep and pebbles constitutes a number system. Such a system only exists when the constituent elements of the control system are given distinctive names according to the precise position of each in a consciously ordered series. This process probably started not with pebbles but with fingers, which automatically constitute—provided the hand is held the same way—an internally differentiated control system, which is what a number system basically is. By naming the elements of this naturally ordered system, and by a simple process of iteration, you have the system of positive integers, and indeed mathematical infinity, in the palm of your hand. Once you learn to count, you can count anything, including the number of times you have counted the same series. All other number systems—the system of positive-and-negative integers, the systems of rational and real numbers, the complex number system—are extensions of the system of positive integers, the so-called 'natural numbers' (which are, in fact, anything but natural in the sense that the phenomena of nature are natural).[16] These extensions of the system of positive integers took many centuries to emerge. There was resistance to the notion of negative numbers, for instance, as late as the eighteenth century.[17] The notion of *negative quantity* seemed counter-intuitive and a contradiction in terms. Language, by contrast, had accommodated negative concepts from time immemorial. Those who would make mathematics the paradigm of human rationality are clearly ignorant of how young mathematics, as we know it, really is.

The creative use of mathematics, however, is not less demanding than the creative use of language in general. But neither symbolism is a self-contained system which may be divorced from that to which it refers. Each is a human creation, serving human needs and purposes in quite unmysterious ways.

What language and mathematics have in common, then, is their original contact with empirical fact and the immense complexity of their later developments. The ways in which they relate to reality, however, are quite different, and the development and utility of the two symbolisms could not be more divergent. Language is a general purpose symbolism by which we refer to anything at all, including mathematics. Its uses are legion, often discontinuous, and are heterogeneous in the extreme, being co-extensive with the entire conscious life of man (and with a great deal of his subconscious life as well). Mathematics, by contrast, is rigorously systematic from the start—this explains the impressive exactitude of mathematical calculation and deduction—and is characterized by the clear demarcation of its areas of use. Despite all this, many people—especially in universities—fail to grasp that language and mathematics are *complementary* symbolisms; that mathematics does not have the same range of reference as language; and that language, and theoretical subjects in the humanities which can be formulated in language alone, do not admit of calculation and deduction of the type which not only occurs in mathematics, but for which mathematical systems are consciously created, by human intelligence.

The attempt to convert language into a calculus, then, is a grotesque anachronism which rests on three errors. The first is failure to grasp that mathematics is a post-linguistic symbolism, and hence not the paradigm of human reason but one of its products. The second is the ancient error of equating logic with deductive inference. The third follows from the second: since strictly deductive inference with apodeictic certainty is possible only within mathematical systems, certain theorists simply equated logic with mathematics. (Whether it was thought that logic was being reduced to mathematics or mathematics to logic matters little, since both terms were carefully left undefined.)

We have already considered the extreme simplicity and purely normative function of the logical principles of theoretical discourse. Mathematics, being a highly specialized form of theoretical discourse, necessarily observes these principles if it is to be valid. This does not mean, however, that mathematics *is* logic or that logic *is* mathematics. It means simply that mathematics is a rational pursuit. Failure to grasp these simple facts has helped create the whole mystique of 'mathematical logic', which has hung like a pall over modern philosophy for the best part of a century, and has given a new lease of life to a seventeenth-century fad: the craving for a universal fool-proof language which would do our thinking for us. It is not language, however, which needs to be rendered proof against folly, but human beings. No language has yet been known to go mad.

The confusion between logic and mathematics has taken various forms over the centuries. In the modern age it goes back to Leibniz, who in 1679 outlined his plan for a 'wonderful universal language' based on the belief that 'there is nothing which is not subsumable under number'. His projected Universal Characteristic would, he believed, prove to be 'an infallible method of calculation' since 'we can assign to every object its determined characteristic number'. The prime utility of such a system would be to supplement 'the miracles of the saints or the conquests of a great ruler' as an 'effective means for the spread of the faith', making apostasy as unthinkable as the repudiation of arithmetic or geometry. Leibniz was inspired in this vision by the medieval Catalan mystic, Ramon Llull, who had earlier put forward a similar ecumenical plan.[18]

This wild notion that human language could be converted into a mathematical calculus is still very much alive, and since the time of Peirce, Frege, and Russell has slowly brought about the virtual extinction of logic, with no benefit to mathematics, and with disastrous consequences for general philosophy. Although the spread of true religion is no longer the motive, strenuous efforts have been and are being made to convert ordinary language into algebra. To this end, certain adjustments were deemed necessary. 'In my universal algebra of logic there is no common noun', Peirce announced—somewhat unnecessarily, since there were no common nouns in algebra in the first place.[19] It was also decided that subjects and predicates were somewhat old-fashioned and should be dispensed with. Russell attached great importance to this novelty. It was repeatedly claimed that the new logic was more 'powerful' than any that had preceded it and would provide a firm foundation for mathematics and natural science (which in fact were getting along quite nicely by themselves). Despite the endless polemics, paradoxes and contradictions which this doctrine engenders—proving at least, as Poincaré said, that it is not completely sterile—it continues to hold academic sway in the modern university. It now bars progress not in mathematics and natural science—whose practitioners treat it with the neglect it deserves—but in the humanities, where superstition is rife, and where any doctrine sufficiently opaque to be incomprehensible is treated with respect.

It would be wrong to suggest that the mystique of mathematical logic, the view that it can set general philosophy on a sound basis, or the notion that language can be reduced to a quasi-mathematical calculus, have gone completely unchallenged. Russell, who did more than any man to propagate this cult or mystique, had by 1931 begun to see the error of his ways. In his *Autobiography* (entry for July 11) we find: 'The best years of my life were given to the Principles of Mathematics, in the hope of finding somewhere some certain knowledge. The whole of this effort, in spite of three big volumes, ended inwardly in doubt and bewilderment.'[20] What is puzzling is to know why, half a century later, so much academic time is devoted to the same fruitless task. Other competent specialists have gone even further. In 1967 Hilary Putnam dismissed all previous 'mathematical philosophy' in a single sentence: 'The various systems of mathematical philosophy, without exception, need not be taken seriously.'[21] In 1974 Hao Wang drew attention to 'the inadequacies of mathematical logic' as the basic tool, not only for general philosophy, but even for the philosophy of mathematics.[22] But long before Boole, Frege, Russell and others had reactivated what we may call Leibniz's folly, Hegel had already shown that the attempt to mathematize language and logic, 'to raise, or rather reduce, logical relations to a calculus', was absurd. He notes that if we merely compare the symbols of mathematics with what they are here supposed to symbolize, namely the concepts and logical relations which are expressed in common language, then the whole exercise 'manifests its own nullity'. He wisely concludes: 'Since man has *language* as the means of symbolization proper to reason, it is an idle caprice to go hunting around for a less perfect mode of expression.'[23] The matter was never stated better. We may forgive Hegel his metaphysical excesses on the ground that he is one of the few modern thinkers—Hobbes, Condillac, Herder and Humboldt are others—to have clearly seen and unequivocally expressed the truth that *language* is the indispensable basis of human *thought*. What to the Greeks was a little too obvious—since *logos* meant both things—has now been virtually lost sight of. The endless spate of modern publications on language, logic and psychology mostly neglect this truth, or are committed to the opposite thesis: that some pre-existent but undefined entity—mind—first creates language and then uses it. The fatal weakness of Hegel's philosophy is that he managed to sustain both theses at once. He, however, had the excuse that at the time he wrote there was no mature biological science to set matters in a proper perspective. The theorists of today have no such excuse.

A consideration of the principles of logic thus brings us to the very core of our subject: to the unique nature of language theory. All theory, no matter how refined or specialized, no matter what field it refers to, is ultimately a use of human language. Man cannot theorize or think rationally at all except through the medium of language. This fact has important consequences both for language theory and for human psychology. What makes language theory unique is that while in all other forms of theory the subject matter is distinct from the symbolism, in language theory we must use language to theorize *about* language. Language theory, in short, is the theory of theory itself, and—most importantly—of its aberrations. One of these aberrations is the notion that language theory is an empirical discipline. This is an error because the stuff that theory and language are made of—symbolization, categories, principles, meaning, interpretation and so on—are not available for empirical investigation as, say, falling bodies are available, or sparks jumping gaps, living tissue, or the behaviour of molecules. Such theoretical categories and principles are none the less important for that: they underlie and support that systematic *understanding* of empirical phenomena which we call natural science. Such theoretical factors underlie not only empiricism, however, but *all* human understanding, including understanding of the role which these theoretical factors—which are linguistic in origin—play in *all* knowledge which is distinctively human. It is here that we find the common ground on which empirical science and the humanities rest, and are thus in a position to establish the equal rationality of both forms of inquiry: despite the spirit of the age which is content to equate reason with empirical science, and to consign the humanities to theoretical chaos, conflicting brands of charlatanry, and almost certain disaster.

The obvious difference between these two forms of inquiry

is that while empirical science is concerned with investigation of empirical phenomena and with whatever measure of human control—technology—such investigation brings in its wake, the humanities are concerned with the no less important task of making provision for the future of the human race itself (without which empirical science would be of little use, and would most certainly cease). Since neither the future, nor the mental faculties of human beings, are empirically given like the phenomena studied in empirical science, they clearly cannot be empirically investigated. Yet intelligent provision for the future is a perfectly common human pursuit, and the nature of human intelligence, as distinct from animal intelligence in general, is perfectly amenable to theoretical understanding. The only condition is that such understanding should be as well grounded and systematic as theory in empirical science. In fact, human understanding of human psychology and human affairs is much less exacting than the laborious and complex investigations of empirical science, as any sane person knows. However, by aping the techniques and jargon of empirical science many theorists in the humanities have managed to obscure this fact, creating the illusion that their institutionalized 'problems' are more mysterious and profound, and quite possibly insoluble. This academic obscurantism aids and abets the more ideological kind. The more complex and chaotic human affairs not only become, but are made to seem, the greater the temptation to succumb to current dogmas of economic and historical determinism, to let events take their course, and to cease even to seek for rational solutions. Yet the dogmas referred to are as metaphysical, illogical and absurd as the moral and psychological determinism on which they tacitly rest, and which amounts to the negation of any human freedom to determine anything whatever. The history of science and technology, and the whole history of human civilization, expose the plain idiocy of these doctrines. Yet such determinism is the sole theoretical basis of the ideologies which divide and threaten the world today. Recent attempts to harness academic linguistics to these conflicting ideologies should alert us yet again to the pressing need for a rational theory of language.[24]

Unexpectedly, perhaps, in a chapter on logic, the psychological, ethical, and even political implications of language theory thus come to the fore. They jointly constitute its chief justification and utility. Language, which has perfectly natural and traceable origins in more primitive forms of semantic behaviour and perception, is the prior condition of the complex of human faculties which we vaguely call 'mind'. Since, therefore, language is implicit in all knowledge, thought and action which is distinctively human, when we theorize about language we theorize about ourselves. Hence, if psychology is ever to become more than the study of animal perception and reflex behaviour, or the study of statistics designed to prove what cannot be proven (since the preconceptions and premisses of the arguments are false); if, in short, human psychology is to throw light on human thought and understanding, then it must relinquish all pretensions to being an empirical science like physics or physiology. If the study of language, which is central to human psychology, is not empirical science, it follows that psychology, as theory of mind, cannot be so either.[25] In compensation for this loss of pseudo-scientific status, however, language theory and psychology acquire a superior epistemological status: for they alone make intelligible the nature and origin of theory as such. Language is the great divide between animal intelligence in general and human intelligence, and the basis of all theoretical understanding, that is, of human reason itself.

The *ethical* importance of language theory is undoubtedly the least understood and the most important aspect of the entire subject. Yet, once understood, it enables us to by-pass centuries of sterile debate on the subjects of free-will and determinism. Historically, only one man seems to have glimpsed the importance of this matter. Condillac, in a private letter, developed a theme already treated in his *Essay on the Origin of Human Knowledge*, and argued that human freedom is a consequence of the acquisition of language (with the extended consciousness and possibilities of reflection that come in its wake).[26] In his treatment of this important subject, Condillac anticipates Pavlov's insight into the essential role of language in the development of human intelligence, his awareness of the fact that language is *sui generis*, and his insistence that human psychology is not to be confused with the study of animal reflex behaviour.[27]

In contrast to such enlightened views, the misconceived and fruitless attempt to make psychology an empirical science carries with it the corollary of psychological determinism. According to this doctrine, there do indeed exist 'laws of thought': not, however, in the sense given to the logical principles we have considered, which are simply the principles to be observed in any discourse which claims to be rational; but in the sense that people speak of the 'laws' of physics and chemistry. The proponents of this doctrine believe even more strongly in 'laws of behaviour' which—if only, alas, they could ever be discovered—would account for all behaviour, animal and human alike. This doctrine, which has long been an academic orthodoxy, implicitly excludes all personal freedom and moral responsibility. Human freedom, symbolic consciousness, and moral action are inseparable concepts, since without conscious purpose and freedom to act or not to act, there can be no moral responsibility. Symbolic consciousness, which emerges with language, is not only a source of theoretical orientation and understanding, but the basis of our ability to conceive and plan projects, often of immense complexity, and then determine the means by which they may be realized. Consciously willed action and co-operation form the basis of all human culture and civilization.

The moral import of an evolutionary theory of language is undoubtedly its major contribution to human self-understanding. In an age when the very concept of ethical theory is challenged this is no small virtue. For the sole aim of ethics is the promotion of rational co-operation in the furtherance of civilized life. Not only does morality need no other justification, but all other conceptions of the subject are, in the modern age, divisive and self-defeating, and can lead only to social conflict and disintegration. This may serve the ends of certain groups who reap benefit from present chaos. It cannot serve the cause of humanity.

We are now in a position to see the absurdity implicit in contemporary misconceptions of Darwinian theory which make no essential distinction between human behaviour and animal behaviour in general. The *reductio ad absurdum* of 'sociobiology' as a theory of human behaviour is that, while claiming to be an evolutionary doctrine, it utterly disregards the distinctive evolution of man and of human intelligence. To eradicate such doctrines and replace them with a genuinely evolutionary theory of language and mind is the fundamental task for education today.

The *political* import of such a theory is simply an extension of its psychological and ethical significance. Politics cannot be divorced from ethics (which concerns social behaviour) any more than it can be separated from economics (which concerns the material conditions of survival). Indeed, social and economic policy is the very subject matter of politics. But the political relevance of a rational theory of language and mind has in recent decades taken on a new significance. We no longer live in a multiplicity of relatively isolated societies but in a world community, and in a world economy. This is a state of affairs thrust upon us by technology and war, and fraught with danger of further conflict between mutually uncomprehending cultures. It is a situation for which we have had no preparation and which the salaried educators of humanity seem determined to ignore. To cope with this situation, all we have at present is a variety of incompatible ideologies, most of which inculcate some form of psychological determinism or fatalistic creed. Academic theory in this field tends either to underwrite such dogmatisms, or to lapse into agnostic lethargy (politely referred to as scepticism).

The only antidote against all such doctrines is valid psychological theory, the prime task of which is to clarify the nature and origin of human knowledge and understanding. This cannot be achieved without a systematic theory of language which alone explains how the distinctively human form of knowledge emerges: by correlating the objects of sense experience with symbolic (i.e. linguistic) norms of our own devising. This process, simple at first, enables us to reduce the ceaseless influx of sensory data to some form of order, to make sense of things, and orient ourselves among them. Once initiated, however, the processes of symbolization, syntactic linkage, sentence construction, and the logical concatenation of sentences into rational discourse, develop by leaps and bounds to produce ever more complex and subtle formulations which provide the basis of theoretical *understanding*, both of human nature and nature at large; and of that measure of rational *control* which we call freedom. It is not here suggested that such a theory will of itself solve all, or any, human problems: only that without such a theory no social or political problems of any complexity can be rationally solved at all. And problems which do not find rational solutions inevitably find irrational ones, which are commonly violent, and often lethal. There can be no human self-understanding until we possess an adequate theory of language: of its origin, development, of its uses and misuses, and of the effects of these on human thought and subsequent action. Only thus shall we understand how language-dependent thought enables us both to lift ourselves by our own bootstraps and hoist ourselves with our own petard. The choice, in either case, is ours.

The epistemological and ethical implications of language theory clearly place it at the centre of human psychology. By the same token, a theoretical grasp of the nature and function of language is a precondition of any mature philosophy. For philosophy is nothing other than theoretical inquiry in the field of the humanities. Its task is to seek coherent answers to the more general questions concerning human life, human knowledge, human self-understanding, culture, civilization and its future. Any proper understanding of these large questions must begin with the more fundamental question of how we come to understand anything at all: and here the function of language is crucial.

It must be stressed yet again that psychology, language theory and philosophy are not and cannot be empirical disciplines like physics, chemistry, or even physiology. The subject matter of the humanities is, in the broadest sense, the human mind, which cannot be empirically inspected. The notion of introspection, which has dominated much philosophy since Descartes, is an unfortunate, pseudo-empirical metaphor. It also has the solipsistic limitation of restricting knowledge of mind to that of one person, and leads to the confusion of *mind* with personal quirks and oddities. In like manner, the notion of freedom as rational choice is commonly confused with its antithesis: mindless activity or mere caprice. But if the mind cannot be inspected it can certainly be understood. What we call *mind* is simply shorthand for all the psychological faculties which the learning of language brings in its train. Supreme among such faculties is human understanding: the ability to categorize and correlate our fleeting experiences, creating a novel symbolic framework of reference with all the functions—designation, statement, social communication, individual reflection or thought, mnemonic and heuristic uses, systematic theory and so on—which appertain to language. Language, mind, reason and human understanding are inseparable concepts. The study of such matters cannot be empirical science: not because they are mysterious, but because they provide the symbolic and theoretical factors which, in conjunction with sense experience, first made empirical science possible.

Finally, it is evident that if language forms the basis of human understanding, the theory of language is the necessary basis of all higher forms of education. Education, properly understood, is not a matter of vocational training, with which it is commonly confused. Much less is education to be equated with indoctrination, with which many would willingly confuse it. Both etymologically and in actual fact, indoctrination is the very reverse of education. Education is essentially concerned with teaching people—or, better, with helping them to learn—how to think rationally and humanely about human problems. Its success or failure concerns us all.

10

Conclusion

> Man is man through language alone. WILHELM VON HUMBOLDT
>
> We must re-examine the whole process of formal education from the point of view of what is the *minimum* knowledge, not the maximum, which must be transmitted if the whole structure is not to fall apart. KENNETH BOULDING
>
> Enlightenment is escape from self-inflicted immaturity. People who remain permanently immature make it easy for others to act as their guardians. KANT

With the principles of logic in the more restricted sense—viewed as the principles of theoretical discourse—the theory of language in its broad outlines is complete. All uses of language are either dependent on, or extensions of, the principles we have considered; or are aberrations resulting from failure to understand these principles. Language theory thus comes full circle. For the basic principle of the most abstract and theoretical use of language turns out to be the originative principle of all language: the normative principle of symbolic, categorial, or logical identity, call it what we will. This is the regulative *a priori* principle which underpins all our thought. (It is not, however, mysteriously embedded in the mind *ab initio* as Kant thought, but springs naturally from the normal use of language, which each person must first learn before he or she can be said to have a mind at all.) Having thus established the continuity between logic in the narrow traditional sense with language function in general, we may now see why logic in the more comprehensive sense must be the theory of the uses (and, of course, the abuses) of language in general, based like all theory on systematic articulation of the principles proper to its subject matter. We are now in a position to recapitulate the most fundamental of these principles, and to reconsider the main obstacles which lie in the path of a co-ordinated theory of human language, knowledge, and mind.

At the outset of this study we noted that principles come in three main varieties—factual, theoretical, procedural—according to whether they concern the basic facts which any given theory has to consider; the theoretical categories which help us co-ordinate the facts and make them intelligible; or the methods best adapted to achieve this end. No one of these three sets of factors can be dispensed with. Without facts there is nothing to theorize about. But without categories there are no intelligible facts. This was the genuine Kantian insight: we can refer to things as factual only because they have been categorized as such in advance. Categories are the basis of our thought. We may not be aware of this, but that is because the language we learn in infancy is what first enables us to think at all. With its categories and uses long since assimilated unawares, language underpins our understanding of common experience. For much of the time such 'unconscious theory' serves us very well. It is liable to cause havoc, however, when we seek to make sense of matters of any complexity, especially matters of theoretical complexity of the kind we are concerned with in the humanities, not least in the theory of language itself. In such areas *unconscious* theory is bound to be abortive, since human *consciousness* is central to the very subject matter of inquiry. At this stage, unconscious categories and procedures need to be raised to full consciousness, to be made fully explicit. To achieve this calls for method: where do we begin, what comes next, how should we proceed now, how does all this tie up? The three different types of principle—facts, concepts, methods—are intimately related, and reciprocally define one another. They do not conveniently present themselves in the order listed, but must be established through critical scrutiny. Error in one area soon contaminates the others. If you get your basic facts wrong, for example, your conceptual principles will be erroneous, and any theoretical method which seeks to co-ordinate the wrong facts with the wrong principles cannot be other than wrong. Much work in the fields of language theory, psychology, and theory of knowledge conforms to this pattern.

What, then, are the factual principles proper to language theory? The 'obvious' answer—the things people say and write—is unfortunately the wrong one, since by the time people are speaking and writing we have left the principles of language far behind. Principles are beginnings. They are the conditions, the preconditions, of what comes later. The chief methodological error in language theory—indeed in human studies at large—is quite simply to begin at the wrong end. Most modern language theory begins by approaching language in all the complexity of its evolved state, and ends with a plethora of descriptive techniques and wild hypotheses, all devoid of any explanatory value concerning the true origin, nature, function and epistemological importance of human language. What we need first to understand is how people came to speak at all, and how language gradually developed from there. By this method we can accommodate the ever-increasing complexities of language development in the right order, as they emerge. Writing, for example, is an intralinguistic development, which clearly presupposes speech, and it is with speech that language theory must begin. The origin of speech, however, takes us beyond language: to the physical, physiological, and psychological preconditions of speech. Once this is grasped—and oddly enough it rarely has been—we are on the right path (which, etymologically, is what the word 'method' implies).

What, then, are the chief physical, physiological, and psychological principles or preconditions of language? They are the obvious facts that speech consists of differentiated vocal utterances, involves the hearing of, and response to, such utterances, and that such vocal utterances are associated with objects of sensory experience: initially with discrete objects of visual perception and human interest. Although many language theorists seem unaware of the fact, language has as much to do with sight and hearing, and with the objects to which words refer, as with the making of noises or with syntax and grammar.

Yet even speech, vocal utterances systematically associated with objects of experience, and so interpreted by others, is quite an advanced stage of language. The theory of language needs to go beyond speech to certain pre-linguistic principles which clarify its origin, and in the light of which we begin to understand its distinctive nature and complexity. We thus move from fairly obvious facts to more theoretical principles: to the consideration of stimuli, signs, and signals.

The essential difference between factual principles and theoretical principles is not only one of complexity. It is also that theoretical principles, being themselves logical constructs, stand in need of logical analysis and interpretation. That speech involves the emission of sound is an obvious fact. Another is that such sound must be heard in order to have effect. The distinctive formation of the human mouth—which permits the effortless production of a limitless number of different articulated sounds—is a simple fact of comparative anatomy. However, to say that something is a stimulus, a sign, or a signal is to say much more than is immediately apparent. These are all associative terms, each of which implies some associated correlate. If such terms are to have theoretical value they must be carefully defined and distinguished. Only thus shall we understand the role which these pre-linguistic factors play in the genesis of the linguistic symbol: the originative principle of human language and thought.

Stimulus is essentially a physiological concept, having to do with animal sensation and correlated reflex action. It makes no sense to speak of perception or semantic interpretation at this level. Sensation, however, is an essential part of all perception. Something must be physiologically registered before it can be the sign of something else. A *sign* is any sensation which is so registered, and which becomes associated with something else as a result of some former link between the two. The *signal* is a different concept altogether. Both stimulus and sign are, in their different ways, passively registered. The signal, by contrast, is emitted: it is a form of *behaviour*, not to be confused with either *sensation* or *perception*. A typical signal is an animal cry. However, to categorize such a cry as a signal implies other things which are quite extrinsic to the cry: for example, that it may be registered by some other creature as a stimulus, and interpreted (no matter how vaguely) as a sign. It is clear, then, that these theoretical principles are closely related, to the extent that they need to be defined largely in terms of one another. To confuse them, however, or to give pride of place to any one over the others, leads straight to theoretical stultification: in language theory, in epistemology, in psychology, and in the humanities in general. Academic orthodoxy in these areas currently offers three bogus options which exemplify such confusion and one-sidedness: a mindless behaviourism which would reduce all human thought and action to a matter of stimuli and reflex behaviour; a vacuous structuralism which sees language as an ethereal, quasi-mathematical system of signs, curiously detached from both external reality and human experience; and the pseudo-biological doctrine dubbed 'sociobiology' which—by-passing millennia of evolution, as well as the obvious perceptual and behavioural origins of language and intelligence—offers implausible and quite groundless 'explanations' of all aspects of human culture in terms of genetic determinism and selection pressures.

The most serious failing of all these doctrines is that they utterly fail to explain what they are supposed to explain: be this human intelligence, the nature and function of language, or human behaviour and culture. Naturally, they also fail to clarify the fundamental interrelations between these three areas of inquiry. There are three main reasons for these failings. First, the general neglect and even ignorance of logical principles, consequent upon the long-standing confusion between logic and mathematics. (This topic has been dwelt on at length in the previous chapter.) Second, the attempt to confer on the humanities the status of empirical science. Third, the persistent refusal to set the problems of human language, knowledge and intelligence in proper evolutionary perspective.

The attempt to equate the humanities—any discipline in which human action, purpose, intelligence and the like are the *objects* of inquiry—with empirical science is both illogical and anachronistic. It is illogical in that empirical science, being a product of human intelligence, necessarily presupposes such intelligence, and therefore cannot be placed on the same logical level. Put in another way, purpose, meaning, mind and so forth cannot be studied like empirical objects,but only by methods proper to their true logical status and complexity. These methods, as Plato and Kant insisted, are purely theoretical, and cannot be empirical or experimental.

But misplaced empiricism is also anachronistic, in that it is based on a misconception of the nature of theory even in empirical science. This misconception is aided by the fashionable illusion that empirical science is a hotch-potch of raw fact and wild hypothesis, ever liable to be subverted by new discovery: rather than a body of systematic theory based on clearly formulated categories and well-grounded principles, and which (despite superficial appearances) develops not by fits and starts, but by carefully controlled extension of those same categories and principles, as and when new data need to be integrated into existing theory. All such categories, principles and resultant theories are symbolic formulations, and hence dependent on the prior existence of language and the mental faculties that come in its wake. Pseudo-empiricism in the humanities thus manages to have the worst of both worlds. It misrepresents the subject matter with which human studies are primarily concerned, and also misconceives the nature of theory of any kind. For while empirical science and the humanities are utterly different in subject matter, what they have in common is that understanding in both areas must be based on explicit categories and principles articulated into systematic theory, the validity of which is judged exclusively by its explanatory and heuristic potential. Because all such theory is a product of human intelligence, and not only expressed in but dependent on human language, it greatly contributes to our understanding of these human faculties, and enables us to escape once and for all from the various crude 'copy theories' of human knowledge which have dominated epistemology throughout history. Neither language nor theory copy or reproduce reality. They do, however, relate or *refer* to the real—and even to the purely notional—in logically complex but quite unmysterious ways: through the skilful use of normative symbolic formulations of our own invention.

The nature of the link between empirical science and our normative theoretical constructs was first stressed by Kant, who thus laid the foundation for a rational epistemology. Kant's insight was developed by such pioneers of modern physics as Helmholtz and Heinrich Hertz. Helmholtz even noted the normative factor present in perception, on which all observation and experimental control ultimately rest; and his notion of 'unconscious inference' clearly anticipates Pavlov's 'conditional reflex', which explains how signs acquire meaning even at the animal level. It may here be recalled that Aristotle also had traced all higher forms of knowledge, animal and human, to a common source: an 'innate faculty of judgment (or discrimination) which we call sense perception.[1]

It should by now be clear why it is absurd to place the study of empirical science and the study of the humanities on the same footing, or to attempt to subordinate the latter to the former. Empirical science presupposes not only empirical phenomena but also an advanced stage of human knowledge. But consciousness, knowledge, mind—the subject matter of epistemology—cannot be studied by the techniques of physics, or even of physiology. It was noted in earlier chapters that Sherrington and Eccles explicitly separate the subjects of physiology and mind, as belonging to utterly different areas of discourse; and also that Einstein saw that the basic problem of human knowledge is located, not in physical theory, but in 'the nature of everyday thinking', of which scientific thought is but a refinement, a development. What few have grasped hitherto is that all thought and all theory depend on complex symbolic formulations, the origin of which is to be sought in human language. To understand human language is to understand human thought.

The other main obstacle to advance in language theory—the refusal to place the related problems of language and intelligence in an evolutionary perspective—is even more anachronistic than the confusion of the humanities with empirical science. The evolutionary method of explaining things in terms of their antecedents, concomitants, interactions, progressive complications and developments was well-established in the humanities long before it was systematically applied to geology or biology. It is not only the method of explanation in history and psychology, but it is a matter of the most obvious common sense in everyday life. Indeed, it must be asked what other method of explanation—as distinct from gratuitous assertion or mere fantasy—can be said to exist at all. This method alone can cope with problems arising from the complex interactions of many heterogeneous factors, problems of the kind constantly encountered not only in biological science but also in human life at large. But equally it is the only method of explanation which can illuminate the immense potential which may flow from some simple and apparently trivial fact or transition. This may be exemplified by the two principles which underlie not only all language and thought, but all meaning whatever.

That anything may become the sign of anything else, that signs may acquire their semantic value by mere association of otherwise unrelated objects in the experience of some creature, was a well-established principle by the time of Aristotle. Only with Pavlov, however, was this principle properly integrated into a systematic framework, related to more basic physiological principles, and shown to be the essential link—but also the transition—between *instinctive reflex behaviour* and the kind of *semantically mediated behaviour* which culminates in human language and intelligence. Likewise, Darwin was the first to establish the principle that animal signalling—semantic behaviour as distinct from sign perception—has purely instinctive origins, quite remote from conscious desire to communicate meaning or intent. Once a form of behaviour is found to produce semantic effects, however, this discovery is soon exploited, both by animals and by human infants. Failure to integrate language theory into a systematic evolutionary framework, in which principles from related fields reciprocally clarify and reinforce one another, has meant that the true significance of these two fundamental principles of language, psychology and epistemology, which have long been a matter of public record, appears to have gone generally unnoticed.

But undoubtedly the greatest absurdity of any non-evolutionary theory of language and mind is the simplistic attempt to explain the most complex of all products of evolution as the necessary result of some single factor, be it an area of the brain, a putative gene, or whatever else. What makes simple cause-effect determinism in the humanities inadmissible is that language, the precondition of any thought or action which is distinctively human, comes about through the complex interaction of the emergent *secondary* functions of many distinct organs, processes, and faculties—anatomical, physiological, perceptual, behavioural—each of which has an independent *primary* function in its own right. Darwin alone seems to have had a firm grasp of the evolutionary importance of secondary functions and emergent faculties. Yet all psychology, even at the animal level, depends on the interplay of many such factors. Human psychology is no exception. It remains firmly moored to the anatomy and physiology on which it rests, as well as to the real world in which human beings find themselves. Any other conception of human psychology is pure fantasy: an aberration of the symbolic consciousness when it runs riot. Properly understood, however, psychology illumines certain momentous transitions which take us beyond blind evolutionary adaptation: first, to behavioural adaptability and animal awareness; then, to human consciousness, intelligence, and that degree of rational control which constitutes human freedom.

Signs and signals are essential *pre-linguistic* concepts. They have, moreover, quite separate origins: perceptual in the case of signs; behavioural in the case of signals. Neither singly nor together do they constitute language. Only when the same uttered sound is regularly used as a signal, regularly interpreted as a sign, and regularly associated with some object of common experience, do we have the makings of the linguistic symbol. Only then can we speak of the origin of language. Moreover, once this stage is reached, many later developments of language are virtually automatic. Vocal signals which communicate meaning, which are also signs through which meaning is interpreted, and which because of their referential utility become stabilized both in form and usage, automatically acquire a normative categorial function, which is the essence of the linguistic symbol, of the basic words of human language. The ease with which the human mouth can form different words and the human ear register the most subtle phonetic distinctions soon creates a network of categorial concepts which aid us in making some sort of sense of our complex experience, by symbolic means of our own devising, under our own control, and capable of limitless extension and development.

Because of their referential and descriptive uses—the most obvious and familiar—it is natural to think that category words are restricted to the objectively given. Although primary, however, empirical categories are also the models for all other categories: most importantly, those which are consciously designed, not to designate that which is, but to determine that which is to be, those which enable us to make rational provision for the future. This future-oriented use of language is most obvious in moral and legal concepts, and in all that has to do with procedural instructions and with practical concepts generally. Human action is by definition future-oriented. But as we saw, this use is already implicit in the heuristic or future oriented use even of empirical category words. The word 'fish' refers equally to those the angler caught and to those he hopes to catch, but of which as yet he has no experience. Equally, all imperative use of language carries an implicit reference to the future, and this long before any grammatical distinction between nouns and verbs. Infants designate and cry for desired objects long before they are acquainted with what we call verbs.

Along with their referential, descriptive and heuristic functions, words automatically acquire a mnemonic function also, laying the foundation both of conscious memory and of critical thought: the ability to distinguish one thing from another not only on the basis of present evidence but in the light of past experience as well. Thanks to the complex symbolic functions of language, things separated in space and time are brought together, for correlation and theoretical scrutiny, in what we are pleased to call the mind, usually with scant regard for the essential role that language plays in the progressive build-up of that mysterious entity. Yet the words we learn not only provide us with a profusion of *analytic* categories ready-made by others: they are the means by which we ourselves learn to categorize, for purposes which range from *ad hoc* convenience to the requirements of scientific theory. But language is also a constant source of innovatory imaginative *synthesis*. Words and word combinations become so firmly associated with that to which they refer, and also with one another, that the mere use of language automatically suggests novel possibilities and situations, more complex and refined modes of thought and action, and with them that awareness of choice and relative value which constitutes human freedom and responsibility. Linguistic reference—the ways in which language relates to other things—is by no means a simple affair like labelling objects given. We do indeed refer to what is there, to the objectively given. But we refer also to what is not there, to what may be there, to what on reflection we may decide should be there. More dangerously we may refer to what could not possibly be there, in the firm belief that it is. Language is a potent source of creative imagination, but also of gratuitous fantasy, and worse: of evil design and its sadistic fulfilment. Once we cross the language barrier animal innocence is lost forever. No other species could perpetrate the persistent and systematic savagery which has dogged human civilization from the start, but which now, with modern technological assistance, is in a position to destroy it altogether. The crude determinism which infests the humanities in the modern university seems designed to bring this about sooner rather than later.

Linguistic reference, then, is a complex affair, and the forms it may take are legion. Much confusion will be avoided, however, if we make two fundamental distinctions: that between *empirical* reference and *modal* reference; and that between *simple* reference or mere designation, and more *complex* forms of reference (from simple predication or statement all the way to extended works of literature, philosophical treatises, and scientific theories). This second distinction is obvious enough: we not only categorize and designate things but go on to say more about them. It is noted here only because of the academic dogma that language originates, not with symbolization and categorial reference to objects of sense perception, but—more miraculously—as a ready-made system of well-formed sentences. This gratuitous belief cuts language off from its natural roots and leaves language theory, and consequently all higher theory in the humanities, enveloped in mystery.

The distinction between empirical reference and modal reference is even more fundamental and important, because it establishes a radical dichotomy even at the level of simple or categorial reference, illuminates the logical complexity of modal reference and thus of language in general, and because virtually all intellectual or theoretical error springs from ignorance of this dichotomy and of this complexity. Empirical reference to the here and now, to objects of immediate sense perception, is the sheet-anchor of language, the primary bond between language and reality on which all other valid uses of language depend, and to which, at no matter how many removes, they refer back. Language is the uniquely human way of making sense of the world in which we live, of coming to grips with our environment by remote control, as it were, and in no small measure of changing it. Language is also the means whereby we become conscious of our own behaviour, and so become capable, in considerable measure, of controlling that also. To make language an escape route into fantasy or a source of determinism is, therefore, entirely to mistake its nature and function.

The theoretical principles implicit in the distinction between empirical reference and modal reference call for some clarification. First, empirical reference is in no sense restricted to empirical science. Furthermore, since by definition all science aims at systematic understanding by way of general theory, it follows that empirical science itself, like all theory, is greatly dependent on modal reference. The notion that empirical science is a matter of pure observation, or that it can dispense with theoretical principles, which are themselves language-dependent, is quite illusory. Turning to modal reference itself, it is clear that the notion of modality cannot be restricted, as it has been previously, to narrow areas of grammar and formal logic. Modality permeates the whole of language. Even linguistic reference to an object of immediate sense experience characteristically comes about by use of a category word or universal. But categories and universal concepts, which have a purely notional existence, may themselves become objects of linguistic reference. When this occurs we pass from empirical reference to modal reference; in this instance, from reference to the real (the object of immediate sense experience) to reference to what is 'ideal' or purely notional. This is the distinction Kant once made between having money in the pocket and having it in the mind. Failure to make this simple distinction is perhaps the main source of confusion and pseudo-empiricism in the humanities.

It is clear, then, that if language begins with empirical reference it certainly does not end there, glued, as it were, to the objectively given. As we saw, we do indeed refer to the objectively given, to what is there, but we refer also to what is not there, to what may be there, to what we think should be there, to what, given certain circumstances, might be there, even to what, as far as we know, could not possibly be there. What follows from all this is that any 'picture theory' of human language and knowledge must be abandoned once and for all. Purely conventional patterns of sound, which moreover differ from one language to another, cannot possibly picture anything: although their mnemonic function does indeed stimulate memory of what is visible, just as they stimulate, by association, memory of any other kind of experience. But apart from a few onomatopoeic words (which, as Herder and many others have believed, may well have been the first), language does not 'copy' reality. Most forms of symbolic reference are quite remote from anything like an image or picture, while many refer not to reality at all—visible or otherwise—but to mere possibilities, or to our own concepts, abstractions and theories. Through a subtle and flexible process of selective reference, which deftly combines many levels of abstraction and degrees of logical complexity at the same time, we are thus able to take stock of present reality, to understand how it came to be, but also to think ahead, to conceive rational alternatives to our present condition, which may later be realized through intelligent action. We can, of course, also make dreadful mistakes unless we acquire critical awareness of how all this comes about.

In the most natural way, so natural that most people remain unaware of it their entire lives, language and language-dependent thought develop *pari passu*. Symbolization (the psychological complexity of which we have noted) establishes the basic bonds between words, sense experience, and thought. The mere juxtaposition of symbols produces syntactic speech and predication, which simultaneously refine our powers of objective reference and analytic thought, and even suggest new possibilities of thought and action. Common speech also moves easily into narrative and descriptive forms of discourse, and these develop, quite imperceptibly, into explanatory discourse and theory. In the process many things can go wrong. The closer the uses of language remain to immediate human experience, mistakes can be most easily rectified. The farther we move in the direction of abstract theoretical discourse, the greater the risk of error. Primitive attempts at explanatory theory, for example, slip easily into myth and metaphysics. The greater the need, therefore, for logical safeguards, for logical analysis, and for the discovery of logical principles by which to regulate theoretical discourse, be it in empirical science or in the humanities. The utility of these principles is purely critical: they enable us to lay bare and eradicate logical equivocation, contradiction, inconsistency, and inconsequentiality. They do not ensure the validity of any theory. They are simply the minimal requirements for any form of theoretical discourse which claims to be rational at all.

In tracking down these principles we found that they are of the utmost simplicity, and that all rest on the most fundamental principle of all: the normative principle of logical identity, which is already implicit in the categorial function of the first linguistic symbol. Since the novel theoretical orientation which symbolic norms make possible is the basis of all that is distinctively human, this principle contains in germ the entire development not only of human language, but of human thought and action (as distinct from reflex behaviour) as well.

At the same time, the development of the symbolic formulations of language out of more primitive forms of semantic behaviour and perception is quite unproblematic. The continuity between pre-linguistic semantics and human language is beyond dispute. And yet, on the normative function that is built into language depend the entire intellectual and ethical life of man and the whole fabric of human science, technology, and civilization. Language is no mere instrument of a pre-existent mind but the means by which mind emerges, the means by which animal intelligence transforms itself into human psychology.

Man is man through language alone. This principle was grasped in modern times by Hobbes, Condillac, Herder, Wilhelm von Humboldt, Hegel, and others. Only after Darwin, however, did it become possible to develop this insight into a systematic theory. Through language we establish purely symbolic norms or terms of reference of our own devising, by which we orient ourselves, in a unique way, amid the ceaseless flux of sense experience. This supplements and radically transforms the purely sensory orientation, based on animal instinct, perception, and memory, which we share with other creatures, but to which they are restricted. Through language we attain both theoretical consciousness, capable of surveying almost simultaneously present, past, and possible future; and also the considerable degree of freedom which we possess: the freedom to create and destroy civilizations, but equally the freedom—were we so minded—to establish a sane world community, based on rational and humane principles.

The chief obstacle in the way of our ever achieving such a goal is to be sought, not in the multiplicity of conflicting myths and ideologies by which humanity has always been divided, but in the virtual breakdown of humane education—as distinct from indoctrination or specialized training—which alone can remedy our present plight. The notion that it will be remedied by blind chance or armed conflict is no longer tenable. Humane education, education fit for the whole of humanity, can be based on nothing less than clear understanding of what it is to be human, of what distinguishes human intelligence from any other kind known to man. Yet when we consider general theory in the humanities we find that not only has this problem rarely been faced, but that academic orthodoxies in this field seem designed to prevent illumination from ever penetrating into this area. This is especially true of the many conflicting doctrines in psychology, epistemology, ethics, politics, and economics. (Despite propaganda to the contrary, economics is not a branch of empirical science, since it concerns not only *material commodities* but also, more problematically, *human decisions* about their ownership, exploitation, and distribution, and about human values, action, welfare, and survival.) The orthodoxies referred to manage to retain an air of modernity by the subterfuge of repeatedly changing the jargon in which their antique dogmas are constantly thrust before the public. In fact, they have all the modernity which they possessed in ancient Greece when they were first marketed in the western world. Basically they are three. A crude naturalism which fails to see any distinction between man and other creatures, or indeed between the study of man and the study of nature at large (in this extreme form the doctrine has been referred to as 'scientism'). An ethereal idealism which refuses to recognize any connection between the human mind and its physical basis. And a bemused scepticism which affects to expose the absurdities of both these doctrines, but in fact borrows from each and is more ridiculous than either. The scepticism of Hume exemplifies this. His *Treatise of Human Nature* is subtitled as being 'an attempt to introduce the experimental method of reasoning into moral subjects'. Not only did he fail in this curious enterprise, but after many introspective 'experiments' in subjective idealism he arrived at the most immoral and unphilosophical conclusions imaginable: that 'reason is, and ought only to be, the slave of the passions', and that human nature must remain for ever an enigma.[2]

Sterile debate between the advocates of these three untenable doctrines is what still passes for philosophical theory, that is, for theory in the humanities. Not the least virtue of a systematic theory of language is that it enables us to bring this centuries-old charade to an end and make way for the more serious business of education for the future.

The disastrous effect of these doctrines, and of the medley of metaphysical doctrines which they underpin, is twofold. First, they block advance to more rational theory in those academic disciplines which most concern the welfare of humanity.Second, they encourage by default the fateful recrudescence of primitive myth, and worse, of conflicting mythologies, in an age of advanced technology. The fact is that their explanatory power is no better than that of primitive myth, and to the mass of humanity is considerably less plausible. We saw earlier that primitive myth, the first attempt at systematic explanation of the whole range of heterogeneous phenomena which are the objects of human experience, was a necessary stage in man's mental development. This however was at a time when isolated cultures sought, each as best it could, to understand and explain the world of nature, and to organize human society in the way best adapted to ensure both internal harmony and security from external attack. But we no longer live in a world of isolated cultures, nor in a world where any explanation of natural phenomena is as good as any other. It is no longer possible to maintain a sceptical stance concerning the destructive potential of modern explosives. Modern communications and modern science have created a world in which such divisions and such illusions are no longer possible. They have forced on us an awareness of our common humanity. Internal harmony and protection from violence are no longer the concern of a multiplicity of isolated communities but of the entire human race. The only way we can become aware of our common human nature, which is a matter of biological fact, and of our common interest in survival, which is a matter of plain common sense, is through awareness of what it is that distinguishes the human race, not only biologically but also psychologically, from all other species. It is human language. Language, which is at once a symbolism, an activity, something we use, understand, and respond to, something we associate, consciously or otherwise, with every form of human awareness, expression, communication and thought, is what makes the human race more than a single biological species. Despite all differences between individual languages, despite all ethnic, cultural, and ideological differences, the possession of language confers on our species a psychological unity also. It is what makes us human.

Plato, then, was perfectly right to suggest that there must be some single theoretical discipline capable of providing not only the theory of itself, and of the other disciplines, but even a critique of bad theory as well. It is the theory of language. For language is the basis of human reason and hence the basis, as well as the vehicle, of all theory whatever: but pre-eminently of all theory of knowledge, of human understanding, of mind. This is no ordinary theory. It concerns what human life is about. But since human reason also begets unreason—and worse, perverted rationality—this unique theory concerns also the greatest question of our age: whether civilized life is to continue to exist at all.

Appendix

A priori. Some prior factor which makes sense experience intelligible. In the idealist tradition, this factor was either external to the thinking subject (objective idealism); or somehow present in the human mind (subjective idealism). In the naturalist tradition, the prior element in conscious knowledge was the result of more primitive unconscious forms of knowledge. Language theory alone can effect a synthesis of these apparently conflicting doctrines. Infants do indeed have experience and knowledge and respond to signs before they learn to speak. As they learn the use of words, these become closely associated with this prior experience, grafted on to it, as it were. This validates the naturalist case. But the idealist theses are also important. The common words of a speech community are indeed initially external to the infant. But as each member of a speech community learns how to use such words (and their various combinations) these become part of his or her psychological make-up. Language alone enables us to *make sense* of our experience. Failure to understand the nature and epistemological function of language leads on the one hand to metaphysics, and on the other to scepticism. Metaphysics is the illusion that there can be rational knowledge which dispenses with experience altogether. Scepticism denies the possibility of any rational knowledge whatever.

Abstraction. Language creates many kinds and degrees of abstraction or abstract reference. Speech begins with direct reference to objects of immediate sense experience. But language also enables us to refer to such objects *without* the check of sense experience; and to many 'things' which could not possibly be objects of sense experience. All such reference is strictly abstract or *modal*. (*See* Reference: empirical and modal.) The main source of *abstract nouns* is the nominalization of words referring to qualities, processes, and relationships. But even a category word which refers to concrete objects takes on an abstract or modal function when used to refer, not to actual objects, but either to the word itself or to the purely notional category (of *any such* objects) which it represents. All linguistic self-reference is modal. Failure to understand the extreme diversity and complexity of abstract or modal reference—by far the greater part of all uses of language—is the principal source of logical error.

Adaptability. A behavioural term referring to functional adaptations, as distinct from the organic adaptations characteristic of a given species. Behavioural adaptability places a high premium on individual intelligence and ability to learn.

Adaptation. A term covering all forms of interrelation and interaction between organism and environment which aid survival. In studying animal adaptation it is imperative to distinguish different kinds of adaptation (e.g. organic, behavioural, perceptual, cultural), and to understand how they develop and how they are interrelated.

Analytic and synthetic functions of language. Human thought, far from merely 'reflecting' reality (a metaphor suggested by visual memory and imagination), is a complex interplay of symbolic analysis and synthesis, in which many objects of reference, levels of abstraction, and degrees of logical complexity may be involved at the same time. This process, which results from the analytic functions of our verbal categories and their limitless syntactic combinations, not only aids understanding of the given, but has constant heuristic potential. Understanding is a matter of looking forward as well as backward.

Association. Any item of experience is liable to signify any other with which it has become linked in the experience of any animal organism. Although exploited in conscious teaching and learning, association is for the most part an unconscious process, the physiological basis of which is the concern of neurology. Association, memory, signification, anticipation (as result of earlier experience) and learning are closely related concepts. Association is the originative principle of all meaning, language, and thought. Although the principle of association was clearly stated by Aristotle, its evolutionary significance was first clarified by Darwin's insight into the origin of semantic behaviour and Pavlov's insight into the origin of sign perception.

Associationism. Simplistic speculation about the nature of association, often conceived in mechanical and deterministic terms, but also liable to veer in the direction of idealism, or toward scepticism.

Associative principles. Theoretical terms which imply the existence of one or more associated correlates: e.g. stimulus, sign, signal, symbol. To refer to an animal cry as a signal may imply intention to communicate, interpretation of meaning, some response on the part of another creature, and so on. The implications of one associative principle—symbolization—are the subject matter of the entire theory of language.

Behaviour. Any animal movement or any aspect of it—inception, continuance, modification, inhibition, cessation—which may be interpreted as a means to some end. Such *ends* are initially quite unconscious, but ends and means may become objects of conscious deliberation and rational choice.

Behaviourism. The attempt to reduce psychology to the study of animal behaviour as manipulated by human beings. The deterministic implications of this doctrine are undermined by its circularity. The doctrine, which has no place for mind, freedom, or human dignity, provides pseudo-scientific support for authoritarian ideologies. (*See* Reductionism.)

Biology. 1. Specialized disciplines such as physiology, biochemistry, genetics. 2. The study of life (Greek *bios*) in general, and more especially its evolutionary developments in a multiplicity of environments.

Categorial. Refers to the categorizing function of verbal symbols. A single word may have categorial value. The term *categorical* is usually applied to declarative statements.

Categorization. The primary function of language. It would be impossible to designate every object of experience with a separate name. Verbal symbols (which are not names) refer to objects, but only in so far as these qualify for membership of some (purely notional) category, designated by a word or words. The categorial use of words is therefore normative. (This was the Kantian insight: concepts to not 'conform' to things, but things must somehow 'conform' to our prior concepts in order to be intelligible.) But categorization is no mystery: it is a natural consequence of the standard use of common words. It is also a continuous process since the same object may be categorized in many different ways, and words are constantly combined (in a limitless number of ways) to create ever new categories of thought. Categories are not classes of actual objects: they are open-ended concepts which accommodate *any* object which is judged appropriate in a given case. (Error of course may occur: there is nothing foolproof about human thought.) Categories may be as general or as restrictive as it suits human purpose to make them. Categorization begins with verbal reference to physical objects, and proceeds with reference to their qualities, dimensions, processes, states, relationships, and the like. In addition to categories that enable us to make sense of the physical environment, there are others—moral, ethical, legal—designed to regulate and enhance the quality of human life.

Causation and causality. *Causation* is a behavioural term: the bringing about of an effect as result of animal or human action. This initially psychological concept was later extended, by unconscious metaphor, to the interactions of impersonal natural phenomena. The term *causality* is best reserved for such events, if we are to avoid two common absurdities: the attribution of a quasi-human agency to the phenomena of nature at large (the pathetic fallacy); and the refusal to acknowledge human consciousness as a determinant even of conscious human action. (*See* Reductionism; Determinism.)

Code. Language is often referred to as a code. This is illogical in that a code is a specialized use or development of language (e.g. legal code, secret code, Morse code), and hence presupposes the whole complexity of language and language-dependent thought. To confuse matters further, the term *code* is often metaphorically applied to animal signalling patterns. These are then 'equated' with language, with the result that language is viewed as not essentially different from birdsong. Such aberrations (and many others) derive from making the disembodied forms of the written language the basis of language theory.

Communication. One of the uses of human language. But (1) there are many other kinds of animal communication; and (2) linguistic communication is quite unlike any other kind, being dependent on symbolization and conceptual thought.

Concept. A psychological term, corresponding to the logical term *category* and to the linguistic term *symbol* (category word).

Conditional reflex. Pavlov's term for the fundamental principle of perceptual learning. Natural reflexes are automatic reactions to stimulation. But any object of perception associated (even unconsciously) with a natural reflex action may come to trigger the same reaction. This is the most primitive kind of signification: the perception of one thing as the sign of another. The sign-dependent reflex is *conditional* on the prior existence of some more basic reflex. Once initiated, however, the process of signification has no limit: anything may come to signify anything else. We thus move into the realm of meaning, interpretation, animal intelligence, human psychology, language, thought, reason, and their consequences.

Conditioning. A neologism for training, inducing patterns of behaviour through manipulation. Animals and humans can be conditioned (i.e made to learn) only because they condition themselves (i.e. learn) without manipulation.

Confusion. Initially a neutral term, equivalent to *unconscious association*. Psychological confusion of one thing with another is the origin of signification. Psychological confusion of one thing with many others is the origin of symbolic categorization and language. Confusion is a precondition of all animal and human knowledge. It becomes a liability, however, at the higher levels of knowledge. The main task of logic is the elimination of confusion at the level of systematic theory.

Consciousness. Psychological terms such as *consciousness*, *mind*, *reason* do not refer to physical entities. But neither do they refer to metaphysical entities. They are abstract words which refer to complex psychological faculties which emerge with the development of conceptual thought. Conceptual thought, in turn, develops as we learn the many uses of language, including the proper use of abstract nouns.

Contradiction. Logical contradiction is self-contradiction, in a given area of discourse. To make incompatible statements is a loose form of contradiction. To make statements which establish an exhaustive dichotomy, such that if one is false the other must be true, is strict contradiction. Partial ignorance and confusion of these three points often lead people to believe that if a point of view contrary to their own is patently false, then their own point of view must be valid. This does not necessarily follow. (Logical contradiction is rarely obvious. Usually it is either delayed, or the result of equivocation, or an infringement of logical implication.)

Copy theories of linguistic reference and truth. Ignorance of the symbolic complexity of language and of its many modes of reference, and ignorance of the complex relationship between language, thought, and reality, have led to centuries of sterile debate (still very much with us) which has polarized in two extreme and equally untenable doctrines. One, naive positivism, maintains that the only meaningful statements are those which directly correspond with fact, allegedly in the same way as a picture corresponds with that which it depicts: all other statements being written off as 'value judgments' and merely subjective. (This doctrine is absurd since millions of meaningful statements do not refer to visible facts at all, but may be negative, or may refer to that which is merely possible or desirable, and may even help us to realize what is merely posited or desired.) The other doctrine, sceptical relativism, would repudiate objective reference altogether, making all knowledge and all linguistic reference a purely subjective matter. Only an understanding of the way in which language mediates between sensory experience and conceptual thought can put an end to this philosophical charade.

Definition. Theoretical definition neither describes how a term is used, or ought to be used, by others. It is a clarification of how a term will be used by a theorist in a given context. To theorize with undefined terms invites all manner of equivocation and veiled contradiction.

Deictic reference. Linguistic reference is chiefly effected by the use of category words. Non-categorial or deictic reference is effected by the use of proper names and certain other words (e.g. he, she, this, that, here, there, now, then).

Determinism. Misplaced empiricism; the metaphysical version of the mythical concept of Fate. The misguided attempt to transfer mechanical models from physics to psychology and to the humanities at large, and the illusion that such models have explanatory or even predictive value. Physical determinism ceases to apply at the level of animal behaviour dependent on the interpretation, and frequent misinterpretation, of signs; and long before we reach the level of human understanding and misunderstanding. Determinism implicitly excludes freedom of choice, moral responsibility, and all ethical and legal values.

Differential function. The symbolic function of language is at once categorial *and* differential. Symbols enable us to refer to a potentially limitless number of differentiated categories, but also to make finer categorial distinctions *within* categories. Contrariwise, we may create more general and complex categories.

Discourse. Sentences concatenated for narrative, descriptive, explanatory, theoretical or any other purpose. The meaning of such sentences depends not only on extra-linguistic fact but also on their intra-linguistic relationship. Hence, to be valid, theory depends not only on factual verification but also on logical coherence.

Education. The chief aim of education is human self-understanding (as distinct, say, from understanding the technologies which are now capable of bringing about human self-destruction). Since language is the most important psychological factor which separates humankind from all other species, language theory is indispensable for human self-understanding and for education. Education is not to be confused with specialist training, ideological indoctrination, or the blight of academic pedantry: much less with the horror of academic charlatanry.

Efficacy: physical, semantic, symbolic. Effects may be produced by physical means. But animals and humans also achieve effects by purely semantic means (requiring little physical exertion, or even none). The use of language immeasurably extends the range, precision, and complexity of possible effects which human beings may bring about. This *symbolic* efficacy (which involves conceptual thought) is quite different in character from semantic efficacy of the kind available to animal life at large, and is wholly dependent on language.

Empirical or physical science. A more precise term than *natural science* for the systematic study of physical phenomena. To be distinguished from the humanities, which are concerned with the equally natural study of human life and psychology, but which call for a different methodology.

Empractic use of speech. We learn our first words in the presence of the objects and events to which they refer. Thereafter we may use words quite apart from that to which they refer. Finally, we may inhibit the utterance of language altogether and use words 'mentally', that is to say, think. The learning and use of mathematics passes through the same three stages. The mental use of language is no more problematic than mental arithmetic. (The latter, in fact, is a special case of the former.)

Epistemology. The theory of knowledge in general and of human understanding and reason in particular. The principles of knowledge are relatively few but fundamental. They become intelligible only in the context of an evolutionary epistemology, which in turn is dependent on an evolutionary theory of language.

Equivocation. The use of the same term with different meanings in a given theoretical context. An infringement of the principle of logical identity.

Evolution. Evolution theory concerns not only the origin of species but also their survival and extinction. Its purpose is the systematic explanation of the findings of *many* scientific disciplines, and of much else which we know about life and nature. All this cannot be accounted for in terms of genetics and blind 'natural selection' alone. There is also conscious human selection: the result of rational choice, but very often also, of irrational thought and action. Ours is the only species which in large measure controls its own destiny. Since all conceptual thought (rational and irrational alike) is language-dependent, an understanding of the origin, nature, development, uses and misuses of language, and of its central place in human psychology, is a prerequisite for determining what course human evolution will take in the future.

Future. One cannot refer to future possibilities as if they were present events or accomplished facts. (*See* Reference: empirical and modal.)

Grammar. 1. A systematic account of the forms and conventions of a given language. 2. Logical analysis of the basic functions which words may perform in any language.

Holophrastic utterance. The pre-symbolic, purely designatory use of vocal utterance, in which a single sound may signify or be a response to many different things.

Humanities. Any field of study in which human consciousness, thought, understanding and so on form part of the *subject matter* of inquiry. The logical complexity of these and related psychological concepts means that the humanities are not amenable to the empirical methodology of physical science.

Idealism. One of the main traditions of western thought, along with naturalism and scepticism. The strength of idealism has always been its recognition of an ideal (i.e. non-empirical) element in human knowledge. Its weakness has been its failure to explain how this ideal factor came into being.

Identity: physical, personal, mathematical, logical. Four quite distinct concepts which are often confused. The same thing, and likewise the same person, may subsist, albeit with changes, over a period of time. (We do not, however, usually confuse people with things.) Mathematical identity refers to the limitless transformations of mathematical values (4 is $2 + 2$, $3 + 1$, $5 - 1$, and so on *ad infinitum*). Logical identity, which is often confused with the mathematical variety, is in fact quite distinct. Logical concepts cannot be transformed in an infinite number of ways, nor do they admit of deduction in the mathematical sense. The principle of *logical* identity is simply that in order to obviate equivocation and confusion the same term must not be used with different meanings in the same theoretical context.

Ignoratio elenchi. Ignorance of what makes an argument fallacious and, by implication, ignorance of what constitutes valid, logically relevant argument.

Implication. Many uses of language imply more than they state. Purely *logical* implication, however, must be distinguished from other kinds: those dependent on modal reference (*see* Reference), and those suggested by the psychological and physical circumstances of utterance. Logical implication is concerned only with what is involved in the use of general and particular statements which are logically related.

Intelligence. At the most basic level, the ability to learn. At the highest level, human self-understanding.

Interpretation. A psychological process implicit in all *signification* and sign-mediated behaviour, in which one thing is responded to as significant of another, or others.

Judgment. At the sensory level, the ability to discriminate. (For Aristotle this was the basis of all higher forms of knowledge.) At the symbolic level, positive or negative predication (i.e. statement).

Knowledge. The philosophical problems which this concept has created result from neglect or confusion of certain facts. The term is the nominalized form of the modal verb 'to know'. *Ken*, *can*, *know* are cognate terms. To know is to be able: to walk, swim, speak, count, remember, reason, and so on. Knowledge may be instinctual; the result of behavioural feedback; or of sign interpretation. These forms of knowledge are common to animal life at large. But knowledge may also be conscious, conceptual, theoretical, rational. Such forms of knowledge are distinctively human, and are dependent on the symbolic functions of language.

Language. As with all theory, the theoretical understanding of language depends on clarification of the principles which make it intelligible. These must explain its preconditions, origin, primary functions, principal developments and modes of reference; and, above all, its psychological importance in human life and thought, its logical complexity, and the aberrations to which ignorance of this complexity gives rise.

Law. 1. A norm of human conduct, either the result of tacit convention or consciously laid down for the regulation of social life. 2. The term is also used, metaphorically, to refer to observed regularities in the study of natural phenomena (the so-called laws of nature). These two meanings are often confused.

Laws of thought. A traditional term for the logical principles essential for the regulation of theoretical discourse.

Logic. 1. In a broad sense, logic is inseparable from the general theory of language, since the logical or normative function of language (which is implicit in the categorial function of our first words) is the condition of its intelligibility and permeates its entire development. (It should be remembered that the term and its meaning derive from the Greek verb 'to speak'.) 2. In a more restricted sense, logic is concerned with the normative principles which regulate abstract theoretical discourse: the principles of logical identity, logical contradiction, and logical implication. Of the many misconceptions of logic, the most common is the belief that it is a 'deductive science'. Since deductive argument (except of the comic sort which 'proves' that Socrates is mortal) is not found outside of mathematics, this misconception led Russell and many others into the trap of thinking logic to be a branch of mathematics. As a result, the concept of logic as regulative of verbal discourse has very largely been abandoned.

Meaning. It is essential to distinguish between pre-linguistic meaning (the semantic behaviour and sign interpretation of animals and infants), linguistic meaning proper (the ordinary uses of language), and post-linguistic meaning (other forms of meaning which *presuppose* conceptual thought, which is language-dependent). It is also important to distinguish between the referential, formal, and psychological aspects of meaning. (*See* Chapter 8.)

Mediation. What distinguishes all higher forms of animal and human behaviour is that they are semantically mediated: not automatic reaction to sensory stimulation, but dependent on the (often delayed) response to signs, signals, and words. These must be interpreted, and are often misinterpreted. Semantic mediation marks the great divide between physics and psychology.

Metaphysics. Gratuitous speculation with pretensions to logical rigour. Since *mind* has long been an object of metaphysical speculation, metaphysics is still often confused with epistemology.

Mind. A psychological term of extreme generality which refers to human consciousness, memory, imagination, intelligence, thought, reason and so on, along with their failings or aberrations.

Misplaced empiricism. Application of the methods of physical science in areas of study where the subject matter is not primarily physical but concerns human meaning, values, purpose and the like. A related error is to hold that these areas of study are not amenable to rational inquiry. (This involves the absurdity of equating human rationality with one of its products: physical science.)

Modality. The main problem area in language theory and in logic. (*See* Reference: empirical and modal.)

Moral concepts. Those which are the distinctive concern of moral philosophy (i.e. the humanities as opposed to physical science), e.g. meaning, purpose, value, thought, mind, and the like.

Mythical thinking. Primitive speculation on matters of human interest and concern, but without adequate information or logical safeguards. Despite their vagaries, myth, and later metaphysics, were initially creative attempts to produce systematic theory. Once they become fossilized orthodoxy, however, both become serious obstacles to more rational forms of theory.

Name and noun. Linguistic symbols are not strictly names of things but names of verbal categories which are used to refer to things. Nouns, like verbs and adjectives, are category words. A name is simply a verbal sign associated with some individual. (*Cat* refers to *any* cat, 'Felix' to *this* cat.)

Naturalism. One of the main traditions of western thought, along with idealism and scepticism. The supreme achievement of this tradition is natural science and human technology. Its major failing to date has been its inability to produce a non-reductionist theory of human psychology and knowledge (on which science and technology depend).

Negation. Although positive and negative statements appear similar, negative statement is logically the more complex. Since negation implies at least the possibility of positive statement, it is a second-order form of reference and strictly *modal*. (*See* Reference: empirical and modal.)

Neoteny. The relative prolongation of periods of biological development. The retention (even into adult life) of morphological and behavioural traits characteristic of youthful or even foetal stages of development, when comparison is made with related species, or with other members of the same species. Neoteny, which has complex repercussions, helps to account for many of the factors (e.g. upright posture, large brain, protracted growth and learning period, language, conceptual thought) which combine to produce a distinctively 'human' nature, radically different from any other. (See p. 39, and ch. 2, n. 20.)

Nominalization. A common source of 'philosophical' problems. Although adjectives, verbs and relational words have logical functions quite different from nouns, we commonly give them nominal status. We thus create problems of the kind: What is knowledge, truth, thought, morality, meaning, value, reason?

Norms: physical, practical, logical. Any device which regulates rational thought and action is a norm. Most obvious are physical norms (e.g. a yardstick or pint measure) and practical norms (e.g. rules and laws). Least obvious are our logical norms: the *verbal categories* which not merely regulate conceptual thought but first make it possible; and the *logical principles* which regulate discourse and theory.

Objectification of subjective knowlege. The symbolic forms of a common language provide us with common categories by which subjective experience and thought may be expressed in terms intelligible to others.

Orientation: sensory and symbolic. Sensory orientation of various kinds is the birthright of animal and human life alike. But only human beings have, as it were, a second string to their bow. They not only register and react to sensory experiences, but also monitor them, categorize them, refer to them, communicate knowledge of them to others, and benefit from the similar knowledge of others by symbolic means. This comes about through the learning and use of language.

Origins of language. Language strictly originates with symbolic reference: the utterance and hearing of category words which refer to things around us. But language has many origins. Symbolic reference has its own origins. Language, which is also the basis of conceptual thought, originates every time an infant learns to speak and think. Each stage in the *development* of language and conceptual thought is itself an origin, which creates novel linguistic and psychological possibilities. (Most speculation on the origins of language is based on simplistic conceptions of its nature and function. When these matters are clarified, theoretical understanding of how language originates, and how it develops, is quite unproblematic.)

Perception of objects and of signs. We often think of perception as recognition (usually visual) of objects. More radical than object recognition, however, is the (initially unconscious) recognition of signs. Singly or conjointly, signs form the basis of object recognition. Sign perception, moreover, is the basis of all *learning*, and thus of all higher knowledge. Signs may signify not only that of which they are part (natural signs), but also, through casual association, anything whatever (fortuitous signs). Of crucial importance in the genesis of language are vocal utterances, which are both uttered as signals and interpreted as signs. Once stabilized by social usage, these become symbols (conventional signs, which are also conventional signals, and conventional *terms of reference*).

Principles: factual, theoretical, methodological. The purpose of all theory—be it in physical science or in the humanities—is not to describe phenomena, but to provide an explanatory framework which enables us to understand the relationships between recurrent phenomena. Theory depends on careful definition of the essential data in a given field of inquiry; on theoretical principles which correlate such data in meaningful ways; and on methods which not only further these ends, but which are capable of accommodating novel data and developments which may supervene.

Reason and irrationality. Since rational thought is a distinctively human faculty, dependent on the symbolic functions of language, it follows that its aberrations (irrationality) are distinctively human also: but amenable to correction through discovery of how they and it (reason) come about.

Reductionism. The paradoxical attempt to treat complex processes or concepts as if they were the simpler ones from whose complications and development they arise. In biology and psychology, reductionism is a major obstacle to theoretical advance along evolutionary lines.

Reference: empirical and modal. The primary form of linguistic reference is empirical, i.e. to objects of immediate sense experience. Empirical reference is often verified or falsified without difficulty. All other reference (and by far the greater part of all language use) is modal, i.e. to things absent, abstract, possible, hypothetical, symbolic, theoretical, and so on. Modal reference is often only suggested, or merely implied, rather than clearly stated. Modality is the main problem area of language theory, since its logical complexity creates limitless possibilities of error, misunderstanding, and false inference (not to mention mendacity, deception and sophistry).

Reification. Since language begins with empirical reference to concrete objects, there is a constant tendency to hypostatize or reify the 'objects' of other forms of reference: qualities, processes, relations, complex and abstract concepts, and even the semantic or symbolic devices by which we refer to all these.

Relativism: psychological, linguistic, cultural. The unavoidable subjectivity of the experience of each individual subject led the ancient sceptics to argue that there could be no certain or objective knowledge. The gratuitous assumption that each different language determines the way its speakers must think led more recent thinkers to a similar conclusion. Others have thought that the different myths and customs of each individual culture determine the psychology of all its members, making cross-cultural understanding difficult if not impossible. If taken together, these illusions conveniently undermine one another. Extreme psychological differences occur within all cultures, and the normative function of a common language is what permits different individuals to understand and learn from one another, and to appreciate the social utility of common standards. Finally, since the logical functions of all languages are identical, it is language alone which creates the possibility of cross-cultural understanding and international concord.

Ritualization. An ethological term for the automatic standardization of semantic behaviour among animals which anticipates the normative function of language.

Scepticism. One of the three main traditions of western thought, the others being naturalism and idealism. The strength of scepticism was to reveal the gratuitous nature of many common-sense assumptions and the untenability of other more sophisticated philosophical doctrines. Its weakness was to infer from all this that no objective knowledge or systematic theory were possible at all.

Secondary function. Many organs and faculties which aid survival take on secondary functions. They also *combine* to produce more complex faculties and forms of behaviour. Language and human intelligence exemplify this principle.

Semantic descent and semantic ascent. Animals mostly utilize the information they derive from signs and signals for the satisfaction of basic needs and interests. Human beings alone have developed the more primitive semantic processes in the direction of conceptual thought and rational theory, on which human culture and civilization depend. Ignorance or perversion of these higher faculties, however, create correspondingly greater hazards for the human species.

Stimulus, sign, signal, symbol. These are all theoretical terms, each of which implies some associated correlate (e.g. animal reaction, behavioural response, interpretation of meaning). Nothing is a stimulus, sign, signal, or symbol *per se*, but only insofar as it is correlated with some such effect or consequence. Stimulus is essentially a physiological concept. Sign is essentially a perceptual concept. Signal is essentially a behavioural concept. Symbol is essentially a linguistic concept, which combines all the virtualities of more primitive semantic processes, but is quite different in kind. Symbols are category words which make possible both linguistic reference and conceptual thought.

Subjectivity. Language is not only the vehicle of objective reference and social discourse but also of subjective consciousness and thought. This *triple function* makes language the unique link between our own thought and experience of the world and the thought and experience of other people.

Symbolization. The originative principle of human language and thought. In using category words (the most numerous in any language) to refer to objects, we implicitly classify these with similar objects, but also differentiate them from others (which may also be categorized and so made objects of linguistic reference). As we build up a repertoire of words with these three basic functions—referential, categorial, differential—the words automatically take on mnemonic and heuristic functions. They serve to refer to, or remind us of, objects not present. They help us identify and designate objects not previously encountered. In the process, we build up a symbolic network of ideas by which we order our experience and orient ourselves in a manner quite distinct from the purely sensory orientation available to animal life at large.

Syntax. Linguistic synthesis. The meaningful *combination* of words not only enhances the analytic function of language, producing both finer distinctions and more complex categories, but also its innovatory or creative potential, suggesting ever new possibilities of thought and action.

Teleology. Only behaviour—the attainment of ends by the adoption of means—is teleological by definition. This is true of the most primitive forms of animal behaviour and of the highest forms of human behaviour (e.g. rational behaviour conforming to ethical principle).

Theory. The primary aim of theoretical discourse is rational explanation, in any field of inquiry whatever. Rational theory is not restricted to empirical science, nor dependent on prediction. It is, however, dependent on an understanding of logic.

Unconscious knowledge. The earliest stages of perception and associative learning are necessarily unconscious processes, since they form the basis of what later becomes conscious knowledge. (Among others, Aristotle, Condillac, Darwin, Helmholtz and Pavlov showed keen insight in this matter.) At the other extreme, conscious knowledge, once assimilated, easily slips back to become unconscious memory. In adult life, we constantly draw on both forms of unconscious knowledge unawares, often to good effect. At the theoretical level, however, this becomes a potent source of confusion and error. Conscious theoretical understanding in a discipline of any complexity is a relatively rare form of understanding, dependent on the systematic correlation of facts and the formulation of logically coherent explanatory principles.

Universals. Universal concepts. The traditional term for the categorial function of language (often viewed as a metaphysical problem or a psychological mystery).

Value. Anything of worth, importance, or interest to animal organisms. At the most basic level, the preservation of life. At the highest level, ethical values which are prerequisites of civilized life.

Value judgments. Since values of one kind or another orient all animal and human life, value judgments cannot be dismissed (as in much academic philosophy) as irrelevant or meaningless. Meaning and value are in fact closely related concepts. Moreover, values are the norms or criteria without which no judgment would be possible at all.

Written language. Writing of any sort is a late development in language: in many cultures it does not occur at all. Alphabetic writing is a much later development. Written language presupposes speech, in all its complexity and with all its concomitants, both physical and psychological. Hence, to make the abstract written forms of one or more languages the basis of language theory—the dominant trend in academic linguistics—is to condemn the subject to sterility.

Notes and references

Titles of classic works are usually cited in English. Reference is made to chapters, sections, or pagination of standard editions.

Chapter 1 The nature of the inquiry

1 Plato, *Charmides*, 167c. The dialogue seeks to define the moral ideal of *sophrosynē*, moderation and self-control. In this context the thesis is queried rather than developed. It is nonetheless the first hint at the possibility of a general theory of knowledge in the western tradition.

2 For the distinction between empirical and purely theoretical inquiry, see Plato, *Phaedo*, 100; and *Republic*, 511. The related but more radical distinction between *perceptual familiarity* and *theoretical understanding* is central to Plato's dialogue *Theaetetus*, and indeed to his entire epistemology. The distinction between natural phenomena and the products of human contrivance is explicitly made in Plato's *Sophist* (265e), but was a basic principle of Greek humanism in general. Neglect of this simple distinction is the main source of misplaced empiricism, reductionism and determinism in the humanities today.

Epicurean emphasis on the importance of language is recorded in Diogenes Laertius' compendium of ancient philosophy (X, 34) and was to re-emerge much later in the work of Hobbes, Vico, Condillac and others.

Aquinas, *De Veritate*, 8, 16, in *Quaestiones Disputatae* (Marietti, Rome, 1964), I, p. 176.

3 'Copy theories' of linguistic reference and truth *versus* sceptical relativism. The most extreme statement of the view that there is a pictorial relation between language and the world occurs in Wittgenstein's *Tractatus Logico-Philosophicus*, 4.014. The sceptical doctrine of Gorgias was transmitted in the pseudo-Aristotelian *De Gorgia* and by Sextus Empiricus. On the persistence of this sterile debate down to the present, see Hilary Putnam, *Reason, Truth and History* (Cambridge University Press, 1981), p. ix, and *passim*.

4 Plotinus and Kant: cf. Plotinus, *Enneads*, IV, 4, 23; Kant, *Critique of Pure*

Reason, B 177. Kant's mysterious doctrine of a 'schematism' which somehow mediates between sense experience and conceptual thought seems to have baffled most of his commentators. The doctrine ceases to be a mystery, however, once we discover its probable origin in Plotinus, who likewise argued that there must be a 'third something' which mediates between the objects of sense experience and conceptual thought, and when we realize that the mediating factor is *language*. Plotinus and Kant were not *aware* that they were stumbling upon the epistemological function of language. Yet language alone can perform this mediating function. Words are not only tied up with objects of sense experience but are themselves perceptible. At the same time they become not only the object but even the vehicle of abstract conceptual thought. Kant's 'schematism', however, designed to bridge the gap between sense experience and conceptual thought, remained for him 'an art concealed in the depths of the human soul', for which he foresaw no natural explanation (B 181–2). But later in the same work he unexpectedly homes on the truth: 'For we can *understand* only that part of our perceptual experience which corresponds to our words', i.e. to our verbal categories and formulations (B 333; cf. B xvi, B 165–7, B 505, where as usual Kant states his revolutionary principle *without* reference to language). Hence the non-empirical *a priori* element which Kant rightly believed to be present in human knowledge is not to be sought in the depths of the human soul but in the normative function of language, whose symbolic formulations provide us with *all* our categories.

Thomas Hobbes, *Leviathan*, I, 4.

Condillac, *Essai sur l'origine des connoissances humaines*, in *Oeuvres philosophiques de Condillac*, ed. G. Le Roy (Paris, 1947–1951), I, p. 36.

5 P. B. Medawar, in A. Bullock and O. Stallybrass (eds), *The Fontana Dictionary of Modern Thought* (Fontana, London, 1980), p. 219.

Chapter 2 Language and evolution

1 C. D. Darlington, 'The inheritance of Darwin', in *Times Literary Supplement*, 20 December 1974, p. 1434. Cf. Wilma George, *Darwin* (Fontana, London, 1982), p. 148: 'After 123 years, Darwinism is still a controversial issue. Much of the controversy is philosophical and semantic.' It would be more correct to say: 'quite unphilosophical and based on total ignorance of semantic theory'. For a critical survey of the chequered history of evolutionary biology, see Ernst Mayr, *The Growth of Biological Thought* (Harvard University Press, Cambridge, Mass., 1982).

2 Wittgenstein, *Tractatus*, 4.1122.

3 Karl Popper, *Unended Quest* (Fontana/Collins, London, 1976), pp. 189, 167.

4 Neuromythology: cf. F. W. R. Walshe in *The Brain and its Functions* (Blackwell Scientific Publications, Oxford, 1957), p. 234. Referring to

'the recurring tendency to create fictitious entities out of certain complex modes of nervous activity', Walshe concludes: 'Common sense, no less than science, cries out against these neuromythological exercises.' The same may be said of the more recent cult of gene-mythology.

5 Konrad Lorenz, *Behind the Mirror* (Methuen, London, 1977), p. 231. (Lorenz's statement is a pseudo-scientific re-affirmation of the *monstrueuse hypothèse* of N. Chomsky.)

6 J. Z. Young, *Programs of the Brain* (Oxford University Press, London, 1977), p. 260.

7 On the symbolic, and not genetic, transmission of culture: cf. Theodosius Dobzhansky, *Evolution* (W. H. Freeman and Company, San Francisco, 1977), p. 451.

8 Charles Darwin, *The Descent of Man* (1871); *The Expression of Emotions in Man and Animals* (1872).

9 This statement is not, of course, meant to undervalue the evolutionary significance of comparative anatomy. For an admirable account of the neuro-anatomical continuities underlying animal and human intelligence, see Stephen Walker, *Animal Thought* (Routledge & Kegan Paul, London, 1983). A central theme of this work is the key role of language in the development of a distinctively *human* psychology.

10 Samuel Alexander, *Philosophical and Literary Pieces* (Macmillan, London, 1939), p. 286.

11 Cicero, *De Finibus*, IV, vi, vii.

12 C. S. Sherrington, *The Integrative Action of the Nervous System* (2nd ed., Cambridge University Press, 1947), p. xxii.

13 Plato and Kant differ in their conceptions of the *a priori*, but the difference is more apparent than real. For Plato, rational discourse is possible because of the objective existence of his transcendent Ideas. But in his *Republic* (596a) Plato lets slip that these Ideas are merely posited and that they correspond to the category words of language. With similar coyness Kant identifies his normative concepts with words on just one occasion (*Critique of Pure Reason*, B 333; but see also his *Prolegomena*, Section 39). The problems of idealist metaphysics dissipate when we grasp that language is a precondition of all our concepts, categories, theory and understanding.

14 Darwin, *The Descent of Man* (2nd ed., 1874): see Chapters 3, 4.

15 The fullest statement of Eccles's views on the mind–brain problem is found in Karl R. Popper and John C. Eccles, *The Self and its Brain* (Springer International, London, 1977).

16 C. S. Sherrington, *op. cit.*, p. xx; and in P. Laslett (ed.), *The Physical Basis of Mind* (Blackwell, Oxford, 1950), pp. 1–4.

17 The distinction between *functional biology* and *evolutionary biology* is expressly made by Ernst Mayr in his *Evolution and the Diversity of Life* (Harvard University Press, Cambridge, Mass., 1976), p. 360. Many 'functional biologists' from Pasteur and von Baer onward have passionately opposed the theory of evolution.

18 Darwin, *On the Origin of Species* (1859), Chapter 11, p. 351: 'I believe, as

was remarked in the last chapter, in no law of necessary development.' All belief in orthogenesis, necessary progress, evolutionary prediction and the like is essentially anti-Darwinian. It is not only the *number* of variables that makes prediction impossible, but their heterogeneity and the haphazard character of their limitless combinations. This is quite unlike the haphazard way drawing pins may fall or that which makes prediction possible in closed systems.

19 Ernst Mayr, *Populations, Species, and Evolution* (Harvard University Press, Cambridge, Mass., 1975), p. 388. Mayr speaks of behaviour as 'one of the vast areas of modern biology . . . in which the application of evolutionary principles is still in the most elementary stage' (p. 7). He also states that 'it is quite likely that speech is the key invention which triggered the step from hominid to man' (p. 386). There does of course exist a vast and ever-increasing descriptive literature on the behaviour of individual animal species. It must be stressed that in this essay we are concerned with general evolutionary *principles* capable of explaining the emergence of animal intelligence, human language, and mind. (For a recent survey of ethology, see Robert A. Hinde, *Ethology. Its Nature and Relations with Other Sciences*, Oxford University Press, London, 1982.)

20 Neoteny refers to the retention of foetal, larval, or youthful traits longer than might be expected from comparison with related species or with other members of the same species. (The neglect of neoteny is the more remarkable in that it is a matter of observation which does not even require acceptance of Darwin's theory.) Neoteny accounts for the most distinctive features of human morphology, as well as for differences between the sexes, between ethnic groups, and even between individuals of the same sex and ethnic group. It also has important behavioural and psychological dimensions. The term was coined in 1884, but the phenomenon was noted earlier by Kovalevsky as explaining the probable origin of the Vertebrates, and is referred to as such by Darwin (*The Descent of Man*, 2nd edn, Chapter 6). The most recent and comprehensive account of *human* neoteny is Ashley Montagu's *Growing Young* (McGraw-Hill, New York, 1981). Stephen Jay Gould's *Ontogeny and Phylogeny* (Harvard University Press, Cambridge, Mass., 1977) is a scholarly history of the subject in general and of the errors to which ignorance of it gives rise. Neoteny accounts for so many 'missing links' (which may never have been there) that Gavin de Beer coined the phrase 'clandestine evolution' in this connection. Cf. *Embryos and Ancestors* (Clarendon Press, Oxford, 1958), p. 31. (On human neoteny as it affects language, see above, p. 39.)

21 Darwin, *The Expression of Emotions in Man and Animals* (1872), p. 355. The most important conclusion of this work for an understanding of semantics and language theory is that all behaviour which acquires a semantic and communicative function has quite distinct natural origins, but that when such behaviour produces beneficial results it may later be voluntarily and consciously put to use. What Lloyd Morgan and Thorndike later saw to be true of behaviour in general,

Darwin had already seen to be true of the most refined—semantic and symbolic—forms of behaviour.

22 Darlington: see note 1 above.

Chapter 3 The nature and origin of language

1 On cutting language down to size: Saussure, father of academic linguistics, was fully aware of the complexity of human language but thought that such complexity was inimical to the quasi-mathematical linguistic 'science' which he hoped to create. He therefore decided that linguistic science must be rigorously separated from any psychological, anthropological or philological factors which might taint its purity. See *Cours de linguistique générale* (1916), pp. 24–6. No critical appraisal of academic linguistics can be undertaken in this volume. (For the author's views on the matter the curious reader may consult review-articles in *Modern Language Review*, 1979, pp. 117–22, and *Times Literary Supplement*, 11 July 1980, p. 785.) There do of course exist countless works on the origin of language: what they mainly have in common is failure to solve the problem. See G. W. Hewes, *Language Origins. A Bibliograpy* (Mouton, The Hague, 1975); J. H. Stam, *Inquiries into the Origin of Language. The Fate of a Question* (Harper & Row, New York, 1976).

2 Darwin: 'Even infants, if carefully attended to, find out at a very early age that their screaming brings relief, and they soon voluntarily practise it' (*The Expression of Emotions in Man and Animals*, 1872, p. 356).

3 Aristotle, *Analytics*, $71^{a}1$; $99^{b}20$–$100^{b}17$.

4 For Democritus the way things either impinge or offer resistance is the basis of all our knowledge. Condillac distinguishes between conscious knowledge, which is language-dependent, and *practical knowledge* 'which governs our actions in a manner we are incapable of observing'. See *Traité des sensations*, in *Oeuvres philosophiques de Condillac* (Paris, 1947–1951), I, p. 298; and below, ch. 9, n. 26.

5 Pavlov: it is to be stressed that Pavlov clarified the evolutionary *origin* of the process of signification. Thereafter anything may come to signify anything else. The principle with which he is usually credited had been clearly stated in 1836 by Hamilton as the law of 'redintegration': 'Those thoughts suggest each other which had previously constituted parts of the same entire or total act of cognition' (*The Oxford English Dictionary*, *s. v.* 'Redintegration'). In Pavlov's Russian the word usually translated 'conditioned' is and can only be adjectival: 'conditional'.

6 Aristotle, *Analytics* $99^{b}35$.

7 I. P. Pavlov, *Conditioned Reflexes*, translated and edited by G. V. Anrep (Oxford University Press, London, 1927), p. 407.

8 Plato, *Cratylus*, 388c. Later (426a) Plato observes that the linguistic specialist who cannot give a lucid account of how the first words came to be is sure to talk nonsense about the rest. This is profoundly true.

9 Aristotle, *De Interpretatione*, 16ᵃ27–30.

10 Mental arithmetic and mental speech. The continuity between overt speech and inner speech or discursive thought was made explicit by Plato and the Stoics. Just how 'automatic, unconscious or subconscious' our language-dependent thought becomes was noted by the neurologist Hughlings Jackson in an article in *Brain* (I, 1878–9), reprinted in his *Selected Writings* (Hodder & Stoughton, London, 1932). See volume II, pp. 167–8.

Karl Bühler, *Sprachtheorie* (Jena, 1934), Chapter 3.

11 Bertrand Russell, *The Analysis of Matter*(Allen and Unwin, London, 1927), p. 152. Cf. Gottlob Frege, *Nachgelassene Schriften* (Felix Meiner, Hamburg, 1969), p. 288. Frege's piece is dated 1924/25.

12 Hegel, *Phänomenologie des Geistes* (1807), ed. J. Hoffmeister (Felix Meiner, Hamburg, 1952), pp. 458ff. Here language and mind are virtually identified. Language is 'das Dasein des Geistes': the form in which mind finds existence. Language is the means by which the self becomes an object to itself—'das sich als Wesen wissende Selbst'—but also, at the same time, to others. Language is the basis of self-consciousness, social consciousness, ethics, law and human society. Behind the jargon and the metaphysical edifice, Hegel's psychology, like Aristotle's, is essentially evolutionary in character. The year 1831, which saw the death of Hegel and Darwin's departure in the *Beagle*, aptly symbolizes the demise of classical philosophy, the many virtues of which are all but forgotten, while its absurdities are, alas, still common currency.

Chapter 4 Stimulus, sign, signal, symbol

1 David Hume, *A Treatise of Human Nature: being an Attempt to introduce the experimental Method of Reasoning into Moral Subjects* (1739), II, iii. In his Introduction, Hume states that any attempt to discover 'the ultimate original qualities of human nature' ought to be immediately repudiated. His statement to this effect is cited at the beginning of this essay. (In context the phrase 'at first' means 'at once'.)

2 Bertrand Russell, *A History of Western Philosophy* (Allen & Unwin, London, 1946), p. 699.

3 Kant's epistemological problem: the formulation of it given here occurs in the second Introduction to Fichte's *Wissenschaftslehre* (1797). This formulation isolates the purely epistemological issue from others with which it is often confused. It also squarely faces the challenge of scepticism.

4 Interpretation: lest this seem too intellectual or hermeneutic a term to be used at the level of animal response to signs it must be said that etymologically all the term means is an interchange of values; and that this comes about in the most natural way, by association and confusion. Confusion, moreover, occurs also at the highest intellectual levels. Interpretation may lead to error as well as to understanding.

5 In an article dated 1896 Dewey exposed the inadequacy of the 'stimulus-

response' approach to human psychology even before it gained academic respectability. See R. J. Herrnstein and E. G. Boring (eds), *A Source Book in the History of Psychology* (Harvard University Press, Cambridge, Mass., 1965), pp. 321–5.

6 Plato, *Phaedrus*, 237d.

7 Hippocratic treatise *Peri technēs*: II, 14–18.

Chapter 5 Speech and thought

1 Vision and hearing. Aristotle (*De Sensu*, 437^a4–17) showed keen insight into the symbolic function of language and the distinctive role of hearing in the development of the human mind. He drew a fine distinction between the direct utility of vision for procuring the necessities of life and the *indirect* role of hearing which, in conjunction with symbolic speech, 'makes the greatest contribution to human intelligence'.

2 Aristotle, *Metaphysics*, 1029^b3–11; Kant, *Critique of Pure Reason*, B 505.

3 Saussure, *Cours de linguistique générale*. p. 24: 'It is quite erroneous to think that the problem of the origins of language differs from that of its permanent conditions'. Saussure erroneously inferred from this that he could ignore the problem of the origin and development of language and resolved to treat it as an abstract formal system. He even held the strange notion that 'the speech apparatus is of secondary importance in the language problem' (p. 26). In this he was influenced by Whitney who believed language to be a mere 'instrumentality' of our 'divinely-given faculties', and that these could have produced 'real language' even if men had been 'unendowed with voice'. See *Whitney on Language*, ed. M. Silverstein (MIT Press, Cambridge, Mass., 1971), pp. 99–102. For proof of Saussure's confusion of language with mathematics, see p. xlii of the same volume.

4 Albert Einstein, 'Physics and Reality' (1936), reprinted in *Ideas and Opinions* (Souvenir Press, London, 1973), p. 290. The relevant passage begins: 'The whole of science is nothing more than a refinement of everyday thinking.' The latter therefore constitutes the real problem of epistemology.

5 Aristotle (*Physics*, 253^a7–18) briefly touches on the influence of the environment (*periechon*) on thought: a topic much neglected by those who view thought as a purely subjective or cerebral affair.

Chapter 6 Discourse and theory

1 Bertrand Russell, *My Philosophical Development* (Allen & Unwin, London, 1969), p. 200.

2 Polybius, *History*, VI, 56. The first systematic study of the *positive* role of mythical modes of thought in the development of human rationality is Ernst Cassirer's *Das Mythische Denken* (1925), translated as *Mythical*

Thought (Yale University Press, New Haven, 1955). This is the second volume of Cassirer's monumental *Philosophy of Symbolic Forms*, the others dealing with language and with scientific thought. This is perhaps the most erudite philosophical work ever written, since Cassirer took in his stride everything from the Presocratics to the philosophical implications of quantum theory,and wrote illuminatingly on these and most other subjects of philosophical interest that come between. If his work has a flaw it is a residual idealism which led him to place mythical thinking, common-sense thought (as expressed in ordinary language), and scientific thought all on the same footing, as products of a pre-existent *symbolic faculty* which remains as unexplained as the traditional concept of mind. Only rarely did he come close to the insight that language is the source of all symbolization and symbolic thought.

3 Aristotle, *Poetics*, 1451^b5–9. Aristotle had before him the example of the classical Greek tragedians whose incomparable achievement was to transform mythical tales of horror, bloodshed and revenge into sublime works of art with ethical content of permanent human value.

Chapter 7 Written language

1 K. R. Popper, 'Epistemology without a knowing subject', in *Objective Knowledge* (Oxford University Press, London, 1972), p. 106.
2 Plato on simplistic materialism: *Theaetetus*, 155e
3 Darwin, *The Descent of Man* (2nd ed.), Chapter IV.
4 Post-verbal nouns. There are, however, exceptions to this rule. Certain psychological terms (e.g. knowledge, thought, understanding) which derive from modal verbs are a notorious source of trouble. See Appendix: *Knowledge*; *Nominalization*; *Reference: empirical and modal.*

Chapter 8 Meaning, reference, categorization, modality

1 Aristotle, *Metaphysics*, 1003^a33–1003^b19. Cf. W. D. Ross, *Aristotle* (Methuen, London, 1956), p. 24: 'The primacy of individual substance is one of the most fixed points of Aristotle's thought—the point at which he most clearly diverges from Plato's doctrine'. (How these two doctrines may be reconciled is a recurrent theme of this essay. See p. 110; p. 137; ch. 9, note 3; ch. 10, note 1; Appendix: *A priori*.
2 Wittgenstein, *Tractatus*, 6.54. The conclusion of this influential work, which is a plea for mysticism, is the absurd thesis (6.53) that only the propositions of natural science are meaningful, and that these have nothing to do with philosophy. Believing psychology to be one of the natural sciences (4.1121) Wittgenstein turned his attention to a putative 'non-psychological self' (5.641), about which he found, not unnaturally, that nothing meaningful could be said.
3 Plato on link between ideas and words: *Republic*, 596a.

4 Plato on the 'network of ideas' as condition of rational discourse: *Sophist*, 259e.
5 Schelling's dictum: see L. L. Whyte, *The Unconscious before Freud* (Tavistock Publications, London, 1962), p. 126.
6 As an example of the theological orientation of modern logic, and of modal logic in particular, see Alvin Platinga, *The Nature of Necessity* (Oxford University Press, 1974). 'The arch-enemy of modal logic is Quine.' Cf. Susan Haack, *Philosophy of Logics* (Cambridge University Press, 1980), pp. 178–94.
7 Aristotle: see Chapter 5, note 1. The role of *hearing* in the genesis of language is treated at length by Herder in his admirable *Essay on the Origin of Language* (Berlin, 1772).
8 Bertrand Russell, *The Principles of Mathematics* (Allen & Unwin, London, 1964), p. 47.
9 The impossibility of empirical reference to the future: Aristotle drew attention to this in a famous passage (*De Interpretatione*, 19ᵃ30) concerning incompatible statements about a possible sea battle tomorrow. This led to a fearsome medieval debate *de futuris contingentibus*, concerning the more serious problem of how to square divine foreknowledge with human freedom of choice.
10 Trivial paradoxes of this sort account for most of the ills of modern mathematical philosophy. Cf. the comments of Putnam and Hao Wang, p. 176, above. Gödel thought such paradoxes reveal 'the amazing fact that our logical intuitions are self-contradictory'. See Hermann Weyl, *Philosophy of Mathematics and Natural Science* (Princeton University Press, 1949), p. 234. What Gödel's intuitions were like we shall never know. What he knew of logic is very little since, as we shall see, such knowledge calls for a thorough understanding of the principles of language: a fact of which Gödel was not even aware. In such circumstances Gödel was not exactly in a position to speak for the logical intuitions of the rest of humanity. Since he has recently become a cult figure this needs to be stated.

Chapter 9 Logic

1 Bertrand Russell, *Our Knowledge of the External World* (Allen & Unwin, London, 1914), p. 42. (See also note 13 below.)
Benson Mates, *Elementary Logic* (Oxford University Press, New York, 1967), p. 1.
Cf. Susan Haack, *Philosophy of Logics* (Cambridge University Press, 1980), p. 242: 'It's good to know (to borrow a phrase of Davidson's) we shan't run out of work.'
2 The notion that people can 'think as they please' and still claim to be rational was briefly dismissed by Bacon (*Essays*, 'Of Truth'): 'Certainly there be that delight in giddiness . . . affecting free-will in thinking, as well as in acting'.
3 Metaphysics as gratuitous speculation: this suggested definition is not

intended to disparage the Aristotelian treatise entitled *Metaphysics*, which also contains much admirable philosophical analysis. The term 'metaphysics' is still often misused as a synonym for epistemology, the theory of knowledge: a subject to which, after Plato, Aristotle probably made the greatest contribution. Aristotle clarified the *psychology* of knowledge as it develops from humble beginnings common to animals and humans. Plato, beginning as it were from the other end, doggedly insisted on the existence of some prior normative or *logical* factor without which rational discourse and theoretical understanding are impossible. How these psychological and logical factors combine to produce human meaning still puzzled Russell in the present century: see quotation on p. 119 and ch. 8, n. 8, above. This does not discredit Russell: other theorists did not even see the problem. The only place where logic and psychology meet is in human language.

4 The miraculous properties of the propositional calculus: cf. I. M. Copi, J. A. Gould, *Contemporary Readings in Logical Theory* (Macmillan, New York, 1967), p. 257. The so-called modal logicians sought to remedy such paradoxes by the introduction of further absurdities.

5 Jan Lukasiewicz, *Aristotle's Syllogistic* (Oxford University Press, London, 1972), p. 47; p. 12.

6 Contradiction: loose and strict. To say that all men are blue-eyed and no men are blue-eyed is a contradiction in which both statements are false. To say that all men are blue-eyed and that some men are not blue-eyed establishes a dichotomy such that if one statement be true the other must be false.

7 Plato on contradiction: *Sophist*, 230b.

8 Aristotle on contradiction: *Metaphysics*, $1005^{b}17$.

9 John Locke, *An Essay concerning Human Understanding*: IV, viii, 3; III, x, 23; II, xxxiii, 19.

10 Bertrand Russell, *My Philosophical Development* (Allen & Unwin, London, 1959), p. 145.

11 W. V. O. Quine, *Methods of Logic* (Routledge & Kegan Paul, London, 1966), p. xiv; p. 43; p. 208.

12 S. Körner, 'The Laws of Thought', in Paul Edwards (ed.), *The Encyclopedia of Philosophy* (Macmillan and Free Press, New York, 1967), vol. 4, p. 416.

13 Russell's statements that logic and mathematics 'differ as boy and man' and that 'mathematics is the manhood of logic' occur in his *Introduction to Mathematical Philosophy* (Allen & Unwin, London, 1963), p. 194. The original edition is dated 1919 but it was Russell's habit constantly to republish views he had long since abandoned. For his view of mathematical logic in 1931 see p. 176, above. His final word on logic is found in *The ABC of Relativity* (Allen & Unwin, London, 1969), p. 135: 'Logic used to be thought to teach us how to draw inferences; now it teaches us rather how not to draw inferences'.

14 Plato on the intermediate status of mathematics: see Aristotle, *Metaphysics*, $987^{b}14$–16. Whatever Plato may have had in mind, many of the ills of 'mathematical philosophy' derive from treating the ideal constructs of

mathematics as if they were empirically given, or from treating mathematical propositions as if they were no different from statements in ordinary language.

15 Richard Dedekind, *Was sind und was sollen die Zahlen?* (1893), p. viii.

16 For a brief account of the progressive extensions of the system of positive integers, see Irving Adler, *The New Mathematics* (The New American Library, New York, 1959).

17 On resistance to negative numbers, see E. G. Phillips, *A Course of Analysis* (Cambridge University Press, 1930), p. 3.

18 Leibniz, 'Towards a Universal Characteristic' (*c.* 1679). English versions in *Leibniz*, ed. P. P. Wiener (Scribner, New York, 1951), pp. 17–25; *G. W. Leibniz. Philosophical Papers and Letters*, ed. L. E. Loemker (Reidel, Dordrecht, 1969), pp. 221–5. Leibniz's inspiration is expressly Cabalistic.

19 Peirce's statement occurs in a jargon-ridden letter—full of cenopythagorean categories, qualisigns, legisigns, sinsigns, rhemes and dicents—to Lady Welby, dated 12 October 1904.

20 *The Autobiography of Bertrand Russell* (Allen & Unwin, London, 1975), p. 395.

21 Hilary Putnam, 'Mathematics without foundations' (1967), reprinted in *Philosophical Papers* (Cambridge University Press, 1975), I, p. 43.

22 Hao Wang, *From Mathematics to Philosophy* (Routledge & Kegan Paul, London, 1974), p. 30.

23 Hegel, *Wissenschaft der Logik*, ed. G. Lasson (Felix Meiner, Hamburg, 1969), II, pp. 257–9.

24 Political linguistics: on this topic see the author's review of books by Geoffrey Sampson in *The Modern Language Review* (1981), pp. 155–8.

25 To state that psychology, as theory of mind, is not an empirical discipline does not of course mean that psychology does not have an important empirical dimension, at the interface with physiology. Language also is clearly rooted in human anatomy and physiology. The main problems of language, meaning and mind, however, are located elsewhere: in semantic theory and epistemology.

26 Condillac, *Lettres inédites a G. Cramer*, ed. G. Le roy (Paris, 1953), pp. 155–8. In his *Essay* Condillac maintained that human thought and reason *and their aberrations* ultimately rest on the association of ideas, mediated by language (*Oeuvres philosophiques*, ed. G. Le roy, I, p. 36). Where others made association the basis of either deterministic or sceptical doctrines, Condillac saw that language-based association was the precondition of critical thought and rational freedom.

27 Pavlov, unlike the behaviourists, did not challenge the concept of human psychology as understood and studied by moralists and humanists down the ages. He did challenge those who failed to distinguish between human psychology and the study of animals. See B. P. Babkin, *Pavlov: A Biography* (University of Chicago Press, 1949), pp. 276–7. There is ample corroboratory evidence.

Chapter 10 Conclusion

1 Aristotle, in the final chapter of his *Analytics*, first outlined the general development of knowledge and drew attention to the fact that rudimentary universals are implicit even in sense perception, on which all higher forms of knowledge depend. The Platonic *a priori* was thus brought down to earth, but Plato's problem was not thereby solved. Kant returned to the problem and re-affirmed that human understanding *presupposes* normative categories and concepts which enables us to introduce meaning and order into the complex and ever-changing world of sense experience. How this came about, however, still remained a mystery. Though strongly influenced by Kantian thought, Helmholtz reverted to Aristotle's down-to-earth approach. Aristotle had made a comparison between perception and an army in rout gradually taking up an orderly formation. Helmholtz saw that perception involves the grasping of constancies and regularities amid the flux of ever changing natural phenomena (*Die Thatsachen in der Wahrnehmung*, Berlin, 1879, pp. 36–9. The reference to 'unconscious inferences' occurs at p. 27). What was then needed was to explain how apprehension of constancy, regularity or identity comes about. This was the achievement of Darwin and Pavlov, with their complementary insights into the origin of semantic behaviour and sign perception. It was then easier to see how signals and signs may take on a primitive categorial function: one thing signifying *many* others. This was a great advance on the vague, albeit valid, principle of association: that anything may come to signify anything else. The more complex symbols of human language, and the limitless possibilities of their syntactic combination, are a natural extension of this semantic process. Language, as we learn to use it, provides us with as many normative categories as we need, and is a prerequisite of all theoretical understanding. Hertz's contribution to our subject—in the Preface to his *Principles of Mechanics* (1894) and elsewhere—was to clarify that valid theory explains neither more nor less than its subject matter, theoretical concepts, logical coherence and methodological propriety warrant. This is true of theory in any field whatever.

2 Hume: see ch. 4, n. 1.

Index of names